THE VIKING CONQUEST *of* ENGLAND

For Dad
1959–2023

THE VIKING CONQUEST *of* ENGLAND

How Danish Monarchs Ruled from 1013-1042

BRANDON MICHAEL BENDER

PEN & SWORD
HISTORY
AN IMPRINT OF PEN & SWORD BOOKS LTD.
YORKSHIRE – PHILADELPHIA

First published in Great Britain in 2026 by
PEN AND SWORD HISTORY
An imprint of
Pen & Sword Books Ltd
Yorkshire – Philadelphia

Print ISBN 978 1 03619 402 4
ePUB ISBN 978 1 03619 404 8
ePDF ISBN 978 1 03619 405 5

A CIP catalogue record for this book is available from the British Library.

Typeset in Times New Roman 12/16 by
SJmagic DESIGN SERVICES, India.
Printed and bound in the UK by CPI Group (UK) Ltd.

The Publisher's authorised representative in the EU for product safety is Authorised Rep Compliance Ltd., Ground Floor, 71 Lower Baggot Street, Dublin D02 P593, Ireland.
www.arccompliance.com

For a complete list of Pen & Sword titles please contact
PEN & SWORD BOOKS LIMITED
George House, Units 12 & 13, Beevor Street, Off Pontefract Road,
Barnsley, South Yorkshire, S71 1HN, England
E-mail: enquiries@pen-and-sword.co.uk
Website: www.pen-and-sword.co.uk

or

PEN AND SWORD BOOKS
1950 Lawrence Rd, Havertown, PA 19083, USA
E-mail: uspen-and-sword@casematepublishers.com
Website: www.penandswordbooks.com

MIX
Paper | Supporting responsible forestry
FSC® C013604

Contents

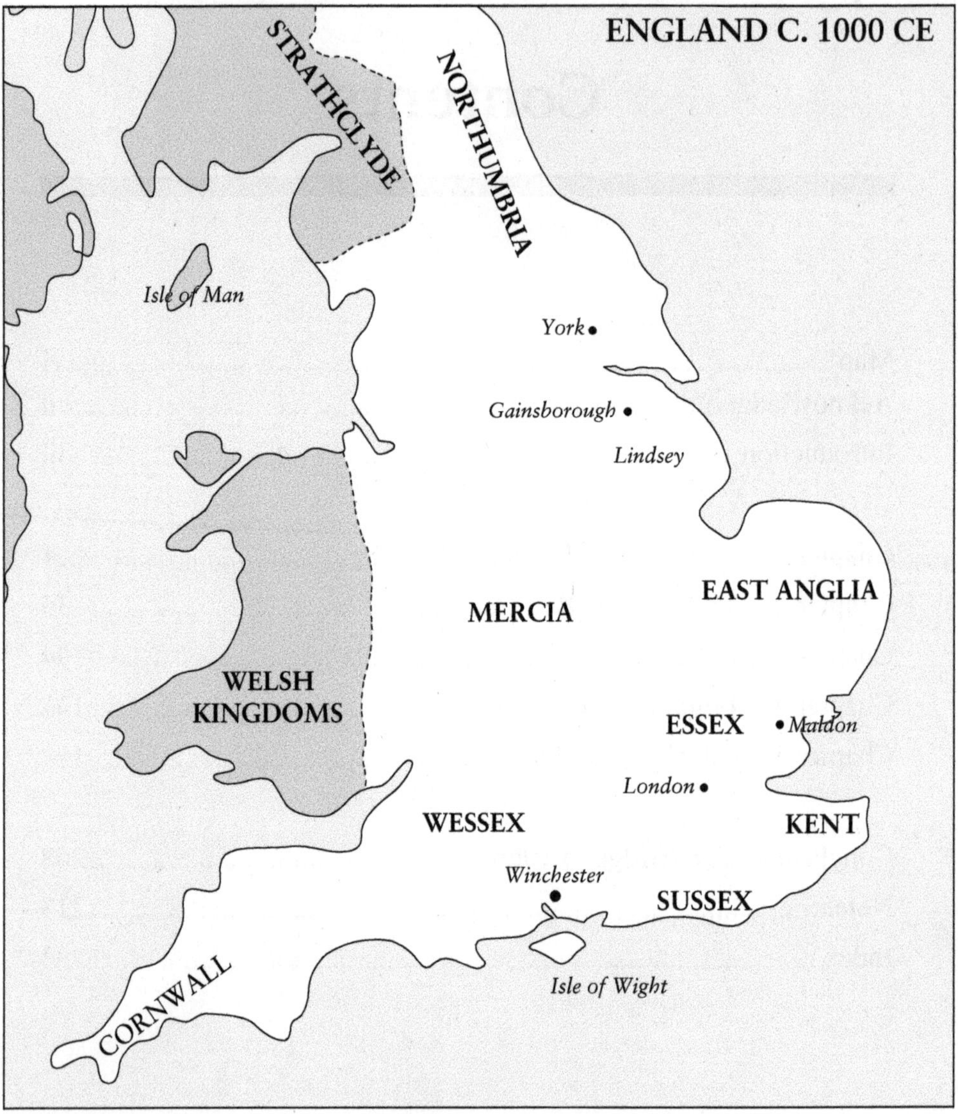
ENGLAND C. 1000 CE
STRATHCLYDE
NORTHUMBRIA
Isle of Man
York
Gainsborough
Lindsey
EAST ANGLIA
MERCIA
WELSH KINGDOMS
ESSEX
Maldon
London
WESSEX
KENT
Winchester
SUSSEX
CORNWALL
Isle of Wight

Acknowledgements

This book could not have been written without the help and support of several people. I wish to express my gratitude to Nicole Marafioti for providing feedback on the chapters about Cnut and his children; Levi Roach for his advice throughout the manuscript, particularly the earlier chapters; Lisa Hoosan, Sarah-Beth Watkins, Charles Hewitt, Sarah Hodder, Jon Wilkinson, and everyone at Pen & Sword for having faith in this book and seeing it safely to the finish line; and finally, my friends and family who have been enthusiastic and supportive of all my writing endeavours. In particular, I wish to thank my wife, Ellen. If she ever tires of hearing about vikings and dynasties, she doesn't let on.

There is an Old English word, *unraed*, that was corrupted into King Æthelred's unfortunate nickname, 'the Unready'. However, originally it meant 'ill-advised', which is a more fitting epithet for him. I have attempted to learn from his example and not be *unraed*, as evidenced by all the wonderful people who have given so much time and effort to this manuscript. Because of this, if any errors remain, they are not the fault of any wicked advisors – they are my own, and I take full responsibility for any mistakes.

Introduction

England's long and winding history is often framed as starting in 1066, when William the Conqueror and his Norman followers defeated the English at the Battle of Hastings. The Norman Conquest is so paramount in English history that the entire complex series of events can be summed up by the year itself – 1066. However, a united England existed nearly a century before 1066, and its ancient West Saxon dynasty was not conquered just once, but three times. This book is about the other two conquests, which occurred in 1013 and 1016 and are collectively referred to as the Danish Conquest. It is a story no less dramatic than that of 1066. It features waves of viking[1] raiders who pillaged England mercilessly in the tenth and eleventh centuries under the leadership of commanders with names like Thorkell the Tall, Swein Forkbeard, and Cnut the Great. It is also a story of great resistance, where the early English kingdom used every tool at its disposal – armies and fleets, financial resources, legislation, and even religion – to resist Norse armies. It is a narrative of purges and massacres, rumours and traitors, and exiles and triumphant returns. At the end of it all, a Danish dynasty ruled England for a generation. England would go from being closely adjacent to Scandinavia to being part of the Scandinavian world itself, something that would never happen again in this way.

The Danish Conquest is a story far too intense to have received so little attention. Part of the issue is that unlike 1066, the Danish

Conquest does not have a convenient one-year phrase to go by. The Danish Conquest took more than one try over the course of three years and was certainly not a singular shift of power. There were so many reversals and changes of fortune that it is tougher to sum up in the same manner as 1066.

Another reason for the Danish Conquest's obscurity is more straightforward. The Danish dynasty that conquered England in 1013 and 1016 lasted fewer than thirty years. The longevity of the House of Denmark pales in comparison to the Normans and their offshoot branches. Danish rule ended in 1042, when the original West Saxon dynasty was back in power, and in 1066, the Normans took over for good. The Danish Conquest has been lost in the commotion, sandwiched between Alfred the Great's ninth-century struggle against the vikings and the later Norman Conquest. That does not make the Danish Conquest any less dramatic or worthy of study, however, nor does it mean that others have not written on the subject before.

Academically focused books like *Swein Forkbeard's Invasions and the Danish Conquest of England* cover this conquest, as do the recent scholarly biographies of Æthelred and Cnut. Jeffrey James' *An Onslaught of Spears: The Danish Conquest of England*, from 2013, represents what might be the first serious attempt to introduce the Danish Conquest to a wide general audience. It was followed by Tore Skeie's *The Wolf Age* in 2018, also for a general audience, which was translated into English in 2021. Eleanor Parker's *A Short History of the Danish Conquest* is also a concise academic e-book for students of the era (unfortunately for me, *A Long History of the Danish Conquest* does not have the same ring to it). Another excellent and recent resource is *Conquests in Eleventh-Century England: 1016, 1066*, a collection of scholarly essays about the Danish and Norman Conquests. General overviews of the Viking Age usually include some information on the Danish Conquest too, but it is rarely the sole focus. While I am fortunate to have enough recent material to work with as I do, it is still safe to say the Danish Conquest has been seriously underrepresented, especially in popular history. If dozens or possibly hundreds of books and documentaries can be produced about the Norman Conquest, then it is time its older, viking sibling received more attention.

Many of the aforementioned books take us up to the conquest's completion (1016), and a few go all the way through the reign of the Danish and English king, Cnut (1016–35), but none of them cover the reigns of Cnut's children in significant detail. My book is partially intended to help fill this gap, as the Danish dynasty in England – along with all its political intrigue – lasted beyond Cnut's lifetime.

As with all conquests, the Danish Conquest does not deal solely with one group or place. While most of the fighting took place on English soil and in English waters, it is also the story of Denmark and its rulers. To a lesser extent, it also involves Norway, Sweden, Scotland, Normandy, Wales, and more. That said, the majority of this book will focus on the situation in England, meaning that the English royalty, nobility, and soldiers will frequently take centre stage. After all, they are the only people present throughout every part of the narrative, the Danes being a close second.

Notes on Sources and Names

Our understanding of the Danish Conquest is dependent on the early sources that discuss it, so medieval chroniclers will be characters in this narrative almost as much as the conquerors and defenders themselves; they are our liaisons to the past, our link to the Danish Conquest.

The sources do sometimes present difficulties, though. Firstly, there simply are not many contemporary or near-contemporary sources from this period compared to, say, the Renaissance or the Early Modern period. Secondly, the ones we do have are often written after the fact (sometimes by decades or even centuries) or by writers with obvious biases and agendas. Biases and delays are not exclusive to medieval sources, of course, but it will still be necessary to occasionally stop and consider how useful a source is. All works of history deal in shades of grey, with probability rather than absolute certainty, but this is especially true for medieval history. I have done my best to be cautious with sources without impeding myself, while also balancing this with the desire to interpret events without being reckless or overly speculative. With an era this remote and comparatively poorly recorded, 'might', 'maybe', and 'probably', are words that simply come with the territory.

As for the sources themselves, there are several that will appear in this book, but one of the most common threads will be the *Anglo-Saxon Chronicle (ASC)*. The *ASC* is not technically one source, as its name might imply, but a collection of different versions recorded in different areas by different writers, although they often address the same events or copy down the same passages. The *ASC* is among the most important set of documents for the Danish Conquest. It provides the structure and timeline of the conquest, and it also relays its basic background and aftermath. It is primarily a year-by-year account of the affairs of England, focusing on the acts of kings, high-ranking clerics, and the nobility, and its many versions were probably composed in churches and monasteries. The *ASC* is not without faults, though: sometimes it mentions a stunningly dramatic event or change of fortune only to leave it hanging with no explanation. Sometimes it singles out individuals, shaming them for cowardice or treachery without much background. Other times, it will word events passively or evasively, making it hard to deduce who was involved in a passage in the first place.

Other important English sources are the documents produced by the royal administration or ecclesiastics, such as charters and laws. Even some wills have survived. These all may seem dry at first glance, but when genuine (as forgery was common), they can provide otherwise unknown details, such as who was at court in which era and who they associated with. They sometimes even refer to events that chronicles omit or were unaware of.

Other sources for the Danish Conquest and its aftermath include texts like *Encomium Emmae Reginae*, *Vita Ædwardi Regis,* and *Gesta Normannorum Ducum*, and John of Worcester's chronicle, all composed in the eleventh or twelfth centuries in medieval Latin.

Even later Norse sagas will be considered occasionally. Due to the late composition of the sagas, and their adventurous, dramatic content, they have not always been considered valuable sources for academic history. That said, they can be valuable as supplementary information, as long as they are treated thoughtfully and carefully. There are many other medieval texts that will spring up in this book from time to time, which are too numerous to outline here.

Names are another tough spot for a book like this, given that it deals with names from various places a thousand years ago. Some of those names have survived into Modern English (Edward, Alfred, and so on), and I have given them modern spellings. A name like Haraldr has survived in multiple languages, complicating things even further. I have rendered it 'Harold' when it involves someone primarily known for his career in England (like Harold Harefoot) and 'Harald' when it involves someone who is more closely associated with Scandinavia (such as Harald Bluetooth). Many names have not survived, though, so I have gone with the most common spellings I see from experts. Swein Forkbeard, for example, can frequently be seen in other variants (like Sweyn and Sven), so in a case like this, I simply had to pick one and go with it. This is the case with many other names in this manuscript.

My aim with this book is to be both scholarly and understandable, to produce something interesting to historians and newcomers alike. This is an admittedly ambitious goal, but one I am willing to attempt because I have seen it work before. In that regard, I owe a great debt to Michael Wood, who I consider the David Attenborough of public history. His books and documentaries on early medieval England served as my introduction to this era, showing me how exciting it could be. Michael Wood indirectly taught me some very valuable lessons about historical writing: it is possible to be both academically thorough and easy to understand, to be simultaneously serious and enthusiastic. If an audience can sense a writer or presenter's passion for a topic, that enthusiasm is contagious. I hope this book can live up to those ideals.

1

A History of Bloodshed

The Danish Conquest took place in the early eleventh century, but England and the vikings had a history that stretched back more than 200 years earlier. Even Alfred the Great's prolonged struggle with the vikings of the ninth century was not close to being the first of its kind, even if it was one of the largest in scale up to that point. The first documented viking raid occurred in 789, as told by the *Anglo-Saxon Chronicle* (*ASC*), and consisted of three ships. The vikings killed the shire reeve, who 'did not know what they were... Those were the first ships of the Danish men which sought out the land of the English race'.[2]

Another version of the *ASC* identifies these 'Danish men' as 'Northmen from Hordaland', in modern day Norway, thus introducing us to one of the most fundamental questions of the Viking Age: who were the vikings and where did they come from? In English sources, viking raiders, whether they come from Denmark, Norway, Sweden, or elsewhere, are often called Danes. Scholars have wondered whether terms like Norwegian and Dane even meant the same thing to the chroniclers as they do to us, given that Norway and Denmark were 'not yet politically unified'.[3] Even if the chroniclers of the time are unclear about exactly who the vikings are, that does not mean we have to be. The term carries all kinds of connotations, not all of which are useful, so maybe it would be best to answer the most fundamental question possible. What do we mean when we say viking? What, for example, separates the vikings from other raiding bands and armies in the medieval period? We know that English lords frequently launched plundering raids into Wales.[4] Early English kings like Æthelstan, Edmund I, and Æthelred II led northern expeditions to ravage areas outside their direct control, presumably to intimidate and exploit those populations, among other reasons. Sometimes these expeditions, such as Æthelred II's attack on the Isle of Man in 1000, involved ships and fleets. Is this not viking behaviour? More or less, it is.[5] Raiding and warfare were endemic in the early medieval world, and the British Isles were certainly no exception. So if this harrying, ravaging *behaviour* is not unique in itself, why are vikings given their own label? Maybe this dilemma helps explain why the vikings are so often described, incorrectly, as a race or ethnicity of people, such as how the Norse outposts in Greenland are often referred to as 'viking' colonies without a second thought. But the vikings were not a race of people. To *go viking* was an occupation and an activity, and in Modern English, the same word is used to describe one who took part in that activity. Should a Danish viking decide to put away his sword and spear, join a monastery, and devote his life to prayer, then he has ceased to be a viking. He is still a Scandinavian and a Dane, just not a viking. The label was not something one was born into or permanently stuck with any more than one was born a scribe. It was an activity, one that had to be learned and could be retired from.

But what, then, separates *viking* from a word like *soldier*? There is heavy overlap, but two of the most distinguishing traits of the vikings were their sailing technology and geographical reach. Every early medieval society had its warriors and soldiers. Only in Scandinavia did those warriors have access to such technologically advanced ships, simultaneously capable of weathering long sea voyages and striking coastal targets with lightning speed. Seafaring technology undoubtedly played a large role in the success of the vikings, but many factors played into the dawn of the Viking Age. Modern writers have argued that the Viking Age was a reaction to aggressive southern neighbours, like the Christianising Charlemagne, who sought to dominate and convert the then-pagan Norse. A later medieval saga claims that overpopulation had something to do with Scandinavians leaving their homeland in search of other places. Another saga dealing with Erik the Red points toward a combination of desperation and opportunism – after being exiled from Norway and Iceland, Erik persuaded a small core of followers to help him establish a colony on the foreboding coasts of Greenland. But Greenland was vast and empty. Aside from isolated skirmishes with the *skraeling* (probably the ancestors of modern day Inuit), the Norse expansion into Greenland was not a violent affair, which is what the term viking would require. Not all targets of Norse expansion were so desolate, though. The British Isles were constantly targeted by the Norse, with a population density exponentially higher than Greenland's. It is not surprising that bloodshed was so often the outcome. So whether the aims of such voyages were conquest, settlement, or simply hit-and-run raids bent on treasure, the technology of the vikings played a leading role in their success. No one else could sail around the known world and beyond (reaching at least as far as L'Anse aux Meadows in Newfoundland, Canada) with such effectiveness.

Although this overview of viking identity is all too brief, we are closing in on a narrower, more precise definition of an oft-misused term. The vikings were not a race, strictly speaking, so much as they were warriors who were Norse. To put it another way, all vikings were Norse, but not all Norse were vikings. The word 'Norse' has some difficulties as well. Some writers use it to refer exclusively to people from Norway, but I usually see it used more broadly, roughly referring to those from Scandinavia and areas heavily influenced by Scandinavia. In this book, I use the second, broader definition and will use 'Norwegian' for people from Norway to eliminate any confusion.

A more important point to keep in mind is that the vikings were not a monolith. One viking band might feud with another or attack an area that had just made peace with a different group of raiders. Only rarely did viking bands coalesce under the leadership of one main chief or king, and English rulers like Æthelred II were all too eager to play viking leaders off one another. Even during the first Danish Conquest in 1013, when the invaders had collected themselves under the Danish king, Swein, other viking chieftains supported the English. So in the final days of the first conquest, London was being defended from vikings by – confusingly – other vikings. There was no overall grand strategy, no master plan.[6] Viking bands followed powerful men like Swein and Cnut because these rulers offered them an excellent chance at glory and riches, not because all vikings had some long-range, oddly-specific goal of ruining England. Large viking coalitions could and did break apart, fragmenting back into rival raiding parties, each with its own agenda. This is why I have avoided capitalising the term viking, except for headers, quotes, and broad terms like Viking Age. Spellcheckers and editors may not like it, but viking is just a term for a Norse raider whose effectiveness was augmented by his technology more so than any fundamental cultural or ethnic difference between him and his neighbours. Sweeping terms like 'Viking society' or 'Viking culture' are misleading. The vikings were one aspect of their society; they should not be confused with the society itself.

Along those lines, even the religion of the vikings is less clear than one might think. At the dawn of the Viking Age, Scandinavia was still pagan – true to the stereotype – and it surely was a point of difference between the earliest vikings and their enemies. The *ASC's* account of the famous Lindisfarne attack of 793 makes it clear that the 'Northmen' cared nothing for the sanctity of the Church, only for its riches. However, the assumption that paganism was a fundamental difference between the vikings and their enemies loses its validity as time goes on, especially by the era of the Danish Conquest. As early as the reign of Alfred (871–899), viking leaders were converting to Christianity. The most famous example is Guthrum, who was baptised in 878 after being defeated by Alfred, who became Guthrum's godfather. It would be easy to overlook Guthrum as an exception to the rule, especially if we accept the contemporary writer Asser's characterisation of the vikings as enemies of 'the Christians'. But more vikings would follow Guthrum's example. In 943, the English king, Edmund I had a similar arrangement with a certain Olaf of York. As late as 994, Æthelred II was able to neutralise Olaf Tryggvason by standing as a sponsor at Olaf's Christian confirmation.

The Christianity of tenth-century Scandinavia could be quite unorthodox, though. Sometimes it existed in a murky transitional state, somewhere between traditional pagan beliefs and Christian orthodoxy. For example, occasionally Christ did not displace Norse gods, but simply became one of them, integrating into their pantheon of deities.[7] While an early English clergyman would see this as missing the point, it does provide a window into the Norse mindset at the time: not all Scandinavians (and by extension, vikings) were opposed to Christianity. Some were happy to call upon Christ and add him to their religious worldview, even if this was not quite what the missionaries had in mind. Even by the early eleventh century, the English sometimes still treated the vikings as heathens (Æthelred's Enham code of 1008, which calls for 'masses against the pagans', is a good example of this). Despite this, it was not a clash of worldviews or a battle of the gods. Swein and Cnut, the conquerors of England, were both soundly traditional Christians, as were many of the men who followed them. Cnut in particular was orthodox in his Christianity (with the only exception being that he had two wives at once) and won praise from his contemporaries who were pleasantly surprised by his piety. Cnut was viewed as a model Christian – and he was also a viking.

And finally, there is another stereotype of the vikings that became popular a few decades ago – the view that the vikings were traders, not raiders. This is an especially fascinating development because it flies in the face of nearly every other viking stereotype. It is also – at least in its more extreme versions – unhelpful. Accordingly, the view of 'the peaceful viking' has seen plenty of backlash and has mostly faded away. Eric John, always known for his ability to turn a phrase, puts it best: 'The Vikings were sometimes traders, just as they certainly were, frequently, raiders. Their trading was on some scale, as evidence from Dublin and York shows. It proves only they were prepared to turn an honest penny as well as steal a pound or two'.[8] The vikings were raiders and traders, not exclusively one or the other. The raiding is the more important part for the purposes of this book, as well as for the medieval chroniclers who had to live through viking attacks.

Those on the other side of the Danish Conquest, the early English (or Anglo-Saxons), were no less complex in their identity. After the fall of the Western Roman Empire in the fifth century, people from several groups – Angles, Saxons, Jutes, Frisians, and others – migrated from continental Europe to the former province of Britannia. They came to Britain as pagan settlers and possibly invaders, competing with the existing British people for land, resources, and political dominance. They gradually displaced the existing British peoples, many of whom moved west and became known as the Welsh. The exact nature of the takeover remains murky; early sources, such as Gildas, treat it as a violent affair of conquest, but this has been challenged by historians over the last several decades. A view of absorption and assimilation has become more common, but the story of continental migration to Britain – and how these groups contributed to modern British DNA – remains unclear and hotly debated.[9] In any case, the incoming peoples, like the later vikings, had a tough time getting along with each other. This is because they were not a monolith either. Even though the genetic contributions of the Anglo-Saxons to the modern English are fiercely debated, the language and culture of southern Britain were forever changed.

By the eighth and ninth centuries, when the vikings first arrived, these groups of Angles and Saxons were thoroughly Christianised, but by no means united. Southern Britain was a patchwork of petty kingdoms that were frequently at war with one another. Occasionally one of these kingdoms, like Mercia under the powerful King Offa, would grow more dominant than the others, only to fade into the background when fortunes changed. Only in the tenth century did something roughly resembling 'the kingdom of England' appear; after surviving the First Viking Age, the West Saxon kingdom, Wessex, absorbed or conquered most of its rivals. The kings of Wessex soon took to calling themselves King of the Anglo-Saxons, and eventually, King of the English. Some of these later kings, especially the more aggressive ones, even took on blustery and inflated imperial titles, claiming to be the Emperor of Britain. The new unity of England was only skin deep, though, and any claim to be Emperor of Britain must have seemed amusing to those living in Wales or Strathclyde. Many early kings of England launched northern and western raids, but ravaging and harrying do not make an emperor. These tenth century English kings were, at best, distant overlords to those outside of southern and central Britain.

By the time of the Danish Conquest in the eleventh century, the English were united under one king, but, just as before, did not always get along with each other. The English nobility often divided up by region or splintered into political factions. In this newly-united England, loyalty to a local lord or magnate could still take priority over allegiance to a faraway king. So these are the English: people of mixed origin who had migrated and settled, been converted, and – after hundreds of years of endemic warfare – been united under one king, but that unity was only skin deep. Not so different from their viking opponents after all. Through the Danish Conquest, England would become intimately linked to Scandinavia, not just on a cultural or geographic level, but in a more formal sense, eventually sharing a king with both Denmark and Norway.

The Viking Age Begins

After that first recorded viking raid from 789, it soon became clear that this was no isolated event. The raids kept coming. King Offa of Mercia mentions pirates in a charter from 792.[10] The vikings' best known early appearance came in 793, though. The 793 raid on Lindisfarne has accordingly become the unofficial starting point of the Viking Age in Britain. The *ASC* speaks of lightning and dragons being seen in the air, followed by famine and a devastating viking attack against defenceless monks.

The setup of this account – dragons, lightning, portents in the sky – makes it clear that the author thought this was a significant turning point in history. Similar signs are recorded for major moments in later entries. For example, after Æthelred II was consecrated in 979, the *ASC* mirrors the imagery of the Lindisfarne attack: 'a bloody cloud was seen, many times in the likeness of fire; and it appeared most of all at midnight'. While these may only be literary devices, they could have been celestial events that seemed portentous in hindsight. The translator Michael Swanton ventures that the 'dragons' in the sky in 793 could have been comets, while historian Marc Morris has suggested they were the Northern Lights.[11] A similar attack occurred the very next year, 794, when 'the heathens' plundered another monastery in Northumbria.[12]

After the viking attacks from 789 to 794, documented raids are spotty for the next few decades, although the minor English kingdoms continued to wage war on each other and their Welsh and Cornish neighbours. It is possible that some Norse raids went unrecorded during this period from which not much writing has survived. Either way, the shock of the initial attacks had left their mark on the early medieval mindset. Writers of the late eighth century, like Alcuin, saw the devastation wrought by the vikings as divine punishment.

The record picks up again in the 830s, and notable encounters between the English and the vikings are recorded for 836, 838, 840–43, and 845. From the 850s on, the vikings are a near permanent fixture in the *ASC*. It was not just English kingdoms that endured such attacks, though. Viking raids occurred all across the British Isles in the ninth century. It could be argued that some of these fleets had greater success in Ireland and what is today Scotland than they did in England. The monastery of Iona was sacked at least four times, and Norse raiders even set up their own kingdoms in some places. The kingdom of Dublin is perhaps the best known of these. Wales was a frequent target too, and medieval Strathclyde and the Isle of Man also became inextricably linked with Norse colonisation and influence. Some viking fleets penetrated into central France, a continual nuisance for Frankish kings. In 911, the Frankish king, Charles III, attempted to permanently solve the problem by ceding an entire duchy to 'the Northmen' in exchange for their loyalty – the aptly named Normandy.

Back in England, the dominant viking onslaught of the ninth century came in the form of the Great Army, or Great Heathen Army, which remained in England in various forms for two decades. The Great Army overran and conquered many of the English petty kingdoms, often overcoming valiant but fruitless resistance. In some cases, Anglo-Saxon kings themselves paid the price. Some died in battle, while some were captured and put to death. In many of these cases, legendary stories sprang up about the horrific way rulers were killed by vikings, such as Ælla of Northumbria, who was killed in 867, being subjected to a ghoulish ritual known as the 'blood eagle'. Edmund of East Anglia, killed by vikings in 870, was later said to have been tied to a tree and shot full of arrows. Some kings chose to flee rather than face such brutality. Burgred of Mercia, for instance, chose exile rather than a violent death. After being confronted with an unusually large viking fleet in 874 (the *ASC* claims it numbered a whopping 350 ships), he abandoned his Mercian throne after a long reign, dying in faraway Rome. Once their opponents had been dispatched or exiled, though, the viking army had little interest in governing directly. They often set up puppet kings with English names to rule in their place, such as Egbert of Northumbria and Coenwulf of Mercia. Coenwulf was famously dismissed as 'a foolish king's thegn' in the *ASC*, although he may have actually been Mercian royalty rather than an obscure landowner who seemed amenable to Norse control. Either way, the likelihood is that these puppet kings had to agree to do the vikings' bidding while the Great Army pressed on, and none of them earned the respect of posterity for it.

Only the West Saxon king, Alfred, managed to hold off the vikings. His tenacious resistance, coupled with his love of scholarship and learning, later earned him the epithet 'the Great'. He is one of just two English monarchs called 'Great', and it is perhaps ironic that Alfred earned his for resisting vikings and that the other, Cnut, was quite literally a viking himself. Alfred's triumph over the vikings in 878 at the battle of Edington is widely remembered as a key moment in the first Viking Age – the first devastating defeat inflicted on a major viking army. After Edington and the following siege of Chippenham, the vikings were driven to the brink of starvation, so their leader, Guthrum, submitted to Alfred. Guthrum converted to Christianity, took the English name of Æthelstan, and became king of East Anglia, never again campaigning against Alfred. Despite subduing Guthrum, the viking problem was by no means solved. Other viking bands continued to be a thorn in the side of Alfred and his successors. But viking armies had changed from being an existential threat to an enemy that could be dealt with and defeated – Alfred had shown they were not invincible. As for Alfred, he eventually changed his title from King of the West Saxons to King of the Anglo-Saxons – a broader, more ambitious title that drove home an important point: Alfred was the dominant player in southern Britain, even bringing the kingdom of Mercia into his orbit. It was not quite a united 'England' proper, but the seeds were sown for his descendants to continue expanding their control.

Alfred passed along the viking struggle to his son and successor, Edward, who also had to deal with a challenge to his throne from his cousin Æthelwold. Æthelwold was the son of Æthelred I (Alfred's older brother) and had a good claim to the throne, especially because there were not many established rules of succession in the Anglo-Saxon and Danish eras of English history. The struggle would foreshadow future succession disputes and only ended when the viking-allied Æthelwold died in battle in 902. With Æthelwold out of the way, Edward reigned until 924 and continued Alfred's strategy of fortifying towns – or *burhs* – so that they could effectively resist attack. Alfred and Edward had preserved their kingdom, bringing it back from the brink of extinction and then ensuring it was well-defended. But internal strife could be almost as dangerous as external attack, which future kings like Eadwig, Æthelred II, Harold Harefoot, and Harthacnut would find out.

'England' as a broader idea, and a political reality, did not fully take shape until the reign of Alfred's grandson, Æthelstan, who extended his control farther and wider than any Anglo-Saxon king before him. Æthelstan would lay the foundations of what can properly be called England, a well-run and wide-reaching kingdom that would again become an attractive target for viking raiders in the following generations.

The Beginnings of a United England

Under Æthelstan, England expanded to roughly its modern size, but due to the messy successions of the West Saxon dynasty, it must have seemed unlikely that Æthelstan would change the course of history. Even though Alfred had gone to great lengths to ensure Edward would succeed him, Edward did not do the same for Æthelstan.

Æthelstan's mother, Ecwynn, vanished from history by the dawn of the tenth century. King Edward then remarried and had other children, shipping Æthelstan off to Mercia, away from the West Saxon base of Winchester. There, the young *ætheling* (prince) was probably connected to Æthelflaed and Æthelred, Lady and Lord of the Mercians – his aunt and uncle. It would appear that Æthelstan, despite his status as the eldest son of the reigning king, was not the most favoured child. Æthelstan made it work, though – this would have been an ideal place for the young Æthelstan to learn the art of war, given that aside from the king himself, few nobles in England had more military prowess than Lady Æthelflaed. She is recorded as ruling alone in Mercia after her husband's death in 911, dispatching armies and constructing *burhs*. Æthelstan got to see effective military policies and practices firsthand.

When King Edward died in 924, the tentatively united realms of Wessex and Mercia were thrown into confusion. At this primordial stage in English history, successions were anything but clear and there were few formal rules. The next king was not chosen by primogeniture, but by the general consensus of a nebulous group of councillors sometimes called the *witan*. They primarily consisted of notable landowners and ealdormen, as well as powerful bishops and abbots. It was not a parliament or congress – it was not even a king's council – and its inner workings are unknown. There are patterns that give us some clues about its practices, though. For example, aside from extraordinary exceptions like in 1066, the *witan* chose the next king from among the *æthelings*, indicating that royal blood was a prerequisite for rule. However, that did not necessarily mean it would be an eldest son, or even a son at all. It could be a brother, cousin, or nephew of the previous king. In 924, the two most prominent *æthelings* were Æthelstan, who was about 30, and his half-brother Ælfweard, who would have been in his early 20s. The limited ability of kings to choose their own successors meant that sometimes rival groups of councillors proclaimed different kings, which may have happened in 924. However, when Ælfweard suddenly died a few weeks later, the tide turned in Æthelstan's favour. Æthelstan was not crowned until the next year, but when the ceremony did occur, he chose a significant location: Kingston-upon-Thames, which sat on the border of the two regions.

The symbolism was obvious, and Æthelstan's initial goal must have been to ensure that Wessex and Mercia stayed united, something that was far from guaranteed. Æthelstan never married, and maybe he agreed to remain single in exchange for the throne, effectively appeasing his opponents in Wessex. Æthelstan's rivals would accept him as king and he would not try to establish his own distinct line. The throne would pass to one of his half-brothers instead. This uneasy compromise would have preserved the young kingdom's unity and allowed Æthelstan to take the throne, even if those in Wessex viewed him as a stop-gap or interim ruler until they could install someone more acceptable. Instead, Æthelstan would become the most powerful ruler the British Isles had ever seen.

With Wessex and Mercia now under his rule, Æthelstan turned his gaze outward. He first sought peace with his neighbours to the north, the viking-ruled kingdom of York, which had close connections to Norse Dublin.[13] Æthelstan married one of his sisters to York's king, Sitric, but Sitric died soon after. In a display of opportunism to rival that of any viking, Æthelstan then seized York for himself. According to the Irish annals, Sitric's demise had also caught the attention of his kinsman Guthfrith (or Gofraid), king of Dublin, who attempted to take York too. It is unclear exactly what transpired, as the *ASC* omits Guthfrith entirely, implying that Æthelstan took York without having to deal with a threat from Norse Ireland. In any case, the end result was that Æthelstan ruled York directly and Guthfrith, if he had indeed attempted to rule York, had to return to Ireland.

Æthelstan's progress continued throughout his reign. He eventually gained power in Cornwall, and he led a massive invasion of Scotland by land and sea in 934, strong-arming the Scottish king, Constantine, into submission.[14] The steady expansion of Æthelstan's holdings must have alarmed the remaining independent rulers of the British Isles. Finally, they combined their strength against Æthelstan in 937, hoping to check the king's ever-increasing power. An alliance of Constantine of Scotland, Guthfrith of Dublin, and Owen of Strathclyde (Cumbria) confronted Æthelstan at a place known as Brunanburh. Æthelstan defeated them in a battle that is recalled as particularly bloody. For those on the losing side, it was a catastrophe. The *Annals of Ulster* call it 'a lamentable and horrible battle' in which several thousand Norse warriors died. For the winners, Brunanburh was a crowning achievement of Æthelstan's reign. It was not the moment when Æthelstan attained control of territory that arguably made him the first 'king of England'. That had been several years earlier. Brunanburh was something even more important: the moment when he was challenged to hold onto what he had won and succeeded. Had the Scottish, Norse-Irish, and Cumbrian alliance triumphed, it could have meant the end of southern English dominance.[15]

Brunanburh is one of the most important battles in early English history, to the point that writing about it nearly constitutes its own cottage industry. There is still intense debate about where it was fought. Barring a monumental archaeological find, it may never be settled, no matter how hard experts and amateurs alike try to tease clues out of place names or reinterpret the lengthy Brunanburh poem found in the *ASC*. But its significance is clear. A united England had been formed and held against the most formidable coalition possible at the time.

The Struggle for Northumbria

Just two years after his great victory at Brunanburh, Æthelstan died. He was unmarried and childless, so he was succeeded by his half-brother, a young man named Edmund who had fought alongside him at Brunanburh. The *ASC* gives his age as just 18 at the start of his reign.[16] Edmund succeeded without any known opposition from the other *æthelings* and began his reign in a fortunate situation – no West Saxon king had ever begun his tenure with so large a territory. In hindsight, thanks to the myriad accomplishments of Æthelstan, Edmund could be viewed as the second king of a united England – not only did he control the traditional Wessex heartland, but he could also add Cornwall, Kent, Mercia, and Northumbria to his list of territories. However, this larger England was still in its infancy, and the British Isles were full of minor rulers who were eager to break it apart, ruling whatever they could for themselves. The *ASC* says that Edmund had received pledges from the Northumbrians recognising him as their ruler, but they were soon 'false to their pledges', choosing an 'Olaf from Ireland' as their king.[17] It would be the first of several quick changes in power as Northumbria became the epicentre of a struggle between the southern English and the wider Scandinavian world.

The Olaf in question was Olaf Guthfrithson, the ruler of Dublin who had fought at the Battle of Brunanburh.[18] Olaf Guthfrithson had an ancestral claim to rule Northumbria because his father had briefly ruled it in 927. From the West Saxon perspective of the *ASC*, the Northumbrians were oath-breakers who chose a heathen warlord as king, but in the Northumbrians' view, Olaf Guthfrithson may have been a far more natural choice. His installation allowed Northumbria to shake off the yoke of a distant southern conqueror, instead returning to the more familiar situation of viking rule – and Olaf was indeed a viking. He was an experienced warrior who had been raiding and plundering throughout Ireland for most of the 930s, not to mention his experience at Brunanburh, even though it ended in defeat. In short, he was a battle-hardened king with a family connection to Northumbria, making him just as appealing as Edmund, if not more so. Olaf's reign over Northumbia was short-lived though, as he died in 941, possibly while raiding in East Lothian, Scotland (a recently discovered skeleton there might belong to him or one of his entourage).[19]

The Northumbrians selected another Olaf to take his place, this one known as Olaf Sihtricson (also sometimes known as Olaf Cuaran). What happened next is uncertain due to a jumble of conflicting information in the surviving sources; the *ASC*, for example, seems to record the following few years in a hodgepodge of non-chronological entries. But the general impression is that Olaf Sihtricson was established as the Norse ruler of York and then led a devastating raid south into Mercia and won control of Tamworth. He had deprived Edmund of Northumbria and now part of Mercia. Edmund then besieged Olaf at Tamworth, but the viking king managed to escape. Then, in an undated entry, the *ASC* records that Edmund neutralised Olaf by standing as his sponsor at Olaf's Christian confirmation. It was a technique that Alfred had used with success and was one Æthelred II would use successfully half a century later, in 994.

Sometime after that, Edmund turned against Olaf Sihtricson and drove him out of Northumbria by force, thus restoring Æthelstan's borders. In 945, Edmund went on the offensive again and invaded the kingdom of Strathclyde, whose ruler had fought against him and Æthelstan at Brunanburh. Edmund died the next year when he was stabbed to death in a brawl, still in his mid-twenties. He had won back everything he had initially lost, but Norse rulers would continue to be a thorn in the side for his successor, Eadred.

Eadred was yet another son of Edward the Elder, probably a couple years younger than Edmund, and his reign began in exactly the same way as his predecessor's. The Northumbrians pledged their loyalty to him only to promptly reject him in favour of a viking ruler. Even the wording in the *ASC* is similar. At Edmund's accession, 'the Northumbrians were false to their pledges', and at Eadred's, they 'pledged themselves to the king, and within a short space they were false to it all'.

Just as Edmund had done, Eadred would reconquer his lost territories. He led an expedition north and ravaged Northumbria in 948, which had submitted to a viking king known as Eric. This figure was once thought to be the famed Eric Bloodaxe written about in Norse sagas, but more recent scholarship has thrown doubt upon this.[20] This Eric of York, whoever he was, had broken apart the conglomeration of kingdoms that Æthelstan and Edmund had fought for. Eadred fought something like a viking himself, though, even sacking a famous monastery at Ripon. After ravaging 'all' of Northumbria, according to the *ASC*, the rear guard of Eadred's army was ambushed by forces presumably loyal to Eric. Eadred then wished to turn around and re-invade Northumbria. Fearing another ravaging campaign (and perhaps more destroyed monasteries), the nobles of Northumbria instead drove out Eric and submitted to Eadred, even paying him some form of tribute or 'compensation'.

This arrangement proved to be temporary, too. Northumbria experienced a chaotic succession of rulers and overlords in the next few years, some Norse and some not: there was Olaf Sihtricson again, Eric again, and finally Eadred again in 954. The *ASC's* entry for 954 records that the Northumbrians, apparently tired of Eric, drove him out and accepted Eadred as their king. A variant of Eric's downfall is recorded by Roger of Wendover, who writes that Eric was 'treacherously killed ... in a certain lonely place which is called Stainmore ... and then afterwards King Eadred ruled in these districts'. Roger places Eric's assassination in 950, which is too early, but it is not hard to believe that Eric was driven out and killed. He was known to be a hard ruler, even by viking standards. Eadred, meanwhile, managed to reclaim Northumbria simply by waiting for Eric to wear out his welcome. In the words of Eric John, 'Eadred liked to see himself as the conqueror of the north. He was really more of a skilful operator than a conquering soldier, which perhaps was what the times needed'.[21]

Eadred had successfully navigated the minefield of war and politics that Northumbria presented him with, and the north remained united with the rest of England from 954 onward. Due to all his accomplishments in keeping Æthelstan's creation alive, one might be surprised to learn that the young Eadred was among the sickliest monarchs ever to sit on the English throne. The first *Life of Dunstan* recalls that Eadred was in poor condition for his entire nine-year reign and suffered from some kind of debilitating digestive problem, which made him suck the juices out of his food and spit out whatever was left.[22] The eleventh-century writer Herman the Archdeacon preserved a nickname of Eadred's, *debilis pedibus*, that means 'weak in the feet'. Exactly what this means is unclear, but for much of the reign, Eadred was not greatly hindered by his digestive issues or his 'weak feet'. Wulfstan Cantor's *Life of St. Æthelwold* records that an active and engaged King Eadred personally came out to measure the foundations and structures of the future Abingdon monastery, a tale repeated in Ælfric's version of the *Life*. These sources also include an amusing anecdote about a time when Eadred brought some rowdy Northumbrians with him to a mead hall, locked the doors, and proceeded to out-drink them over the course of an entire day.

But Eadred could not hold off his ill health forever. He began to withdraw from public life in the final years of the reign. Earlier in the reign, Eadred had personally accompanied armies into the north, but by the end, he did not even witness his own charters.[23] He largely handed control of the government to his chief administrator, the quickly ascending Abbot Dunstan, a sign that the later stories of Eadred's debilitating illnesses have a basis in reality. The king died in 955, leaving behind a will that serves as a snapshot of England as it existed in 955. Eadred's will sets aside '1,600 pounds, to the end that they [the people of England] may redeem themselves from famine and from a heathen army if they need'. The threat of a viking incursion deep into England – or their recovery of Northumbria – was still a strong possibility, and Eadred followed Alfred the Great in believing that sometimes it was worthwhile to pay off a viking army if it would buy time to organise a more coherent response. This practice was known as offering tribute but was sometimes pejoratively called 'Danegeld' by later historians who disapproved of the practice and inaccurately viewed it as a solution in its own right. The practice of giving tribute to vikings would become a fixture of the years leading up to the Danish Conquest, but it could sometimes be used quite effectively, as future chapters will bear out. Alfred and Eadred saw nothing shameful about it, and even William the Conqueror would one day offer tribute to a viking king.

To return to the immediate circumstances of Eadred's will, this dying king ruled an England that was not even a generation old. It could break apart at any time, especially due to viking ambition. Northumbria in particular had experienced such turnover in the span of a decade that historians struggle to count exactly how many people ruled it and for how many times. Olaf Sihtricson, Eric, and Eadred ruled it at least twice apiece. In hindsight, more than a thousand years later, Eadred's final years marked the point when viking control over Northumbria ended. He could not have known his reign would kick off a generation of peace and stability after almost a century of near-constant viking conflict.

Today, Eadred is seen as one of many short-lived, oddly-named kings who ruled before the Norman Conquest. Among those who specialise in Anglo-Saxon history, Eadred is occasionally mentioned, but he is almost never a sole focus of study. Usually, he is simply a stop-gap between the 'golden age' reigns of Æthelstan and Edgar. This is unfortunate, because Eadred ruled during a pivotal time in early English history, when the achievements of Alfred, Edward the Elder, and Æthelstan could have been lost. Æthelstan enjoys such a great reputation partly because rulers like Edmund and Eadred ensured his legacy – northern expansion – would survive. Æthelstan is regarded as the first king of a united England because he had worthy successors, whereas previous dominant kings like Offa of Mercia did not, so their achievements were almost immediately lost. Later, Edgar's prosperous reign (959–975) owed a lot to the tenacity of Edmund I and Eadred. Had Eadred lived longer, maybe his reputation would be similar to Edgar's. Both kings were closely associated with Dunstan and embraced the abbot's vision of Benedictine reform, and Eadred even showed a militaristic side by leading armies against a viking king – something Edgar never had to do. But in any case, Eadred did not live on, so power passed to his young nephew, Eadwig.

English Factionalism

Eadwig was only 15 or so when he rose to power following his uncle's death. This was a precarious age for an Anglo-Saxon king. He was old enough that he could theoretically rule on his own, but also young enough that a regency, or something akin to it, would not be out of the question. Æthelred II was younger than Eadwig (probably aged 10–12) at his accession and had an informal regency, whereas slightly older teenage rulers like Edmund I and Edward the Martyr apparently did not (the House of Wessex had no shortage of child rulers in the tenth century). As for Eadwig, he seems to have ruled alone from the start, but there are signs of a struggle.

Accounts of the reign vary in the amount of detail they give, but all signs point to a serious conflict between Dunstan and Eadwig. The most famous story, from the *Life of Dunstan*, says that Eadwig abandoned his coronation feast to 'cavort' with a young lady and her mother. Dunstan found the trio and was outraged. In return, Eadwig drove him into exile. This story is not found in the *ASC*, but the *ASC* does say Dunstan was exiled in 955 or 956 (different versions disagree on the year). The salacious tale of the threesome on coronation night comes from a text whose main purpose is to honour Dunstan, a man that the king exiled, so of course it has a motive to make the king look as bad as possible. 'The vitriol and scurrilous gossip poured on Eadwig' and his allies 'should be placed at the door of their enemies (such as Dunstan) and their propaganda machines in the form of traditions of houses that these ecclesiastics were associated with'.[24] However, this was not the only major conflict Eadwig would have with a man of the Church; Archbishop Oda dissolved the king's marriage at about the same time. According to the *ASC*, this happened because Eadwig was too closely related to his wife, Ælfgifu. She may have been a descendant of Æthelred I of Wessex (Alfred the Great's brother); if true, this would mean Eadwig and Ælfgifu were third cousins once removed.[25] A later Anglo-Saxon law code, *Æthelred VI*, says that people should not marry if they are within four generations of common descent. The fact that Eadwig and Ælfgifu were related was a convenient technicality, because the dissolution of the marriage almost certainly had more to do with politics than following the letter of the law.

Oda and his allies were instead trying to suppress a rival line of the House of Wessex that had been out of direct royal power since the ninth century. This branch had produced the rebellious *ætheling* Æthelwold, who fought Edward the Elder for control in the early 900s. Ælfgifu, as a well-to-do member of this branch, was trying to reintegrate their interests with the main line of West Saxon kings, and surely not everyone was happy about this. The salacious threesome story, the exile of Dunstan, and the conflict with Oda could all be manifestations of an underlying anxiety about the king's marriage, which could upset the power balance at court.

But while the conflicts with Dunstan and Oda make it look like the ecclesiastics were out to get the king, Eadwig was not unpopular with all churchmen, and we must not paint too broadly over these factions. For every movement, like Dunstan's Benedictine reform, there is a counter-movement that wants to squash it. Eadwig found support among clerics who were hostile to Dunstan and his brand of monastic reform. One of the king's allies was Bishop Ælfsige of Winchester, who later rose to prominence as Archbishop of Canterbury under Eadwig. Ælfsige had good reason to oppose the celibate trappings of monasticism – he was married with children.

Another common, if over-simplified, factor that contributed to Eadwig's alleged bad behaviour is that he was doing what teenagers do – rebelling against the status quo. Dunstan was part of the old guard.

Eadwig was not Eadred. There is almost certainly more to the story than teenage angst and rebellion, though. Judging by the prominent role of Glastonbury, Dunstan's base, in royal administration, Dunstan had grown accustomed to having total control during the waning years of Eadred's reign. Decades later, Dunstan would continue to heavily influence successions and royal administration. He was clearly a driven man who wanted, perhaps even demanded, to be at the centre of royal and ecclesiastical politics. Not even multiple ousters could dissuade him (he had also fallen from favour in Æthelstan's reign). While we can never know his personality with any certainty, especially due to later legends that sprang up, his constant involvement in national affairs is telling. It could be that Dunstan expected to maintain his iron grip on royal affairs, especially due to Eadwig's age, but that Eadwig simply would not stand for it, siding with people like Bishop Ælfsige instead. The result was an exiled abbot, an angry archbishop, and a widening gulf between the reformers and their opponents.

Eadwig's reign was also notable for the unusually large number of grants and diplomas issued, which has contributed to the image of a young, grasping ruler who was desperate to win – or even buy – support from important figures. Viewed more charitably, the flurry of charters from Eadwig's early years, though unusual, could instead be interpreted as 'a great intensity of rule' from an active king.[26] Viewed from 956, without the benefit of hindsight, Eadwig's position may have looked fairly strong – thanks to a large number of land grants, the new king had his own friends and newfound allies, as well as established churchmen like Ælfsige, who helped him resist Dunstan's influence and reforms. Also to his credit, Eadwig did indeed win his power struggle against Dunstan. Dunstan would never again influence affairs at Eadwig's court. However, it was a victory with consequences. Eadwig's posthumous reputation would be tarnished by writers who were sympathetic to Dunstan, as well as to Benedictine reform generally, who found Eadwig to be a convenient target to blame for Dunstan's hardships, ignoring the possibility that Dunstan himself may have pushed matters too far with the new king rather than learning to work with him. Consequently, these writers circulated tall tales that became infamous, such as the threesome story, that attempted to explain Dunstan's sudden downfall during Eadwig's reign. Remnants of a more favourable reputation still survive, though, such as from Æthelweard the Chronicler, who records that Eadwig gained the nickname 'All-Fair' for his attractiveness and says he 'deserved to be loved'. Henry of Huntingdon also summarises Eadwig as a 'praiseworthy' king who enjoyed 'good fortune'.

❋

Two years after Eadwig came to power, the Mercians installed his younger brother, Edgar, as their king. Eadwig retained Wessex and his status as the senior ruler. It was a remarkable development – England had been partitioned and was now ruled by two teenagers. Edgar, thumbing his nose at his older brother, made a bold move by recalling Dunstan and instating him as a chief advisor. When Eadwig died in 959, Edgar ended up succeeding to the whole kingdom. Different versions of the *Chronicle* explain Edgar's accession differently, though. One implies that Eadwig and Edgar had ruled jointly all along from 955. Another explains that Edgar became king of only the Mercians in 957. Yet another implies that Eadwig ruled alone from 955–959 and that Edgar only became king after Eadwig died. The middle option is taken the most seriously by academics, with Eadwig being sole king from 955–57, Edgar ruling Mercia from 957–59, and then Edgar gaining all of England after 959.

Even though we do not know the specifics of why this remarkable division of royal power occurred, the *ASC* does give the impression that Eadwig's first two years in power had seen their share of controversy. He had caused political upheaval by exiling Dunstan, and then the king had been humiliated by Oda when his marriage was dissolved. Even leaving the threesome story aside, chaos did seem to follow Eadwig around. Whether it was his own doing, beyond his control, or a bit of both is unclear.

Likewise, the reasons for splitting the kingdom in this way are hard to deduce. Traditionally, this split has been seen as a contentious one, a wedge between brothers and regions of the kingdom. In this interpretation, Eadwig lost control of Mercia and the north because his administration was too chaotic, scandalous, or both to retain the loyalty of the entire court. However, this view has been significantly revised in recent decades, and a new possibility has emerged: that this split was designed and very much intentional, not the result of a revolt at court.[27] The framework of an amicable split can make some sense when leaving behind the baggage of the assumption that England is one entity that should not be subdivided. In 957, just twenty years past Æthelstan's victory at Brunanburh, the concept of a united England was still new and relatively untested. It was also more common for brothers to succeed to the throne among West Saxon royalty, not sons, further strengthening Edgar's chances of being Eadwig's designated heir. The era of English primogeniture was still a long way off, and the (now unmarried) Eadwig may have been returning to established West Saxon succession practices by assigning his brother a sub-kingdom to govern on his behalf. If this is the case, then Eadwig was not losing support, but engaging in succession planning now that his marriage had been dissolved. Another detail that adds credence to the 'friendly split' idea is that Eadwig does not seem to have resisted Edgar's accession in Mercia.

Still, the cause of the kingdom's division is unclear. If one chooses to accept an 'unfriendly split' between the two, Eadwig's lack of resistance could still make sense. Perhaps Eadwig knew he did not have the support to reclaim Mercia through negotiation or force. Conceding to the Mercians might have been an act of self-preservation by Eadwig and his inner circle. They surely knew it was still common for unpopular rulers in the British Isles to be ousted, assassinated, or even forcibly retired to a monastery (that must have been the last place Eadwig wanted to end up!). Eadwig may have known he had backed himself into a corner, and some modern historians still see the 957 division of England as an emergency measure, not a planned one – a reaction to an 'unstable government and a court in deep crisis, and we may well suspect that many important men were frightened by how quickly things were slipping beyond their ability to control them'.[28]

Whatever the backstory, by the end of 957 Edgar was clearly positioned as heir apparent. Eadwig's marriage had been annulled, so he could not be expected to produce acceptable heirs, and now a huge swath of his kingdom was in Edgar's hands. Although the last two years of Eadwig's reign passed without recorded scandal, his position was weakened by the death of his old ally, Archbishop Ælfsige, in 959, while trying to cross the Alps to retrieve his pallium in Rome. Eadwig met his own sudden death later that year, aged just 19, which must have seemed very convenient to Edgar and Dunstan. His cause of death is unknown, but he had made a lot of powerful enemies in just four years. That is all we can say about it.

At first glance, Eadwig's brief but erratic reign might seem unrelated to the Danish Conquest. However, just as with Æthelstan's accession in 924, Eadwig's tumultuous four years in power prove just how fragile English unity was in the tenth century – an uncomfortable truth that will be vital to understanding the Danish Conquest and the factors that contributed to it. England during these earliest years can almost be thought of as a conglomeration of sub-kingdoms who all recognised the same overall king.[29] Under a strong, politically savvy ruler like Eadred, it was possible to hold factions in check and bring territories back into the fold when they rebelled. During the complex and confusing developments of Eadwig's administration, English unity was so delicate that it fractured after only two years. Whether this was by design or by disaffection is almost beside the point because either way, it means the kingdom could be divided up by regional differences in response to political rivalries, succession questions, or both – factors that would be at play throughout the approaching Danish Conquest. Had Eadwig and Ælfgifu had children, 'it would have increased the likelihood that the partition of 957 would become permanent'.[30] Lofty concepts of rulership and English identity could be important, but the attitude of Anglo-Saxon government was above all pragmatic.

Upon Eadwig's death in 959, Edgar succeeded to Wessex, uniting England once more. At his side was Dunstan, the domineering reformer whose influence grew exponentially upon Edgar's decision to recall him from exile. First, he was made a bishop by Archbishop Oda, the same man who had annulled Eadwig's marriage. Oda appointed Dunstan to the see of Worcester, but that was not enough. Oda made Dunstan Bishop of London, too, allowing him the controversial privilege of holding two sees at once. After Oda's death, Dunstan himself wished to become Archbishop of Canterbury, but first he had to overthrow the incumbent archbishop, Byrhthelm, whose appointment had been one of Eadwig's last acts. Dunstan ousted the archbishop with apparent ease, sending Byrhthelm packing to his former see of Wells. The point had been made. Dunstan was back and more powerful than ever. Thanks to the patronage of Edgar and a series of very timely deaths, Dunstan's turnaround was complete by about 960 – Eadwig was dead, Archbishop Ælfsige was dead, Archbishop Byrhthelm had been ousted, and Edgar was sole king.

After this early phase of intense political upheaval, Edgar's reign matured into one of remarkable prosperity. The political disputes of the reign focused mainly on monastic reform, not on successions or invasions. Edgar's reign provided a decade and a half of stability, and stability was something unusual in tenth century England. Edgar was also lucky in many ways. The 957–59 division of the kingdom had not been fatal. Had the vikings returned at exactly that time, it could have meant the end of unified England as a political reality and as an idea. Part of this 'luck', as mentioned previously, is because Edmund and Eadred had done a lot of dirty work that Edgar never had to, meaning that although the kingdom had divided itself between brothers, outsiders like Eric of York had already been defeated. This absence of direct external pressure allowed King Edgar to promote the monastic reform that won him a good reputation among his celibate but powerful allies, which is no small achievement given his alleged habit of seducing nuns. The lack of outside pressure also gave Edgar the time to put together his mighty fleets, which he used to intimidate his neighbours by display of force. In 973, Edgar supposedly got several sub-kings to row him down the River Dee, as if they were his lowly servants or shipmen. At about the same time, Edgar treated himself to a second coronation, this one more imperial in character. Edgar saw himself as the Emperor of Britain.

Aside from the showmanship of the famous River Dee spectacle and the re-coronation, little from Edgar's reign has remained in the modern consciousness, other than the general impression that it was a brief 'golden age' before the chaos of the Danish Conquest. Frank Stenton made the iconic remark that Edgar's reign was 'singularly devoid of recorded incident'.[31] At least for armed conflict from 957–975, this assessment is almost true. The *Annales Cambriae* records an undated English raid into Wales, which has been approximated to 968, placing it in Edgar's reign.[32] The king also 'ordered all Thanet to be ravaged' in 969, although the passive wording implies the king himself did not take part. Probably due to this piecemeal military record, Edgar's reign has even been seen as a time of 'atrophying military infrastructure'.[33] However, the showing on the River Dee, harrying campaign in Thanet, and possible Wales raid complicate this interpretation, which may fit better with the reign of his successor, Edward. The *ASC* also includes a curious reference to Edgar as 'bold in battle' and a 'dispenser of treasure to warriors'. These could be nothing more than tropes of good kings that were then placed onto Edgar. However, it is also worth considering that

Edgar was engaged in military affairs enough to conceivably be seen as a patron of warriors, even if the phrase 'bold in battle' is a gross exaggeration.

Edgar died suddenly in 975, still in his early thirties. The *ASC* openly mourns his passing and includes a poem in his honour. Had Edgar lived into his fifties or sixties, as a few members of his dynasty managed to do, he would have endured the full brunt of the viking invasions in the coming decades.[34] Although it may sound harsh or counter-intuitive, dying young was probably the best thing possible for Edgar's historical reputation. He died at the height of his power, frozen in medieval memory as the strongest possible version of himself. It is possible that those who lived through Edgar's reign, like our anonymous chroniclers, were aware of how good things were. However, the chaos of later eras emphasised this even more, causing Edgar's reign to be idealised. To later observers in more turbulent situations, Edgar's reign probably stood out *because* of its non-eventfulness, not in spite of it.

Edgar's reign was so comparatively calm that it would be tempting to say it has little to do with the Danish Conquest, aside from serving as a control method of what England looked like without external pressure. This is not entirely accurate, however, because Edgar's reign is linked with the Danish Conquest in some important ways. Under Edgar, England remained organised and efficient, particularly where coinage is concerned, which would help his son Æthelred raise huge sums of cash to stay afloat in the face of viking invasions. Perhaps even more significantly, Edgar's embrace of monastic reform, influenced by Dunstan and another particularly zealous bishop, Æthelwold, helped embed a style of 'penitential kingship' that would influence how following generations of rulers and writers alike viewed the kingdom's fortunes. Edgar's circle, like many in early medieval Europe, began to emphasise that God rewarded and punished nations based on their morality. This view compounded the 'halo effect' around Edgar, making his rule look especially sound, but it also affected the way his son Æthelred behaved in the face of serious crises. Because Edgar and Æthelred both embraced this worldview, it makes sense that Æthelred would purge and punish advisors at critical moments when England was at its lowest points – clearly Edgar and Bishop Æthelwold would have believed that misfortune was the result of wickedness. With this example from his father and his tutor, some of Æthelred's more bizarre decisions over the coming decades will begin to make sense.

The moment Edgar died, things went right back to normal, and 'normal' in this case is a euphemism for political chaos. He had left no known preference for who should succeed him, although such a decision would not have been his alone. Kings were made by their supporters, and unanimous support was far from guaranteed.

Edgar had at least four children with three women, leaving a complicated and undesirable situation for those who had to reckon with his sudden demise. Even the most incisive modern historians regard Edgar's marital record as 'extremely difficult to unravel' and containing 'a number of scandalous stories ... about King Edgar's predilection for young nuns'.[35] In spite of the confusion that persists around Edgar's relationships, it is generally thought that his oldest child was Edward, born to a woman named Æthelflaed who may or may not have been Edgar's wife. The king had a daughter named Edith with a former nun named Wulfthryth, but repudiated Wulfthryth shortly after Edith was born. Wulfthryth seems to have gone back to consecrated life and became an abbess, and Edith was later viewed as a saint.

Finally, with the powerful Queen Ælfthryth, Edgar had two more sons. The older was named Edmund and the younger was Æthelred. While Edgar had been alive, Edmund seems to have been favoured in some circles as the 'most' legitimate son, leapfrogging the older Edward and outranking his younger brother Æthelred. However, Edmund predeceased his father, leaving a messy situation with the remaining three children. There was the older but less favoured

Edward from the first relationship, and Edith from the second. From the most recent and most prestigious marriage, there was Æthelred, although he would have been very young, possibly looking at a decade-long minority.

There is a much later but possibly meaningless tradition that claims Edith was offered the throne a few years later, in 978. It is doubtful she would have been in play in 975 either, as early sources say nothing of an Edith claim in 978, let alone three years earlier. This leaves Edward and Æthelred as the remaining claimants in 975. Edward had the advantage of being older, but Æthelred was the son of an anointed queen and had routinely been listed in front of Edward in charter witness lists. Clearly Edward was a black sheep of the family, but he had powerful allies. Dunstan supported him, which can even be seen in a contemporary genealogy produced at Dunstan's monastery. It shows Edward listed above his half-brothers – a jarring change from how other sources arrange the names. The issue threatened to divide the kingdom again, which would have been a real possibility considering that it had happened not even a generation earlier. However, perhaps wishing to avoid a 957-style split, the nobility eventually coalesced around Edward, who was crowned by his main champion, Dunstan. Late sources like John of Worcester and William of Malmesbury claim this was by no means a unanimous decision though, going so far as to claim that Dunstan hastily assembled a partial group of councillors and bishops, who were sympathetic to him, and had Edward crowned before his opponents could object.[36] This allegation is refuted by a much earlier source, though: one of Æthelred's own charters says that Edward had actually been acclaimed unanimously.[37] In any case, the era of King Edward had begun, and he would be known to history as St Edward the Martyr.

With an epithet like 'the Martyr', perhaps we would expect Edward to be one of those beardless, cherub-like saints in Renaissance paintings, maybe with an arrow in his chest. There are a few accounts that seem to support this, at least until they are scrutinised. In *Gesta Regum Anglorum*, William of Malmesbury praises Edward as wise beyond his years, a young man who mirrored his father's piety, although William was writing long after Edward's sainthood was already established and he appears to be checking typical hagiographical boxes. In some cases, it appears that information about Edward's saintly personality has been outright fabricated. The most egregious example is a recurring quote from 'Theodoric Paulus' that says Edward was 'a young man of great devotion and excellent conduct'. Theodoric says Edward was 'wholly Orthodox', although the word 'Catholic' is sometimes substituted, and that he 'loved God and the Church'. A search for Theodoric Paulus quickly turns circular. His name only brings up that quote, and that quote is the only thing attributed to him. Whoever invented Theodoric even forgot to give him a profession, era, or nationality. He only exists to provide a fictitious quote about King Edward, but judging by the widespread repetition of the quote, the attempt has been successful.

Part of the reason someone like Theodoric Paulus had to be invented was because there are early, authentic sources that say Edward was anything but saintly. The case of Edward 'the Martyr' further illustrates why nicknames cannot be trusted, which will become a common theme. Edward was apparently an angry and violent young man. His profanity and aggression worked against him during the succession dispute, as *The Life of St. Oswald* (written *c.*1000) tells us that many preferred the younger Æthelred because 'he was gentler in speech and deeds'. Edward, on the other hand, was not just cruel to his enemies, but also to his own supporters. Edward 'inspired in all not only fear and even terror ... not only with words but even dire blows, and especially his own men dwelling with him'.[38] This account is especially significant because it was written at the same time Edward's cult was being vigorously promoted by the royal family. Such disturbing behaviour is unlikely to have been mentioned while Edward's star was on the rise – unless, of course, it was widely known. Given Edward's more ambiguous rank and frightening behaviour, maybe his accession says more about the political acumen of Dunstan than anything else.

The *ASC* gives a terse account of Edward's reign. A comet appeared. There was a famine. A building collapsed during a meeting, which left many important people dead except for Dunstan, who survived by 'standing on a beam'. The climax of the reign was its end: the young king was assassinated on March 18, 978. The most popular versions of the story claim that the murder happened while Edward was visiting his stepmother Queen Ælfthryth and his half-brother Æthelred at Corfe Castle, where he was stabbed to death by Æthelred's supporters (and in some versions, dragged along the road by his horse). A later retelling by Henry of Huntingdon has Queen Ælfthryth personally plunging the dagger into poor King Edward. A sermon by Archbishop Wulfstan, written around 1014, also preserves an otherwise unknown tradition, saying Edward's body was burned after the assassination.

However, the accounts in the *ASC* are far plainer. They say that 'no worse deed' was done than this murder, and they do set the murder at Corfe, but they do not place Ælfthryth and Æthelred there. The method of assassination is not specified, and the killer is left unnamed. One version laments that Edward's 'earthly relatives would not avenge him', passing some shaded judgment on the royal family, but just as soon relates that Æthelred, now King Æthelred II, assumed the throne amid 'great rejoicing'. Given this version's immediately favourable treatment of Æthelred, it is unlikely the annalist viewed him as a suspect. So why do much later versions blame him and his mother? Perhaps it is as simple as needing to fill in a blank space; the *ASC* does not identify a murderer, so later writers did. After all, the last king to be murdered, Edmund, has his killer identified – it was an outlaw named Liofa.[39] Why not Edward? Later scribes apparently corrected this glaring omission by blaming the people with the most to gain. However, blaming Æthelred doesn't make much sense due to his age. He was no more than 12 at the time, and possibly as young as 10, making it doubtful that he would be in a position to orchestrate his own coup. His mother is also an unlikely candidate. Although some modern writers have theorised that Queen Ælfthryth was in an 'anti-monastic' camp that gathered around Æthelred, and that this partially motivated the murder, this does not hold up to much scrutiny. She had in fact been part of the monastic reform movement, not one of its opponents, which led Simon Keynes to remark that she 'in particular fits badly in anti-monastic clothes'.[40] Ælfthryth's association with the murder also owes much to the 'wicked stepmother' trope that persists to this day.[41] Although it makes for a less colourful story, the only fair answer is to concede that Edward's killers are unknown.

What we do know for certain is that Edward was not given a proper royal burial until nearly a year later, making him an anomaly among early English kings. He was initially buried in Wareham, near the site of his assassination at Corfe Castle. Early commentators agreed that this internment was hasty and improper: the *ASC* says that Edward was buried without honour, while *The Life of St. Oswald* says that the corpse was brought to the home of a commoner and laid to rest without any Christian rites. In 979, nearly a year later, Edward's body was exhumed and relocated to Shaftesbury Abbey, finally receiving the honourable Christian burial that a king was expected to have. Stories later cropped up about divine retribution for the king's killers, one of whom was struck blind.[42] This divine vengeance, though, was necessary because Edward's killers ultimately went unpunished by earthly authorities. The murderers, although we do not know who they are, could have been politically powerful, and Æthelred may have been in no position to displace them so early in his administration. He owed his very position to them. However, it is possible that they made amends in other ways, such as by the payment of *weregild* – a fee that legally atoned for an individual's death, climbing in harshness in accordance with the slain person's rank.[43] Whether Edward's *weregild* was paid or not, medieval chroniclers clearly felt that any efforts to punish the killers were insufficient. The assassination of an anointed king was a dark cloud that loomed over Æthelred's reign, and Æthelred himself became a leading advocate of Edward's developing cult. In the short term, the killing put a permanent end to the 'Edward versus Æthelred' question, but in the long run, it ensured that the factionalism of the 970s lived on.[44]

Despite its obscurity, the short and turbulent reign of Edward the Martyr again highlights how divisive and unstable the early English kingdom could be, just as the earlier reign of Eadwig had. It also reinforces that Edgar's reign was an exception, not the rule, because the infighting that had plagued earlier reigns resurfaced immediately once Edgar was dead. That infighting would become an even more serious problem for England in the coming decades, not because the nature of factionalism changed, but because England would come under serious external pressure. If England was to weather the impending storm, the magnates would all need to unite around their king. The vikings were on the move.

2

The Vikings Return

The vikings returned to England in the 980s, the dawn of the 'Second Viking Age', but surprisingly little is known about their origins, intentions, and politics. The view from Denmark in the late tenth century (to pick the region that eventually had the largest impact) is not nearly as clear as the one from England. Even though English annals for this era are often biased toward recording military and ecclesiastical affairs, many of them were drafted relatively soon after the events they describe. Charters from the king's own administration provide an even more immediate and detailed look into the workings of late tenth-century England. In contrast, many of the Scandinavian literary sources that deal with this time come from centuries later. Historians are more reliant on other evidence, such as archaeological findings, to supplement these sagas and legends, although the narratives themselves are sometimes helpful. A rough picture of early Denmark's rulers has emerged from this evidence, although the most tantalising question of all – why the vikings decided to attack to England in the 980s – has more answers than one might imagine.

In the late tenth century, the area that would become Denmark was coalescing into one entity under a line of ambitious Scandinavian rulers who had rapidly expanded their territory in the preceding decades.[45] This dynasty goes by many names: the House of Denmark, the Jelling Dynasty, the House of Knýtlinga (the House of Cnut's Descendants), and others. One imaginative dynastic origin story comes from Saxo Grammaticus in *Gesta Danorum*, who writes that the dynasty was founded by an ancient ruler named Dan, who became the namesake of the Danish people. The more historically-grounded view is that the House of Denmark was founded by a figure known as Harthacnut I, followed by his son, Gorm the Old, although Gorm's historicity has been called into question by modern scholarship.[46] Gorm and Harthacnut, if they were both indeed historical members of the House of Denmark, were the grandfather and great-grandfather of Swein Forkbeard – the man who would conquer England.

Swein's father, Harald Bluetooth, is more firmly grounded in history, and his reign was a pivotal one in Danish history. Reigning from approximately the late 950s to the mid-980s, Harald was a dominant warlord who gained enough centralised control over Denmark to build impressive military encampments, such as the ring fortress of Trelleborg, the remains of which are still visible.[47] Harald was likely the first member of the line to convert to Christianity, with the famous Jelling runestone – one of the dynasty's namesakes – boasting that he controlled Denmark and Norway and converted the Danes to Christianity. Politically, Harald became the paramount figure among the many chieftains in early Denmark. In that sense, the early Danish kings were little different than the West Saxon rulers who were consolidating control over England in the mid-tenth century.

Sometime in the 950s or 960s, around the same time his father was establishing control over Denmark, Swein Forkbeard was born into this ascendant dynasty.[48] As the son of a notable Christianising king, Swein himself was a Christian; it is a common misconception that Swein was a pagan like the vikings of earlier ages. Some medieval chroniclers, like Adam of Bremen and Thietmar of Merseburg, denigrate Swein as a heathen, but modern scholars uniformly agree Swein was raised Christian and seems to have remained so.[49] Adam considered Swein a villain, which helps explain his portrayal, and also mirrors a wider trend for enemies of Scandinavians to generalise them as pagans even if this was no longer the case. In England, for example, the charters of Æthelred II and the writings of Archbishop Wulfstan II of York are notable for blanket-labelling their Scandinavian opponents as heathens, while later chroniclers like William of Malmesbury erroneously claimed Harald Bluetooth's children were pagans.[50] It is accurate to say that many Scandinavian leaders in previous centuries had been pagans, such as those faced by Alfred the Great in the 800s, but this was rapidly changing by the eleventh century. Aside from the fact that it makes little sense for a child of Harald Bluetooth to be pagan, there are medieval sources that support the notion that Swein was Christian. The *Encomium Emmae*, a relatively early source written in the 1040s, portrays the adult Swein as an ideal Christian who advised his son Cnut to zealously practice the faith. We need not go so far as the idealised portrait of piety from the *Encomium*, which has the purpose of glorifying Emma of Normandy and Cnut's dynasty, but it is probably closer to the truth on this matter than Adam of Bremen is.[51] Swein's Christianity is important to note because it is not just medieval writers who frame the conflict between England and Denmark as 'Christian versus pagan'. Some modern bestsellers do too, even though the majority of academics reject this. After overthrowing his father in the mid-980s, Swein raided throughout northern Europe in the following decade, with campaigns recorded in Frisia and the Isle of Man.[52] Swein was far from the only viking leader active near England and represents only the most prominent figure in a very broad pattern.

This brings up the question mentioned at the beginning of the chapter: why did the Second Viking Age occur? The old myth that vikings attacked England because they somehow 'sensed weakness' after the reign of Edgar does not hold up well. The theory quickly runs into problems when one realises that no viking attacks are recorded during the reign of Edward the Martyr, who was a boy king, and that viking attacks were recorded all over the British Isles. It would be vastly overstating England's importance to assume that every viking attack was about England rather than about what vikings could gain from the wider pattern of hit-and-run raiding. While the English certainly would have felt like the protagonists of their own story, there is no indication that vikings were fixated on England in particular at this stage. Over the years, several explanations have been offered for the resumption of widespread raiding in northern Europe, and they all probably had an impact to one degree or another. One contributor is thought to be the disappearance of Arabic silver from Scandinavian trade, thus necessitating other sources, such as England, that were rich in silver.[53] Another crucial factor is that the ascendant Jelling Dynasty in Denmark may have pushed aside some of its rivals, who sought their fortunes and glory elsewhere. Broader factors – an unseasonably warm climate, improved sailing technology, and pure opportunism – likely played a role, too.

The uptick in raiding activity in the late tenth and early eleventh centuries occurred during a favourable climatic era, the Medieval Warm Period. Norse outposts had already been established throughout the British Isles (Dublin and the earlier Kingdom of York are notable examples), but their exploration soon stretched much farther. Perhaps aided by calmer seas with less pack ice, Norse sailors reached the edges of the known world, beating Christopher Columbus to North America by several hundred years. Norse colonies were established in Greenland by about the year 1000, with two prominent settlements on its western shores.[54] Despite the common joke that Greenland's name is an early example of false advertising (an allegation likely inspired by *The Saga of Erik the Red*), the Greenland of 1000 would have indeed been much greener than today.[55] Norse settlers pressed even farther at this time, describing a land of flat rocks that was probably Baffin Island in modern day Nunavut, while recent analysis has shown that the Norse settlement at L'Anse Aux Meadows in Newfoundland was constructed from trees felled in 1021. Scandinavian coinage has even been found as far south as present day Maine, although the finding remains controversial.

The warmer climate undoubtedly aided this impressive and unprecedented pattern of exploration, but it was also made possible by advanced sailing technology that ranked among the best in the European world. Some Norse longships could carry nearly a hundred men and still sail quickly and nimbly. 'Long, sleek and flexible, they "snaked" through the waves at speeds which could easily exceed trading craft'.[56]

Finally, the simplest explanation for the resumption of viking attacks is sheer opportunism. With Denmark becoming more centralised, the seas becoming less icy, and sailing technology reaching new heights, is it any wonder that Scandinavians decided plunder their silver-rich neighbours? This behaviour is obviously not unique to the era or region. The Norse pirates who were known as vikings were simply better at it than anyone else.

Æthelred Comes to Power

Back in England, after Edward's assassination in 978, the throne had passed to Æthelred II, who was now the only surviving son of King Edgar. He was the latest in a long line of young kings – Edmund had gained the throne at 18, Eadred at about 22, Eadwig at 15, Edgar at 14, Edward at 16, and Æthelred was 12 at most. He had a different temperament than his predecessor, though. Whereas Edward was portrayed by a contemporary as unstable and vicious, Æthelred had the disposition of a king. *The Life of St. Oswald*, written during Æthelred's reign, preserves an early description of the new king as 'young in years, graceful in manners, beautiful in face, and comely in appearance'.[57] In his own history, John of Worcester includes a similar summation of the king's character and appearance. Even a late Norse saga echoes this, portraying the adult Æthelred as generous, dignified, and 'a good prince'.[58] After dealing with Edward, the powerful figures of England probably felt some relief that they had a king who could work with his leading men and take their counsel. Indeed he did, although the effects of this behaviour were not always positive.

Given these favourable descriptions, it may come as a surprise that this is the same Æthelred who would be known to posterity as Æthelred the Unready. It would be easy to assume that Æthelred's nickname refers to his youth and inexperience, but 'Unready' has nothing to do with that, as he would go on to record one of the longest reigns in early English history. The nickname itself is inaccurate, giving us our second king in a row with a misleading epithet. It turns out that unready is a mistranslation of an Old English word, *unraed*, that means ill-advised. *Æthel-raed* meant 'noble-counsel' in Old English, while *unraed* meant 'no-counsel' – an Old English pun. There is no hard evidence that the name was used during the king's lifetime, although some scholars have posited that it could have been contemporary.[59] More importantly, the nickname is a clue that some of those leading men, from whom Æthelred was so willing to take advice, were not the best of counsellors.

Although Æthelred would eventually be on the losing side of the Danish Conquest, at the time of his accession the conquest was nearly forty years away. The early and middle portions of Æthelred's reign were stable and prosperous. Many of the key figures in Edgar's reign, like Bishop Æthelwold and Queen Ælfthryth, remained in power in the early 980s.[60] Even the elderly Dunstan was still around, intervening in royal politics as late as 986, just two years before his death. The factions were still there, of course, but the early portions of the reign resemble Edgar's rule far more than they resemble the lead-up to the Danish Conquest. The absence of a figurehead to rally around also helped prevent any active opposition to Æthelred's administration.

There were no Cousin Æthelwolds running about, no half-brothers like Ælfweard (Æthelstan's rival) to get in the way. The 980s were arguably a calmer period politically than the mid- and late-970s had been.

There were omens, though. One version of the *ASC* says that in 979, the year after Æthelred succeeded to the throne, there were fiery portents seen at night, not unlike the 'dragons' that had preceded the first appearance of the vikings. Clouds as red as blood were visible over England at night, but they would vanish by sunrise. These could be dramatic details that were written into the account with hindsight, making England's downfall appear prophetic, but these meteorological displays may not be the work of a creative scribe. Other possibilities have been put forward, such as that this entry describes a southerly sighting of the aurora borealis.[61]

The *ASC* mentions that Æthelred was not consecrated until 979, but there was no great urgency. England was peaceful and prosperous, and there were no rival claimants to the throne to inspire a hasty ceremony. In all likelihood, the relative lack of external and internal pressure meant that the ceremony could be planned out well in advance and done properly.

The first sparks of renewed viking activity, however, occurred early in Æthelred's reign. The *ASC* reports that in 980, a small pirate fleet ravaged the coasts, such as in south-eastern England, where Kent was targeted. Farther west, 'Southampton was sacked ... and most of the citizens killed or taken captive'. A 'northern fleet' also attacked Cheshire. The 'northern' ships that raided Cheshire may be distinct from the fleet that attacked Kent and Southampton (which is only called 'a naval force', without specifying its origin). The Cheshire fleet, owing to its target in the northwest, may have come from the Irish Sea area, perhaps from the Isle of Man, Strathclyde, or Ireland.[62] If so, it would be the first of many such attacks that originated from the area early in Æthelred's reign.[63] However, references to Swein Forkbeard raiding the Isle of Man in the 990s mean that it was certainly possible for Scandinavians to target these western areas.[64]

The attacks of 980 were the first recorded pirate attacks on English shores in decades, but they had little to do with the later conquest. The D and E versions of the *ASC* (though lacking the detail about citizens being killed or captured) specify that the fleet that attacked Southampton was made up of just seven ships, a total that pales in comparison to the end stages of the conquest, which saw fleets of forty or more ships pass between different leaders like pawns on a chessboard. Even on the English side, fleets could number in the hundreds.[65] Furthermore, it is not actually stated that this fleet of seven ships was a 'viking' one. Normally when the *ASC* refers to viking attacks, it will use words like 'Danish' or 'northern'. It is generally assumed that the Southampton attack was a viking one, even if not from Scandinavia itself, and this is probably the most reasonable judgment to make; it is not, however, a given. The Cheshire attack, on the western fringes of Æthelred's realm, may in fact be the first instance of renewed viking (i.e., Scandinavian or Norse-influenced) attacks on England since it is explicitly said to be 'northern'.

More raids occurred in 981, but the origins of the attackers are again left out of the *ASC*'s entry. Their target was the southwest, with Devon and Cornwall being sacked, including the monastery of St Petroc in Padstow, Cornwall. These details bring to mind the earliest viking raids on record, which also targeted monasteries. This fleet may have originated from a similar region as the Cheshire ships of 980 (possibly the Irish Sea) judging by the choice to raid in the western portion of the British Isles. The year 982 saw another raid, albeit with a fleet numbering a mere three ships. Their identity though is certain: 'three ships of *vikings* arrived in Dorset and ravaged Portland'.[66] After this, there is no mention of pirate activity in the *ASC* for another five years. The attacks of 980–82, dramatic as they would have been to those in the areas directly affected, were evidently minor and haphazard events that warranted mentioning in the *ASC*, but had no known long-term effects. No response from King Æthelred or his regency was recorded, and perhaps none was needed.

The problem had been small in scale and unpredictable, and it fizzled out within a few years.

The attacks of 980–82 fit well within the broader context of neighbouring realms raiding each other regularly on minor scales. For example, the English themselves were launching raids into Wales during this time, such as a ravaging campaign in 983 and a vague 985 entry in the *Annales Cambriae* that says 'Idwal was killed by the English'.[67] Welsh kingdoms were subject to both English and viking aggression, it seems.

In 984, the powerful Bishop Æthelwold died, and the young king seems to have used the opportunity to his advantage. A decade later, Æthelred remembered Æthelwold fondly as someone who gave good counsel.[68] In 984, though, Æthelred was between 16 and 18 years old, of similar age to previous independently-ruling kings like Edmund, Eadwig, and Edward. Æthelred may have felt it was time to do the same and rule on his own, especially as the mid-teens generally appear to be the transition to adulthood in the medieval era.[69] There are signs of upheaval as the young king moved to establish himself. From 984 until 993, Queen Ælfthyrth disappears from witness lists. In 985, an ealdorman named Ælfric was expelled from office after a tenure of just two years.

The king probably also got married in the mid-980s, although the details are poorly recorded. One source names his royal wife as Ælfgifu but says she was the daughter of an ealdorman, Æthelberht, whose existence is otherwise unknown. Another leaves her unnamed but says she was the daughter of an Earl Thored, for whom there are some historical candidates. This patchwork information means that it is possible that Æthelred was married twice in his early years: to Ælfgifu and to an anonymous daughter of Thored. However, Æthelred's recent biographers think it is more likely that these sources combine to refer to the same woman: Ælfgifu, daughter of Thored.[70] Soon there was a series of royal births in quick succession. The king had several children by the early 990s, with at least four known sons and two daughters: two of the sons, Æthelstan and Edmund, would become significant in the later stages of the Danish Conquest. The daughters from this era were named Ælfgifu and Edith.[71] All the sons were named after previous kings, a pattern that would continue with Æthelred's younger sons Eadwig and Edgar. With the exception of an Egbert placed between Æthelstan and Edmund, the male names follow the chronological order of historical West Saxon kings, many of whom were discussed at more length in the previous chapter. The two known daughters were also given historically significant names, with Ælfgifu possibly being named after her mother, although she also shared the name with two previous royal wives, those of Edmund I and Eadwig. Edith, meanwhile, may have been named for Æthelred's half-sister Edith of Wilton, who had died in 984 and was soon regarded as a saint. Some of these children were brought up by their grandmother Ælfthryth, a clue afforded us by the will of the eldest child, Æthelstan: he recalls that his grandmother 'brought me up', and that he also had a 'foster mother', Ælfswith. Even though Æthelred himself could have barely been in his twenties by the end of the 980s, he and his wife had ensured that there were many potential successors to the throne, which is significant because just a decade earlier, Æthelred had been the last male of his direct line.

In 986, around the time this young royal family was being established, Æthelred led his first military campaign by ravaging the diocese of Rochester, apparently in response to a land dispute between the see and the king. The old Archbishop Dunstan made one final appearance in royal politics by urging Æthelred to back down, offering him 100 pounds of silver as tribute.[72] Ian Howard thinks Æthelred led one more campaign near the end of this period, in 988, based on charter evidence, although this is far from certain.[73] None of these events were particularly unusual, of course. Kings like Æthelstan, Edmund, Eadred, and Edgar led or ordered ravaging campaigns, including within England. Æthelred was shaping up to be a relatively ordinary king who was more occupied with regional politics and enforcing his will than he was with vikings. After all, from 983 to 987, vikings were nowhere to be found in Æthelred's England.

The next raid did not occur until 988, when the *ASC* says Watchet was attacked by a force of unknown size and origin. This time, the invaders were confronted: 'Goda, the Devonshire thegn, was killed, and many fell with him'. *The Life of St. Oswald* may also refer to this same incident when it remarks that 'a very severe battle took place in the west, in which our countrymen, who are called Devonshiremen, strongly resisted and obtained the victory of a holy triumph, thus gaining glory. Many of our side fell, more of theirs'. These two sources combine to give the impression that Watchet was attacked, but the raiders (possibly vikings from the Irish Sea again, judging by the westerly target) were successfully resisted. It was not a victory without serious casualties, but with help from forces from nearby Devonshire, further damage was prevented. It may seem surprising that the English managed to confront and defeat these probable vikings, but if the attack was on a similar scale to earlier ones (perhaps three to seven ships), it seems less unlikely. And apparently it was successful – no other raids are known for 988.

The years 989 and 990 marked a return to the calmness of 983–987, with no viking attacks mentioned in the *ASC*. As usual, there was some drama internally in the mid- and late-980s as ealdormen rose and fell from favour and clerics died and were replaced, but from the vantage point of the year 990, Æthelred's England was not in a bad position. There had been more viking activity than in the reigns of Eadwig, Edgar, and Edward the Martyr, but the raids themselves had been isolated and small in scale. This is a significant point considering that popular history often portrays Æthelred's reign as a disaster from start to finish, marred by serious incursions for nearly forty years. Æthelred himself is often accused of trying to buy off vikings with tribute payments rather than fighting them. In reality, over Æthelred's first twelve years on the throne, not a single tribute payment was made to vikings, and incursions were stopped by local resistance on at least one occasion (Watchet in 988). As will be discussed later in the chapter, Æthelred's government also took steps to fortify sites in the south and west of England – the areas most affected by the raids of 980–990 – and even areas farther inland like Oxford, whose fortifications date from *c*.990.[74] It demonstrates a foresight rarely credited to Æthelred or his administration: the raids were not severe enough to impact England as a whole yet, but Æthelred was taking steps to refurbish defences throughout the kingdom anyway. By 990, Æthelred had already reigned longer than many of his predecessors had, so the popular caricature of the shortsighted ruler who solved problems with money falls flat unless one entirely ignores the period of 978–990.

Another important consideration is that England was not merely a victim of warlike aggression at this time. It was also an instigator, as the 983 and 985 *Annales Cambriae* entries showed. The king himself was on the move militarily as well, flaunting his royal power by ravaging Rochester just as previous strong kings had harried within England to maintain order or get their way. The 980s were ordinary rather than extraordinary in this way, but the early 990s would see the first major invasion of England that warranted a response from the king himself: a ninety-three-ship fleet that threatened England and culminated in the Battle of Maldon.

In 991, these ninety-three ships amassed off the eastern English coast and sacked Ipswich before turning toward Maldon, a town about thirty-five miles to the southwest. According to the A manuscript of the *ASC*, these vikings were led by the Norwegian warlord Olaf Tyrggvason. While Olaf would go on to win greater fame in England and beyond, there is another figure who may have been in the mix in the invasion of 991: Swein Forkbeard, the king of Denmark who would spearhead the conquest of England decades later. The *ASC* only mentions Swein in connection to one campaign in England in this decade, in 994, but a charter of Æthelred's from the 990s strongly implies that Swein was in England on more than one occasion in those years. It says, 'It was many years before Æthelric died that the king was told that he was concerned in the treacherous plan that Swein should be received in Essex when he *first* came there with a fleet; and the king before many witnesses informed Archbishop Sigeric of it…'[75] The chronological details provided in the charter – that Æthelred learned of the plot to receive Swein during the tenure of Archbishop Sigeric – tell us that Swein was in England on more than one occasion between 990 and 994. Perhaps he accompanied or supplemented the Maldon army with his own fleet from Denmark.[76] It is also possible that the charter preserves evidence of an otherwise unknown assault on Essex, perhaps one that took a back seat to the Battle of Maldon.[77] Either way, we can now throw Swein's hat into the ring for 991 as well.

As was the case at Watchet, the viking army was confronted by a regional leader; Byrhtnoth, ealdorman of Essex, arrived to defend the fortified town of Maldon. He 'came against [Olaf] there with his army and fought against him; and they killed the ealdorman there and had control of the field'.[78] A rather different account can be found in the *Liber Eliensis*, which portrays the episode as two battles in 991, one in which Byrhtnoth is victorious and one in which he is defeated and beheaded.

However, the events of Maldon are most famously relayed by the fragmentary poem that now bears the battle's name. *The Battle of Maldon* survives in 325 lines, and although there is no way to know how much more has been lost, it offers a glimpse into how the battle was remembered in England. In the poem, Byrhtnoth readies his men for battle and rebuffs the vikings' offers to be bought off. The viking messenger calls out: '...it will be better for you all that you buy off an attack with tribute, rather than that men so fierce as we should give you battle. There is no need that we destroy each other, if you are rich enough for this. In return for the gold we are ready to make a truce with you'. Byrhtnoth's immortal reply ensured that the vikings would not receive tribute without a fight: 'Hear you, searover, what this folk says? For tribute they will give you spears, poisoned point and ancient sword, such war gear as will profit you little in the battle'.[79]

Byrhtnoth dies a hero's death in the poem, and many of his closest companions follow him to the grave. Those who flee, on the other hand, are named and shamed. The poem reads like propaganda – the characters in the poem are from all over England (soldiers from Essex, Mercia, and Northumbria are mentioned), but when they unite to face a common foe, it is to protect 'the home of Ethelred'. Many of them embody the ideal warrior spirit: tribute should not be offered without a hard-fought struggle; the bonds of lordship are so strong that one must be willing to give his life in battle for his lord if need be; and those who flee are not only cowards, but also considered to have betrayed their lord. One such character, Godric, 'turned his back on war, forsook the hero who had given him many a steed'. He and his brothers, who also fled, had not 'remembered all the favors that [Byrhtnoth] had done them for their good'. The Maldon poem, idealised as it may be, illustrates the most foundational aspects of lordship and warfare, where boasting on the mead bench had to be backed up with loyalty in the battlefield.

Sometimes the significance of a historical event is overstated as a 'watershed moment' or 'turning point' in hindsight. The Battle of Maldon does represent an escalation of hostilities, though. The Norse army at Maldon was nowhere close to toppling the English kingdom (Thorkell the Tall's invasion of 1009–1012 is a much stronger candidate for that), nor did it seem to want anything more than loot and tribute. But at the time, its strength was unparalleled. The attacking fleet was more than ten times the size of the next largest to appear within living memory. It was also possibly the first fleet of the reign to originate from Scandinavia proper, rather than the Norse-influenced regions bordering the Irish Sea.

After the defeat, Archbishop Sigeric 'the Serious' advised King Æthelred to pay tribute to the vikings.[80] It was the first time that Æthelred paid tribute, often inaccurately called 'the Danegeld'. A millennium later, it was anachronistically compared to the twentieth-century policy of appeasement. However, it is better understood as coming to terms after military efforts have already proven unsuccessful. In 991 (as with all subsequent tribute payments under Æthelred), the English only paid off the vikings after trying more forceful methods first. The English had been defeated with heavy losses after a battle (or after two battles, if the *Liber Eliensis* is to be trusted) before the archbishop convinced the king to pay tribute. The king thus did not act contrary the famous speech attributed to Byrhtnoth. The English did not freely and peacefully offer tribute, as Olaf's messenger was lobbying for. Only after the battle did it make sense to pay up, and in doing so, the English did not violate any of the norms of the time. As mentioned earlier, kings like Alfred had used tribute, while others like Eadred were prepared for it and left no indication that it was shameful or unkingly.

Scandinavia and the Irish Sea were not the only thorns in England's side, though. Across the channel, the nascent duchy of Normandy was causing problems for Æthelred, although the exact nature of their enmity is unclear. In March 991, Pope John XV sent out a letter to 'all the faithful' that summarised a peace agreement between Æthelred and Richard I of Normandy. The letter says that the Pope sent one of his legates, Bishop Leo of Treves, to England to seek a resolution to the hostility. After summoning his leading counsellors, Æthelred agreed to 'a most firm peace'. The king sent an entourage to Normandy to relay his decision, which Richard accepted. Unfortunately, the cause of the conflict is not mentioned in the letter, but it was serious enough that the Pope was aware of it and actively sought to quell it. It is traditionally assumed to relate to the viking raids on England – such as if Normandy had been offering shelter to vikings – but this raises other questions. Why would the Church, all the way up to the Pope, be involved in arbitrating a dispute over trading stolen goods or offering shelter to pirates? Even at the pinnacle of the Danish Conquest, twenty-five years later, the papacy did not intervene. Given the Church's involvement, the arbitration treaty is more likely about pilgrims or other Church affairs.[81]

Another connection to Normandy comes nearly a decade later, in 1000, when the *ASC* says that vikings left England for Normandy. Around the same time, Æthelred sent a naval force to ravage Normandy. Finally, in 1002, Æthelred married Emma of Normandy, whose brother was by then Richard II. The general picture that emerges from the early 990s to early 1000s is one of suspicion and sporadic conflict between England and Normandy, which could be resolved through diplomatic means. Normandy and England would remain allies – although possibly uneasy ones – all the way through the Danish Conquest.

After dealing with the defeat at Maldon, a tribute payment, and a peace negotiation with Normandy, Æthelred turned his focus to military affairs. He decreed in 992 that 'all the ships that were of any use' should be collected at London so that they could be used to trap the vikings out at sea.[82] This entry is often read in a dismissive light, as if the annalist knew that Edgar's once-impressive fleet was no longer in fighting shape nearly fifteen years into a successor's reign. However, even though the chronicler was writing with the benefit of hindsight, it is possible that the entry instead refers to an emergency request for *any* suitable vessels to assemble, whether they were technically part of a 'naval force' or not. Tenth- and eleventh-century writers may not have even categorised them differently; historians like Ryan Lavelle and Hirokazu Tsurushima have noted 'the likelihood that there was no clear distinction between "naval" and "civilian' vessels" in the first place'.[83] Whether the entry is referring to a decaying royal fleet or a broader call for civilian ships to join the effort, there was no time to construct a naval force from scratch. Æthelred had stopped the immediate damage with his tribute payment, but he needed to act quickly.

His emergency fleet failed to accomplish its ambitious goals, however, which the *ASC* blames on an ealdorman, Ælfric, warning the vikings in an act of deliberate treachery. Supposedly Ælfric fled from his own camp, but not before he sent a messenger to warn the vikings of an impending attack, allowing them to escape. Ælfric did not lose his rank and served through the end of the reign though, meaning that outright treachery is probably an exaggeration of his offence, whatever it was. The ealdorman was also present at a sea battle later in 992 that led to his temporary capture, so clearly he was not always slinking away from conflict. In any case, the *ASC* makes it clear that Æthelred's emergency fleet of 992 failed to bring the vikings to heel. It did succeed in slaying the crew of a single enemy ship, and it later brought the vikings to battle at sea (the same event that led to Ælfric and his ship being captured), but the encounter was a defeat for the English. Æthelred's administration was attempting to solve the viking problem with warlike measures, but their results were mixed at best. They managed to locate and engage their opponents at least twice that we know of in 992, but failed to deal them any lasting damage.

The bloodshed continued in 993, when a viking army sacked Bamburgh and wreaked havoc throughout Northumbria and Lindsey. The *ASC* records that 'a very large English army' was then collected, led by three men named Fraena, Godwine, and Frythegyst, but that these leaders fled just as the army was ready to do battle. The king himself was not with this large army, and may not have even been involved in its assembly, due to the great distance between it and his bases far to the south. It has often been pointed out that the area Æthelred had to defend was much larger than the territory Alfred had to cover a hundred years earlier, meaning that it was not possible for the king to be involved in (or even immediately aware of) every encounter between local forces and highly mobile viking armies. As such, the king had to depend on subordinates to act as the first line of defence, a practice defended by his contemporary Ælfric the Homilist, and this also helps explain his decision to delegate leadership of the fleet of 992 to four individuals: two secular magnates and two bishops. In the chronicler's view, it was the lack of competence of these subordinates that undermined the king's often sensible commands – Æthelred himself is almost never criticised, but the next rung of leadership is frequently shamed for its incompetence and cowardice.

In 994, England again was under attack, this time by a force led by Swein Forkbeard and Olaf Tryggvason. With ninety-four ships at their disposal, these great warlords of Scandinavian history descended upon London. The besieged Londoners resisted successfully, forcing the vikings to abandon the effort and head to the coasts and the open country where they could ravage unimpeded. Æthelred again ordered that a tribute payment should be offered, although the implications of this one were more significant. The bargain struck between the king's administration and the viking leaders was less of a bribe this time and more of a mutually beneficial agreement. The vikings would be given money and provisions, but Olaf was to become Æthelred's Christian godson. It was a tactic that Alfred had famously used against the viking leader Guthrum in the ninth century, and Æthelred took a page out of Alfred's playbook by binding Olaf close to him. Olaf also agreed that he would never again visit England's shores with ill-intent, a promise that he kept.[84]

A relevant document from this time, known as *II Æthelred,* gives us a glimpse into the sort of agreements that English kings could make with viking armies. It also reveals something innovative about Æthelred's strategy. Besides the tribute and confirmation, which were methods conspicuously borrowed from previous successful kings, Æthelred was trying something different. A contingent of the viking force would switch sides and defend England against other viking raiders, and the document 'reads more like a contractual agreement for mercenary troops than a peace treaty'.[85] The strategy of hiring one's enemies as mercenaries does call to mind the methods used in the late Western Roman Empire and eventually West Francia.[86] However, the use of mercenaries was not common practice among early English kings, with Alfred as a possible exception.[87] For the most part, 'it was not until the end of the tenth century that the English state began to hire mercenaries in earnest'.[88] If Æthelred's regime is sometimes accused of being unimaginative in response to the viking threat, the decision to hire some of them as mercenaries is a notable exception, evidenced by the rarity of this strategy in the preceding centuries.

The context of *II Æthelred* even helps make sense of the Maldon poem's portrayal of the vikings of 991. In the Maldon poem, they are not presented as bloodthirsty, mindless barbarians, but as a reasonable, calculating opponents. Leonard Neidorf has argued that because the poem was written in the context of the diplomatic agreements between Æthelred and the vikings in the mid-990s, such as *II Æthelred*, the Maldon poet had to be careful not to openly oppose any of his own king's commands.[89] *II Æthelred* states that damage inflicted prior to agreement must not be avenged.[90] If the Maldon poet knew of these details, as Neidorf argues, it could explain the relatively benign portrayal of the viking messengers and army in the Maldon poem. At the time of writing, these warriors had probably already come to terms with the English, and Olaf Tryggvason himself became Æthelred's godson in 994, presumably undertaking his campaigns in Scandinavia with Æthelred's approval, if not outright support. The Maldon poet obviously had incentive not to demonise them.

Olaf was received by Æthelred with much pomp and ceremony, and after his confirmation as Æthelred's godson (and a hefty tribute payment), he departed for Norway. There, he set about accomplishing Æthelred's real strategy: dividing his enemies. Swein is glaringly absent from the *II Æthelred* agreement, and it could be that Æthelred was unable to forge the kind of permanent bond with Swein that he had with Olaf. It could also be that Æthelred never intended to, and that he wished to turn these allied vikings against each other. Non-English sources record that there had been bad blood between Swein and Æthelred long before the Danish Conquest. A Scandinavian saga asserts that Swein once swore to kill or oust Æthelred before three winters had passed, while Adam of Bremen alleges that Swein had been exiled from Denmark at one point and sought refuge in England, only for Æthelred to rebuff him.[91] On the other hand, the bond between Olaf and Æthelred was strong enough that it was mentioned in a Norse saga of Olaf. It recalled that Æthelred's son, Edward the Confessor, would reminisce about how his father was good pals with one of the bloodiest vikings of all time: 'King Edward did not forget the friendship which had been between King Ethelred his father and King Olaf Tryggvason. King Edward made it his custom on the first day of Easter to relate to his chief men and courtiers the saga of Olaf Tryggvason ... out of the very same book which Olaf himself had sent to King Ethelred from Jerusalem'.[92]

All these tales of exile, boasting, and saga-reading may be legendary, but they illustrate the pronounced difference between Swein and Olaf in relation to England. They also correctly highlight that England operated within the Scandinavian world, rather than outside it, where English kings were honoured in sagas alongside viking heroes and exchanged gifts with some Norse warlords while others plotted against them.

After his confirmation, Olaf left England, and he soon began a protracted war in Norway, a kingdom that Swein also claimed. Olaf and Swein had gone from co-leaders of a triumphant army to bitter enemies, and Æthelred was the wedge between them. The English king was funding (directly or indirectly) Olaf's Norwegian campaigns, a tactic that 'succeeded utterly', in a medieval example of dividing one's enemies.[93]

Swein also left after the agreement of 994. He was a long way from Denmark, but he did not head home immediately. In the *Annales Cambriae*, Swein is recorded as leading an attack on the Isle of Man in 995, a viking attacking a viking-influenced region.[94] Swein's target illustrates an important point: most 'viking' regions were not allied with each other, instead viewing their counterparts as rivals. There was no grand strategy that pitted all vikings against all the English. The vikings of the Isle of Man had most likely been among those who attacked England in the 980s and 990s, but that did not mean they were immune from attacks by the king of Denmark. This was an age when any king was happy to exploit a weaker neighbour, an era when strong leaders dominated lesser ones. Swein's ambitions were great, even at this early stage, where he had won great treasures in England only to set off to the Irish Sea in search of more.

Back in England, Æthelred came face to face with the opportunistic nature of other vikings as well. The protection offered by his Norse mercenaries was only temporary. From 997 to 999, a viking fleet was again active along the southern coast. The *ASC* makes no mention of the king's mercenaries opposing them. In fact, this fleet probably included some of them, a detail provided by John of Worcester and accepted by historians like Marc Morris and Levi Roach.[95] We can only guess whether the entirety of the mercenary fleet suddenly decided to attack or whether they simply joined a group that had arrived from the Irish Sea or Scandinavia. Whatever their composition, their itinerary was well recorded in the *ASC*. They spent 997 raiding in Devon and Cornwall, but this was not merely an attack on the English; Wales was fair game, too. Soon they turned back toward south-western England and went up the River Tamar until they were possibly repelled at Lydford, which was heavily fortified.[96]

Lydford's earthworks had been in place for at least a century and may have been a deterrent for the pirates of 997, but Æthelred also took measures to refurbish other sites in the 990s and early 1000s. An English mint was moved to an Iron Age hillfort at Old Sarum in Wiltshire; Shaftesbury, Dorset was renovated; strategic coastal sites such as Hastings, Sandwich, and Dover were established or significantly refurbished. Farther inland, Oxford was also given defensive upgrades in this era – an insightful decision given that Oxford would be attacked later in the reign. Archaeologist Jeremy Haslam notes that these systematic defensive efforts '...belong to this phrase of royal aggrandizement and renewed military preparedness in the last decade of the tenth century, which represented a heightened level of royal authority'.[97]

The viking fleets may have stepped up their game since the 980s, but so had the English. Putting aside the fact that the fleets of the preceding fifteen years operated independently of one another, clearly England had become an attractive target. Vikings were able to successfully raid England and Wales in a hit-and-run manner, and they were at their most successful when managing to avoid local levies and fortified towns, especially as those towns were becoming increasingly well-defended. In the following decade, the pattern of success in the open country and along the coasts, but only mixed results against towns and *burhs*, would become more pronounced.

While the *ASC* does not explicitly mention any English resistance against the invaders in 997, a diploma from that year called S 891 provides a clue that the king did take immediate measures to stop the vikings. The diploma mentions that the king summoned 'the whole army' that year – a stark reminder that it can be dangerous to argue too much from the *ASC*'s silence.[98] Even though the effects of this English army are unknown, S 891 does show the king resorting to military solutions during a time when he is rarely credited with doing so.

For the next year, 998, the *ASC* itself concedes that the 'English army was often assembled against them'. Despite this persistence, the *ASC* adds that 'as soon as they were to have joined battle, a flight was always instigated by some means, and always the enemy had the victory in the end'. In 999, this viking fleet was active farther east, sailing up the Thames and Medway before laying siege to Rochester.[99] An English army from Kent tried to lift the siege, fighting against the vikings at Rochester, 'joining battle stoutly'. After this initial good showing, the Kentish army fled. The E version of the *ASC* claims that this was because they did not have as much support as they should have – perhaps an annoyed reference to the king's absence. As for the king, he too decided that the vikings should be opposed on both land and sea. While not a seafaring king like Cnut the Great, Æthelred repeatedly emphasised the importance of ships throughout his reign. He had constructed a fleet in 992, hired one *c.*994 that likely turned against him, and gave orders for another one to assemble in 999. It would certainly not be the last time the king was associated with ship fleets. However, it appears that the 999 ships never got out of the harbour to begin with. The *ASC*'s entry for this year includes a lengthy diatribe about the fleet's mismanagement, complaining that the endeavour was plagued by constant delays that frustrated the shipmen and wasted money. The chronicler includes few details about the land component the king had ordered, other than that they, along with the ships, had no impact on the vikings. These delays allowed the vikings' strength 'to increase', perhaps referring to a missed opportunity after the battle at Rochester. By failing to strike while the iron was hot, the English allowed the vikings to recover their strength with no further resistance.

Not everything was trending downward in 990s England, though. Perhaps surprisingly, Æthelred's reign was a time of significant literary output, with some of the most notable Old English writers springing into action at approximately this time. Ælfric of Eynsham, one of the most prolific writers of his era, was active in the 990s and 1000s, as was Wulfstan of York, who is best known for his energetic homilies from the early eleventh century. More familiar to the modern reader is the epic poem *Beowulf*, whose surviving manuscript is generally thought to have been produced in Æthelred's long reign. Although the poem itself is probably centuries older than this copy, the events of Æthelred's reign likely served as a convenient backdrop to *Beowulf's* themes of war, invasion, and monstrous dangers. Many of the famous writers and works from Æthelred's reign were surely influenced by the ongoing viking incursions, including the aforementioned Wulfstan, who was often concerned with the end of the world.[100] The sheer volume of their output, however, shows that the situation could not have been as hopeless as popular history would lead one to believe. Even during the escalating attacks of the 990s, England was stable enough for writers to produce works of all sizes and themes that are still enjoyed today.

Among the most interesting tactics Æthelred used in the 990s and onward was his own piety. Æthelred became openly introspective, demonstrating a style of 'penitential kingship' in his surviving diplomas. Æthelred began to reflect on some of the mistakes of his youth. He regretted his 986 raid on Rochester, confiscating land from churches, and taking advice from corrupt ministers. Æthelred, whose name meant 'noble-counsel', was admitting that he was *unraed*, or badly counselled. Seen in isolation, this may only appear to mean that the king had grown up and was demonstrating more maturity. In connection to the viking attacks, especially the significant ones like Maldon, it has a deeper subtext. Æthelred had been tutored by Bishop Æthelwold and taught (to put it simply) that a ruler's personal morality affected the state of the kingdom. God could punish nations whose people or rulers acted sinfully, a mindset that was not exclusive to tenth-century England.[101] This general view can be seen in other kings, such as Louis the Pious of France, and in later medieval chroniclers like William of Malmesbury.[102] During the very first wave of viking attacks in the 790s, the famous scholar Alcuin had produced a series of letters with the same overall theme: the people's immorality was leading God to punish them with viking raids. With this in mind, it is a very real possibility that Æthelred perceived the viking attacks of the 980s and 990s, large and small, as a divine punishment.

The remorseful language in Æthelred's charters was not just for show – it appears to have been genuine, as the king backed up his words with actions. Throughout the 990s, he restored land that he believed he had taken unfairly. He removed advisors who had taken advantage of his youth in the 980s. His mother, Queen Ælfthryth, returned to a prominent position at court by 993, after nearly a decade of absence.[103] The king's uncle, Ordulf, (Ælfthryth's brother) was prominent in this era and would remain so until his retirement in 1006. Ordulf had also attested charters prominently in the 980s, albeit more intermittently, but the importance of Ordulf's circle was 'unmistakable' by 990.[104] A sign that points to the king's sincerity is the inclusion of potentially embarrassing or incriminating details in charters from this era. Æthelred repeatedly stresses his youth as an explanation for his previous behaviour, pointing out that his maturity has allowed him to see that he has sinned against God and the Apostles – and he fears their judgment. While the emphasis on his youth serves as something of a mitigating factor, the king also has plenty of blame for previous advisors: counsellors Ælfric, Wulfgar, and Æthelsige are named and shamed. However, Æthelred also accepts the blame and moves to restore lands and rights he had unjustly taken.

This surprisingly specific and personal turnabout shows that Æthelred himself was involved in crafting the messages of these charters; he was not merely following the lead of ambitious clerics at court. Most stunningly, and unusually for a monarch of this era, this means we likely have something of the king's 'voice' preserved for posterity. The charters themselves employ different styling and wording throughout, meaning they are almost certainly the work of different draftsmen. Roach notes that 'the only significant similarities are to be found in the narrative sections discussing Æthelred's misdeeds and even here the similarities are mostly thematic... That these ideas came from the king himself therefore seems probable'.[105] Æthelred may have even had some competence in Latin given his upbringing and education.[106] Even if the king did not necessarily dictate these passages word for word, he was obviously involved in their production and messaging.

This public effort to atone for one's sins (and perhaps restore divine favour) may seem foreign to some modern readers, but in Æthelred's time, it was seen as a wholly rational approach. It is also important to note that it was not the whole solution. Æthelred sometimes receives more flack than he deserves for trying to 'pray away' the vikings, but it was only one part of a many-pronged strategy. Military resistance through ealdormen like Byrhtnoth was the first line of defence, but diplomatic successes like *II Æthelred* and the eventual confirmation of Olaf, a shakeup of royal advisors, revamping fortifications, and the king's own piety were parts of an overarching effort to improve the state of the kingdom.

The king's prayers were seemingly answered in the summer of 1000, when the viking fleet of 997–99 left for Normandy. Despite the damage they had caused along the southern coasts, they disappeared without an obvious reason. No tribute payment is mentioned. No agreement was struck. No decisive defeat was inflicted on them. Perhaps the English army and fleet of 999 were more effective than the chronicler lets on.[107] Either way, the vikings' departure gave Æthelred's administration a chance to regroup and reconsider its strategies. Many of the fleets that had plagued his coasts in the preceding twenty years had come from the Irish Sea, and this most recent one had departed for Normandy. These details help explain the new, aggressive Æthelred present at the start of the next millennium. No longer would he be content with reactive measures. Beginning in the year 1000, the English king was on the move, striking wider and farther than any English king since Æthelstan.

Æthelred Strikes Back (1000-02)

> *All the host of the generous and dauntless Prince fears England's Lord as a god, and the sons of men do homage to Ethelred.*[108]
>
> Fragment of a Scandinavian poem in honour of Æthelred

After the fleet of 997–999 left for Normandy, Æthelred did something seemingly out of character. According to the *ASC*, he marched north to Strathclyde (or Cumberland) with his army in 1000 and 'ravaged very nearly all of it'. A naval force was supposed to rendezvous with him there, but was unable to do so, raiding the Isle of Man instead (John of Worcester clarifies that it had been blown off course). It is not known what the fleet's ultimate goal had been, whether they were primarily present for supply reasons or whether they were supposed to link up with the king's land force for a more ambitious purpose. Either way, raiding the Isle of Man (which, like Strathclyde, was heavily Norse-influenced at this time) ensured that even if the target itself had changed, the fleet could still inflict damage on a viking outpost.[109]

Leading armies is not something Æthelred had done previously, other than during the harrying campaign against the see of Rochester in 986. The Strathclyde campaign had higher stakes, though. Strathclyde was much farther away from Wessex than Rochester was, and it was enemy territory. Because many viking raids originated from there, scholars often interpret Æthelred's campaign of 1000 as a response to this. Else Roesdahl writes that 'King Æthelred himself plundered heavily in north-west England and the Isle of Man, presumably in order to crush the Scandinavian peoples there'.[110] Æthelred's biographers and experts of medieval Strathclyde have followed a similar line of reasoning.[111] Another of Æthelred's biographers, Ryan Lavelle, points out that the king may have had more abstract goals in mind, even though it was an 'audacious attack'. Æthelred was emphasising that he, like his father Edgar, had wider, perhaps even imperial, ambitions: 'We can get a glimpse of the bigger picture in which the king saw himself. This was an English identity which manifested itself in conquering others, a king over other kings...'[112]

There is no indication in the medieval sources that the fleet met with any kind of resistance on the Isle of Man, but there is a clue that the king's army in Strathclyde met with some opposition. Henry of Huntingdon, a twelfth-century chronicler, mentions that Æthelred's 'very heavy army ... overcame the Danes in a great battle, and in ravaging he laid waste nearly all of Cumberland'.[113] Henry is only rarely consulted by experts of Æthelred's reign, and for good reason: he repeats many of the most dubious and far-fetched tales about the king and was writing over a century later. His obvious bias against the king makes him suspect. However, Henry's portrayal of the Strathclyde campaign is oddly triumphant. The detail about the successful 'great battle' is not found in other sources, and Henry omits the potentially embarrassing detail about the fleet going off course. Henry's distaste for Æthelred is well-known and problematic, but his flattering portrayal of the king 'overcoming the Danes in a great battle' seems bizarre when considering these biases. Could Henry have had access to useful details about this campaign (much like how John of Worcester included details about the fleet being blown off course) that were otherwise unrecorded? Henry's depiction of Strathclyde as 'the Danes' especial lodging place', is also surprisingly accurate and in line with the views of modern scholars, who frequently recognise its Norse connections.[114] It is worth considering that the Strathclyde campaign involved more than mere raiding and foraging and that a battle between the English and Cumbrians took place, resulting in a lopsided English victory. The very fact that this detail comes from

Henry means that it needs to be taken with a pinch of salt (or perhaps an entire cup of salt), as it could be little more than another example of colourful storytelling. However, Henry does get the context of the situation – that Strathclyde was a hostile area – correct, and it would hardly be surprising for an English invasion to be met with resistance, perhaps by some of the same warriors who were normally on the other side of the pillaging.

Battle or not, the Strathclyde campaign was a success, and it is possible that Strathclyde's rulers would have recognised Æthelred as their overlord in the succeeding years.[115] At the very least, Æthelred was 'removing its capacity to fight back', by systematically ravaging nearly all of the region.[116] Although its history is poorly recorded, the kingdom of Strathclyde collapsed at some point in the following decades. The other (accidental) target, the Isle of Man, was likewise in an unfortunate position following the campaigns of 1000. It had been raided by Swein Forkbeard, the future conqueror of England, just five years before Æthelred's fleet did the same.

Strathclyde and the Isle of Man were not Æthelred's only targets at this time, though. The king also reportedly sent part of his fleet to ravage the Contenin peninsula in Normandy. A Norman writing in the 1070s, William of Jumièges, recalls that Æthelred's fleet attacked Normandy and sought to capture Duke Richard II. Richard II was the son of Richard I, who had agreed to peace with Æthelred in 991. The *ASC* notes that the vikings of 997–99 departed for 'Richard's kingdom' in 1000, referring to Richard II of Normandy, which allowed Æthelred time to strike at the northwest. It is not stated directly, but the implication may be that Normandy was a staging point for England's enemies. This could help explain the king's decision to send a fleet to essentially conduct 'a Viking raid in reverse' on Normandy.[117] According to William of Jumièges, the raid on Normandy was not a success. A local noble named Nigel repelled the English with a coalition of peasants and women, a detail intended as an insult to the masculinity of the English attackers.[118] The English were driven back to their ships and had to return to England in shame. William does not provide an exact date for the attack. Historian Eric John placed it in or before 991, seeing it as a precursor to the papal agreement between England and Normandy in 991.[119] However, Richard II was Æthelred's target, not Richard I, which would place the attack after Richard I's death in 996. The Normandy raid must have also taken place before Æthelred's marriage to Emma of Normandy in 1002, as the two territories were allied from that point on and were still on friendly enough terms in 1013 to serve as Æthelred's place of exile. Æthelred's biographers place the Normandy attack sometime in 1000–1002.[120]

However, given the late composition and flamboyant details of the story, its reliability is suspect. It also suffers from chronological problems, as the 'Nigel' who led the Norman defences did not actually come to power until the 1020s.[121] That said, the core of the story is likely authentic, meaning that Æthelred probably did conduct some type of raid on Normandy around the turn of the millennium.[122] It fits well within the overall context of long-running tensions between England and Normandy from 991 to 1002 (which is a conservative estimate because we do not know how much earlier than 991 the two had been at odds). The biggest looming question is why the *ASC* does not mention it, given that the chronicler seems to relish in English defeats. That question cannot be answered, but it is worth remembering that while the *ASC*'s military focus is broad, it is not exhaustive – a good example is how the *ASC* says nothing of Æthelred summoning his army in 997, but charters from that year reveal that he did so.

More significantly, the Normandy attack, *c.*1000, could have helped prompt Æthelred's marriage to Emma in 1002. Richard II may have repelled an English invasion once, but with Æthelred enjoying military success elsewhere in the early 1000s, there was no guarantee that Normandy would be so fortunate next time. It was more strategic to make peace with Æthelred and gain prestige by marrying into an ancient royal dynasty that had ruled Wessex for centuries. Normandy had also successfully used diplomacy to reconcile with England just a decade earlier.

As nebulous as the conflict between England and Normandy appears to us due to the lack of specifics in the sources, Æthelred's marriage to Emma highlights how seriously he took Normandy as a potential friend or foe. It was unconventional for early English kings to marry outside of the English nobility, and Æthelred's first wife had been from a noble English family. That first wife, Ælfgifu, barely left a mark on the historical record, and it is not known what became of her. Perhaps she was quietly set aside due to the political realities of the era, when the king had to seek a higher profile bride to quell the tensions with Normandy. Another possibility is that she had died in the preceding few years. Her legacy would be much stronger than her obscurity would lead one to believe, though. She was the mother of several royal children, of course, but she even gave her name to her successor: Emma went by Ælfgifu once she married Æthelred. Perhaps Emma chafed at taking the name of her predecessor, being 'effectively a living memorial to Æthelred's dead first wife'.[123] That said, it is unclear whether the name was forced on her or whether she adopted it on her own. If the latter is true, it would also make sense. Ælfgifu was an English name with royal connotations, setting aside the awkwardness of it being her predecessor's name. Future royal wives would also go by Ælfgifu, as future chapters will bear out, making the name almost permanent at court.

As for this 'new' Ælfgifu, Emma of Normandy, she was probably much younger than Æthelred. Her year of birth is unknown, as is Æthelred's. Æthelred was roughly in his mid-thirties at the time of his marriage to Emma in 1002. Emma herself was probably no older than her early twenties, given that her last child, Gunnhilda, was born about twenty years later. She may have been significantly younger, perhaps in her mid-teens. Given that Emma would eventually write Æthelred out of history in her *Encomium*, popular history has often assumed that she must have resented her first husband. We cannot know how Emma felt about her husband, however, seeing that she left no direct reference to him whatsoever (not even a negative one!), and that her importance at the time of the *Encomium*'s writing hinged on her connection to her second husband, not her first. What we can be certain of is this: the match was highly strategic for both sides. Normandy gained prestige through its connection to the House of Wessex, and England neutralised any threat Normandy posed, whatever it might have been, while gaining a powerful ally. Together, Æthelred and Emma helped stabilise the relationship between England and Normandy. They had three known children, Edward, Alfred, and Godgifu, who would help shape European politics in the next several decades. Godgifu, whose name meant 'God's gift' in Old English, married two successive counts in France and lived until at least the 1040s. Alfred would briefly become a player in the confused succession crisis that broke out in England in 1035–37. Finally, Edward later became king of England, ruling from 1042–1066, and is better known as the Edward the Confessor of 1066 fame.

Even before her children were born, though, Emma helped fill a hole in the royal court. Æthelred's mother, Queen Ælfthryth, had been the dominant female player in England for decades. She had first been married to King Edgar, then was notably one of Æthelred's chief advisors (essentially a de facto regent) during his minority. Following her expulsion from court in the mid-980s, she had been welcomed back in the 990s, where she remained at her son's side until her death sometime between 999 and 1002.[124]

The vikings' absence at the turn of the millennium had allowed Æthelred to go on the offensive, but in 1001, they were back. The *ASC* recounts that a fleet landed in Hampshire and marched inland, where they were confronted by a small English army. Instead of fleeing at the sight of a fierce opponent, the king's reeves fought and died against the vikings in Hampshire. The annalist may have had access to better information about the battle in Hampshire, as the entry includes some surprisingly specific details: eighty-one Englishmen died against the vikings, but the vikings suffered heavier losses. Nonetheless, the *ASC* concedes that the vikings controlled the field at the end of the battle, implying this was due to their greater numbers rather than to superior skill. It is a rare example of the *ASC* being forthright about how effective local English levies could be in Æthelred's reign. The Hampshire battle also highlights just how small some armies and raiding parties could be in this era, where a hard-fought defeat led to only a few dozen casualties. It also provides perspective for just how large fleets and armies would grow in the coming decade, when rival forces would number not in the tens or hundreds, but perhaps up to 10,000 per side. The end stages of the Danish Conquest would be a huge escalation, but in 1001, battles and skirmishes could still be surprisingly small. These were not the events that would lead to England's downfall. Viking raids were no longer a mere nuisance, but it would be equally misleading to say that the English kingdom was in mortal danger.

The strength of English resistance continued later that year when vikings tried to besiege a fortification on the River Exe. The king's network of fortified *burhs* again proved too strong, with the vikings retreating after a 'courageous' English defence – another surprisingly optimistic detail from the normally gloomy *ASC*. The vikings had been seriously weakened at the battle in Hampshire, and beaten back at the River Exe, so they had to resort to pillaging in the open countryside. They may have been purposely pursuing a policy of avoidance after their setbacks in 1001, a strategy that would be mimicked by different viking armies later in the decade and even through the conquest itself more than fifteen years later.

But another English army assembled and directly engaged the vikings yet again. This time, however, it was a clear-cut defeat for the English. The battle occurred at a place called Pinhoe, and after defeating the English, the vikings were free to ravage unimpeded again. The carnage was bad enough that Æthelred ordered a tribute payment to disperse the raiders in 1002, his first known tribute payment since 994.

As usual, though, Æthelred had more tricks up his sleeve than mere tribute-giving, and some of those tricks were sinister indeed. One of the darkest episodes in English history occurred on November 13, 1002, when the king and his advisors ordered the death of 'all Danes' in England in response to a plot against Æthelred. The king had been told that the Danes would faithlessly betray him and take his life, as well as those of his councillors. In response, Æthelred decreed that all Danes would be slain. This event transpired on the feast day of a now-obscure saint, Brice of Tours, giving the slaughter its name: the St Brice's Day massacre.

For all the drama surrounding St Brice's Day, little is known of what it actually entailed. The *ASC* simply says that Æthelred commanded that all Danes be slain in response to the aforementioned plot. Written just a few years after Æthelred's death, these passages of the *ASC* are (for medieval sources) chronologically close to the events they describe. There is an even earlier source, though, written just two years after the massacre itself. A charter of Æthelred's from 1004 mentions that a church in Oxford, St Frideswide's, had been destroyed during the St Brice's Day massacre. Written in the king's voice, the charter says that it was 'well known' that he ordered the deaths of all the Danes a couple of years ago, who were 'sprouting like cockle among the wheat' – a reference to the New Testament parable of the wheat and the chaff. When some of the townsfolk of Oxford took refuge in St Frideswide's, it was burned to the ground. In the charter, the king orders it to be rebuilt, but expresses no remorse for the loss of life. If anything, he (or the draftsman) sounds proud of what he sees as a justified event.

These are the two most valuable sources for the St Brice's Day massacre – they are both describing events shortly after they occurred, and the latter came from an incredibly close source: the king's own court. But they leave much unsaid. Aside from burning buildings, we know nothing of how the king's orders were carried out. We also don't know how many people were killed or exactly who was targeted. Later on, medieval writers like William of Jumièges recorded legends about St Brice's Day that are so cartoonishly gruesome that they likely tell us more about the imaginations of twelfth century clerics than they do about events that took place in 1002. They emphasise the deaths and torture of women and infants, with the king's agents acting with almost unimaginable cruelty. These details may make for a dramatic story, but they do not necessarily make good history.

Even when turning back to earlier and less embellished sources, the episode is confusing. Taking the *ASC*'s wording of 'all Danes' at face value is almost impossible. Although it was more common in the twentieth century to view St Brice's Day as outright ethnic cleansing, this view has sharply fallen out of favour in recent decades. There is no way Æthelred's administration could have killed everyone of Danish descent in England. Their numbers would be far too large, especially in the northern reaches of the kingdom, and it would have been impossible to tell who was sufficiently 'Danish' considering that it had been well over a century since Scandinavians had settled in England in large numbers around the time of Alfred's reign. In the intervening generations, many had surely intermarried with the local populace and had offspring who were, for all intents and purposes, English. So if not 'all Danes' were killed, who were the targets? We know from Æthelred's charter that the killing extended into Oxford, a border town between what was thought of as northern and southern England – but this still tells us only a little about the victims.

Archaeology may provide an answer. At sites in Ridgeway Hill, Dorset, and St John's College, Oxford, archaeologists have discovered mass graves from the early eleventh century that may be the remains of St Brice's Day victims. The victims were males who grew up in Scandinavia, and all were in young adulthood. They had been systematically executed, lacking the defensive wounds that would be expected from death in battle or by ambush. They are also notable for what they are not: none of them are women or children, and none of them were second, third, or fourth generation Scandinavians. All of them had grown up in Scandinavia. Finally, the locations themselves make the association with St Brice's Day almost irresistible. Dorset was a frequent target of viking raids, and Oxford of course caught the attention of historians who realised that Oxford was specifically noted by Æthelred's charter as a site of the massacre. However, the range of possible dates for the burial sites is wide enough that a link to St Brice's Day is far from certain. Surely the residents of areas like Dorset would have captured and killed raiders without a royal directive if they could. The Oxford bodies also blur the line between Æthelred's reign and earlier ones and may instead date from Edgar or Edward the Martyr's time (although this would raise even more questions, given that there were no known viking incursions during their reigns). More importantly, though, these findings have altered the perception of St Brice's Day, steering historians in an even more different direction than their twentieth-century predecessors.

Rather than St Brice's Day being a paranoid attempt at ethnic cleansing, it instead looks like Æthelred was very selective about who he was targeting: those who were actively raiding or his own viking mercenaries. Perhaps he had figures like Pallig in mind, an English-allied viking who abandoned his pledges to Æthelred as soon as his old raiding buddies showed up. This narrower view also helps make sense of the *ASC*'s details about St Brice's Day being in reaction to a plot against the entire royal administration. Ordinary English people of Danish descent would be in no position to pull off a coup or overthrow like this, so this detail was often written off as a half-hearted defence of the king's ruthless actions. But if St Brice's Day was about hired swords from Scandinavia, the detail makes sense: mercenaries may indeed have been a genuine threat to the king and his circle. If this interpretation is correct, then it suddenly seems possible that Æthelred caught wind of a real plot and decided to beat them to the punch.

Nonetheless, the St Brice's Day massacre was still a brutal, bloody event that appalled later medieval writers. This sinister order also came after the most actively militaristic period of Æthelred's life to that point, showing that perhaps the king had grown overzealous in his efforts to stamp out resistance. But when remembering that the king may have received intelligence of a tangible threat from his mercenaries, it becomes less perplexing to see why Æthelred orchestrated such a drastic culling of Scandinavians in England. One can understand the king's motives without agreeing with them, after all.[125] St Brice's Day was perhaps the most extreme example of Æthelred's burst of activity at the turn of the millennium. Just as with his military expeditions to Strathclyde, the Isle of Man, and Normandy, Æthelred was using force to get his way, 'whether he used direct methods or underhanded ones'.[126]

If Æthelred had died at this point, in the early 1000s, his legacy would be far different than the one normally attached to the 'unready' king.[127] By 1000, Æthelred had overcome the influence of unscrupulous advisors and matured into a king who carried on his illustrious father's vision of penitential kingship. At the same time, his expeditions into faraway lands like Strathclyde and the Isle of Man mirrored the militaristic kings of the past, like Edmund I and Æthelstan, both of whom were famous for their northern campaigns.[128] His attacks were even further ranging when considering that he sent an expedition to Normandy as well, which may have been a catalyst for his prestigious marriage to a Norman bride. Even St Brice's Day shows a king who was far more aggressive than he is normally thought to be. But unlike several of his immediate predecessors, who all died young, Æthelred had another decade and a half to live. There would be fleeting moments of triumph for Æthelred and his kingdom in the coming sixteen years, but the overall trajectory would be a steep slope downhill – towards viking conquest.

The *ASC* records Swein's sudden reappearance in southwest England in 1003. First he stormed Exeter, which resulted in widespread destruction in the *burh* – a rare instance of a viking army toppling a fortified town without suffering setbacks or losses. From there, Swein's army marched through Wiltshire and east to Hampshire, where they were confronted by an English army raised by Ælfric, Hampshire's ealdorman. As Byrtnoth had demonstrated at Maldon in 991, ealdormen were supposed to be the first line of defence against hostile armies, ideally raising local levies as soon as possible. Unlike Byrtnoth, though, Ælfric did not earn himself a reputation for bravery in 1003. He had been blamed for sabotaging the king's fleet in 992, and his son Ælfgar had been blinded by the king in 993, so perhaps the ealdorman had lost the benefit of the doubt. The chronicler blames him again in 1003, saying he pretended to be ill and began vomiting. Ælfric may have had a genuine reaction to the impending battle, or maybe he was truly ill, but the *ASC* automatically interprets his incapacity as an act of betrayal. The passage also preserves an Old English maxim that must have seen heavy use during Æthelred's reign: 'As the saying goes, "When the leader gives way, the whole army will be much hindered".' And hindered they were. Ælfric's army split up and Swein was able to ignore them, ravaging through Wilton and Salisbury with impunity. King Æthelred, contrary to his reputation for solving problems with money, did not organise a tribute payment to disperse the raiders. The *ASC* does not say whether the viking army overwintered in England, but neither does it record it leaving between 1003 and 1004, so it may be that this army stuck around all winter, a drain on local resources.

1004 found Swein further east, bringing his ships to Norwich in East Anglia. The *ASC* says that Swein's army 'completely ravaged and burnt the borough', in classic viking fashion. A local leader named Ulfcytel, whom John of Worcester calls an ealdorman of the East Angles, took the opposite approach of Ælfric. He decided to buy off Swein, who had appeared so suddenly that Ulfcytel had no chance to assemble his men. But Swein's men were false to their pledges and began raiding despite a truce between them and Ulfcytel. Ulfcytel responded by ordering Swein's ships to be destroyed while the vikings were away, an order that apparently failed, although the chronicler does not say why.

Ulfcytel soon proved himself to be more mettlesome than his counterpart Ælfric of Hampshire. In the wake of a broken truce and a botched attempt to disable Swein's ships, Ulfcytel hastily assembled what army he could. Three weeks later, Swein's men returned to their ships, where they were blocked by Ulfcytel's army. In this case, the leader would not 'give way' as Ælfric had. Ulfcytel offered battle, and contrary to the behaviour of some later viking armies, who preferred avoidance, Swein obliged. The battle was a fierce one, with many falling on each side, including 'the flower of the East Anglian people', probably referring to many promising young thegns who perished on the battlefield. The chronicler gives no indication of winners and losers, only saying that 'the Danes would never have got back to their ships', if the East Anglian army had been at full strength. As the chronicler frames the battle, Swein's men said that 'they never met worse fighting in England than Ulfcytel dealt to them'. Given the *ASC*'s almost universally bleak portrayal of English military affairs at this time, it is remarkable that Ulfcytel's encounter with Swein is not somehow twisted into an embarrassing defeat. While the annalist stops just short of saying it was an English victory, it very well may have been characterised as such by a less pessimistic writer. However, in a closely-run contest like this one, perhaps it was hard to tell winners from losers when both sides had suffered such devastating casualties.

More interesting is the chronicler's comment that the East Anglian army was not at 'full strength'. This could merely refer to Ulfcytel being unable to raise levies as he wished, given that he had made peace first, only to find that peace broken. However, it is hard to read this passage and not think of the wider picture. Three weeks passed between the broken truce and the battle, yet no further help had arrived. Ulfcytel was on his own. Although it is correct that Æthelred's England was far larger than Alfred's of a century earlier, it may have been a great disappointment that the king himself did not bring an army. After all, he had recently been at the head of a large and apparently triumphant army in 1000 and had personally ordered out his levies in 997 and 999. Where were these levies when Ulfcytel needed them?

In 1005, the situation changed, but not necessarily for the better. England was struck with a famine so severe that the chronicler says it was the worst anyone could remember. The brief but sombre entry notes that the viking fleet went back to Denmark that year and says little more. The two events were likely related. Swein probably saw that staying in England was becoming untenable due to the food shortage, and his army had been seriously weakened by their encounter with Ulfcytel the year prior. Throughout his life, Swein seemed to have an impeccable sense of timing, appearing and disappearing at exactly the right moments. His army had plundered throughout England for the better part of two years, but with battle scars and a famine, it was time to cash in and head back to Denmark.

The campaign of 1003–05 was the first time Swein had been active in England in nearly a decade – a gap that has given rise to some colourful stories that attempt to explain why. In popular history, Swein's campaigns of 1003–05 have commonly been framed as a reaction to the St Brice's Day massacre, turning Swein's bloody ravaging into a noble revenge story. Supposedly Swein's sister, Gunnhilda, had been murdered in the 1002 massacre, along with her husband, Pallig – the disloyal ally from 1001 who had rejoined his viking companions. At first glance, this story provides a convenient and tidy explanation for Swein's campaigns: he had no choice but to avenge his sister and brother-in-law's death and to punish the king who ordered the atrocity. However, although it is a near-universal explanation in popular sources, the story holds no water when held up to scrutiny. The story of Gunnhilda being caught in the massacre appears in the twelfth century, when the St Brice's Day massacre was already attracting legendary accretions and turning into more of a tall tale than a historical event. Experts of the period are not even certain that Gunnhilda ever existed. Worse for this story is that Pallig, Swein's alleged brother-in-law, is known to have willingly left to join the viking fleet, with no indication that he soon died. The chronicle is always eager to mention disloyal nobles who were punished, so it is surprising that Pallig's punitive death in 1002 would not be mentioned. And while it is dangerous to argue from the *ASC*'s silence, as noted before, this may be an exception; the *ASC* is generally well-informed on noble assassinations and mutilations, and sometimes even seems to gloat at their well-deserved demises. Fittingly, most historians of this era are highly sceptical of the notion that Swein's campaign of 1003–05 was revenge for his sister's death.

There are more practical reasons for Swein's reappearance in 1003, mainly that he was no longer distracted by rivals in Scandinavia. Æthelred had turned Olaf Tryggvason into a godson and ally in 994, which had the byproduct of turning Swein and Olaf into foes. Swein finally got his chance to rid himself of Olaf in 1000, when he defeated Olaf in the sea battle of Svolder, which probably took place in or near the Baltic Sea. Badly outnumbered and facing certain defeat, Olaf supposedly chose to jump into the waves in full armour rather than face defeat or capture. With Olaf defeated and drowned, Swein had freed himself from a longstanding rivalry. It also meant that the time

Æthelred bought by dividing his enemies had expired. Although it is possible that Swein knew some of the soldiers killed in the St Brice's Day massacre, it is also possible that Swein had nothing to do with them and that the later chroniclers are connecting dots they should not be. The death of Æthelred's ally Olaf, and the allure of loot and prestige, is probably a better explanation for Swein's re-emergence than a personal revenge story that is only recorded in late and confused narratives.

With Swein finally gone after the famine of 1005, Æthelred was left to reflect on all that had gone awry recently. Perhaps the only bright side for the English people was that a tribute payment had not been necessary this time. However, given that a viking army had toured the country for two years and the kingdom had been struck by a serious famine, it looked like England was experiencing punishments of biblical proportions. That seems to be how the king interpreted it, anyway. In order to purify the kingdom, Æthelred orchestrated another purge. It was at least the third such event of the reign – after the court turnover of the early 990s and the St Brice's Day massacre – and it would not be the last. As noted earlier, Æthelred, like many medieval monarchs, believed that the state of his kingdom reflected the morality of its leaders and inhabitants: God could and did punish wicked, sinful nations. Apparently England was one of them.

Æthelred was God's anointed king, and thus the kingdom was stuck with him. As the homilist Ælfric of Eynsham (Æthelred's contemporary) pointed out, 'No man can make himself king, but the people has the choice to choose as king whom they please; but after he is consecrated as king, he then has dominion over the people, and they cannot shake his yoke off their necks'. By this logic, Æthelred was irreplaceable even if he was part of the problem. Although England occasionally had multiple, simultaneous kings in the tenth and eleventh centuries (such as formally from 957–59 and nominally from 1035–37), this did not involve 'undoing' kingship after a formal consecration.[129] Assassinations of anointed kings like Edmund I and Edward the Martyr were viewed as especially heinous. In theory, once a king, always a king. But if the next rung of leadership was not pleasing to God, they were fair game and would have to be replaced – one way or another. A system where the king is a permanent fixture but all others can be evil influences is, unsurprisingly, a perfect recipe for the many purges that erupted in Æthelred's long reign.

So began 'the palace revolution', as Simon Keynes coined it. The most dramatic casualties were an entire noble family in 1006 – according to the *ASC*, Ealdorman Ælfhelm was killed, while his sons Wulfheah and Ufegeat were blinded. John of Worcester claims that this was the handiwork of a new but quickly-rising figure, Eadric Streona, who would go on to be a central player in the drama of the Danish Conquest. According to John, Eadric had invited Ælfhelm to a great feast and arranged for Ælfhelm to be assassinated during a hunt. Shortly after this, Ælfhelm's sons were blinded at Cookham – the same place Æthelred himself was staying at the time. It is as close as John gets to directly blaming Æthelred for the backhanded ouster of Ælfhelm's family, but most readers will take his hint.

Although the *ASC* sometimes provides context for the downfall of other nobles, it provides no such hints for Ælfhelm and his sons. However, Æthelred may have been suspicious of the north in general, given that he rarely visited the region without an army. Perhaps his worries were well-founded, given that Northumbria had openly campaigned for Scandinavian kings in living memory, during Eadred's reign. On the other hand, Æthelred's violent and reactionary solution can only have bred more fear and distrust between the north and its distant southern king. Indeed, Ælfhelm's assassination would have long-reaching consequences, both during the Danish Conquest and beyond.

In the *ASC*, another thegn, Wulfgeat, loses his property during the same purge of 1005–06. He had been a prominent witness in charters since the 990s, alongside Æthelred's influential uncle, Ordulf, Ælfhelm's sons, and a south-western minister named Æthelmaer. Notably, Ordulf retired to Tavistock (a monastery he had founded) in 1005, perhaps encouraged to accept a monastic life rather than be removed by force. Maybe his status as the king's kinsman saved him from a grislier fate. The aforementioned south-western noble, Æthelmaer, also retired from court life at this time, saying he wished to oversee his monastic community at Eynsham, although it is also possible he sensed the coming storm and got out before the king could move against him.[130] Levi Roach has pointed out the irony that Ordulf and Æthelmaer's undoing may have been caused by the very belief system that they had advocated for fifteen years earlier – the same ideas to which they owed their prominence. 'Penitential ideals were a double-edged sword in medieval politics. Equating worldly success with religious purity might inspire reforming zeal when the going was good, but had a tendency to backfire (often quite spectacularly) when things took a turn for the worse.'[131]

The year 1006 brought new challenges for the English kingdom, too. According to *De obsessione Dunelmi*, Malcolm II's Scottish army besieged the city of Durham. It was confronted by a previously obscure lord named Uhtred of Bamburgh (who loosely inspired the character Uhtred of Bebbanburg from *The Last Kingdom*). It was a rare English success, with the Scottish army routed and their heads placed on spikes. Although the *ASC* does not mention a battle against a Scottish army in 1006, its omission is not surprising when considering the chronicler's biases. A triumph over an invading army does not fit the *ASC*'s narrative for the middle and later portions of Æthelred's reign, where military affairs went from bad to worse and even strong showings (like Ulfcytel's stand against Swein in 1004) are not tallied as victories. Additionally, while the chronicler is happy to devote line after line to London during these years, the *ASC* shows a disinterest in – or ignorance of – northern affairs by comparison. A different source, The *Annals of Ulster,* does mention Uhtred's victory of 1006, and the account in *De obsessione Dunelmi*, while chronologically confused, seems to be describing the same event.[132] The aftermath saw Uhtred entrusted with all of Northumbria, which was either already vacant after Ælfhelm's murder or would be very shortly. Uhtred was also rewarded when he became Æthelred's son in-law, marrying Ælfgifu, one of the king's many daughters. Uhtred's victory in 1006 probably earned him his nickname, 'the Bold', and highlights two crucial points about England in the mid-1000s: Æthelred was willing to reward leaders who successfully resisted invasion, and English levies could still function well enough to defeat rival armies, even if the *ASC* would have us believe otherwise. Uhtred's stand had no direct connection to the invasions from Scandinavia, but it did prevent further chaos and show that the *ASC*'s picture of events is not always complete.

Even if the Scottish invasion had been dealt with handily, the vikings would not stay away for long. After departing during the famine of 1005, a large viking fleet returned to England's shores in 1006. Although the *ASC* does not specifically say that this was the same fleet led by Swein, the phrasing at the end of the entry for 1005 and beginning of 1006 is telling. The end of the entry for 1005 says, 'the fleet … let little time elapse before it came back'. The entry for 1006 says, 'Then after midsummer the great fleet came to Sandwich, and did just as they were accustomed', strongly implying this is the same group from 1003–05, likely with Swein involved once more.[133]

Unlike the events of 1003–05, when the English seriously weakened the viking army on at least one occasion and did not pay tribute, they had less luck this time. King Æthelred ordered his armies out to pursue the vikings all autumn, raising levies in Wessex and Mercia, but they had no success bringing the vikings to battle. Eventually the strain of having two armies at large in the country was too great, and the English levies were dismissed by the winter of

1006. The viking army made their base on the Isle of Wight but also spent their time burning down Wallingford and camping at an ancient landmark called Cuckhamsley Barrow, waiting for an English army to confront them. None did. Finally, another English army was levied near the end of the year in 1006, although the *ASC* does not say by whom. This second English force of 1006 promptly lost a battle at the River Kennet and dispersed, leaving the vikings to rampage unimpeded again. The king, for what it is worth, is recorded as taking his Christmas food rents in Shropshire around this time – perhaps a subtle way for the chronicler to disapprove of Æthelred's absence in the field. More importantly, this may have been when Eadric Streona – the man who allegedly assassinated ealdorman Ælfhelm – made his best impression on the king. Shropshire was his territory, and his meteoric rise would begin in earnest the next year.[134]

Æthelred and his counsellors were now faced with the same issue that had confronted them in 994: a massive viking army rampaging through the kingdom, with seemingly no options left to stop them. Tracking them down with a massive force from Wessex and Mercia had failed. A second levy confronting them in battle had failed. There was no 'act of god' to force them out like the famine of 1005 had. It was time to pay tribute, 'hateful thought it was to all of them'.[135] Arranging tribute payments has been seen as a hallmark of Æthelred's reign, but up to this point, it had been avoided more often than not. No tribute payments were recorded to the small raiding fleets of the 980s. Tribute had been paid in 992 and 994, but not for the raiders of 997–99, 1001, or 1003–05. In 1006, though, the king and his council felt it was prudent to stop the senseless damage given that militaristic methods had failed. Æthelred made an offer to provision the vikings with food until the payment itself could be delivered, which they accepted. The financial transaction itself was completed in 1007, with a staggering £36,000 handed over, according to the *ASC*.

After receiving his tribute payment, Swein largely disappears from the historical record again. However, he may have been shipwrecked off the Welsh coast in about 1012 — one of the few clues about his whereabouts between 1007 and 1013.[136] Perhaps he was returning to his earlier pattern of raiding near the Irish Sea when he was stranded in Wales. As this chapter has borne out, places like Strathclyde and the Isle of Man were both allies and victims of viking fleets in the early eleventh century. Whether Swein was returning to harass or collaborate with these territories is unknown, but his presence near Wales or the Irish Sea in 1012 would hardly be unexpected. Presumably he would have also spent some of the intervening years ruling Denmark in person.

With the vikings paid off and finally out of the country, the *ASC*'s entry for 1007 is short. The only other detail it provides is a succinct one – the elevation of Eadric Streona to ealdorman of Mercia – but one whose significance cannot be understated. Although Eadric's first notable appearance was during the assassination of Ælfhelm of York, he is known to history before this, in a more minor capacity. He came from a more modest noble family that sometimes attested Æthelred's charters, with Eadric himself first appearing at the very bottom of a 1002 charter. His quick rise in the late 1000s saw his influence expand exponentially, especially after the fall of Ælfhelm's family, whose southern Northumbrian influences were previously in Eadric's way. The king would eventually catapult Eadric to the front of charter attestations by 1012, ahead of more senior ealdormen.

Æthelred, ever suspicious of established noble families like Ælfhelm of York's, had chosen to promote a new man in Eadric. The king knew as well as anyone that old, powerful factions were a threat to the kingdom; he owed his very throne to the overzealous members of his own faction murdering the figurehead of another. Æthelred's father Edgar had likewise benefited from a faction that formed against King Eadwig in the late 950s. Æthelred's removal of several powerful nobles during the court purge of 1005–06 and his elevation of Eadric can be seen as efforts to purify the kingdom spiritually, but they served another function, too: they were likely intended to stunt the feuding and disloyalty that was endemic in early medieval English politics, especially during a precarious time of viking incursions. If an established noble family failed to defend the kingdom or was suspected of collaborating with enemies, then they would be replaced by newcomers with more incentive to do the king's bidding.[137]

Eadric certainly fit the bill. He was from a less distinguished background, so he owed his unexpected prominence primarily to the king himself, rather than to longstanding regional or familial ties. In return, he showed unwavering loyalty to the king during his first several years as ealdorman of Mercia, proving his worth by conducting some of Æthelred's most grisly assassinations and ousters. By the last stages of the Danish Conquest in 1015–16, Eadric's influence would grow to such an extent that his allegiance, or lack of it, made and unmade kings. His unscrupulous rise and tendency to appropriate land earned him the nickname 'Streona' – Old English for 'the Acquisitive' or 'the Grasper'. Even without acting as Æthelred's enforcer, it is possible he would have earned the same nickname by virtue of being seen as a social climber. His presence as the most prominent ealdorman from 1012 and onward cannot have endeared him to his more established counterparts.

In 1007, Eadric was merely a promising thegn who could be trusted to do whatever the king said, and he was rewarded with oversight of Mercia. Eventually he even became the king's son in-law when he married Æthelred's daughter, Edith. The king did not know it yet, but he had created a monster. But what was it about Eadric that endeared the king to him? Eadric, after all, would become synonymous with duplicity. He may even be one of the influences behind the *Lord of the Rings* character Grima Wormtongue, the corrupted advisor to King Theoden. While Grima's characterisation is probably a composite of many historical figures and literary tropes, it is not hard to see him as an Eadric analogue. Æthelred himself may have influenced Tolkien's portrayal of King Theoden, the once-sluggish ruler who leads a period of renewed military effectiveness near the end of his life.[138] There is obviously more to the story than an old king being seduced by a classic evil advisor, however. Clearly Eadric had qualities that made him stand out in positive ways. Æthelred's biographer, Levi Roach, concludes that the king must have liked Eadric on a personal level, not just as an enforcer or advisor.[139] Later writers like John of Worcester and William of Malmesbury emphasise Eadric's intelligence and charisma in the same breath as they condemn his treasonous acts. Although these late depictions could be doing little more than squeezing Eadric into wicked advisor archetypes, it is also possible that they preserve nuggets of truth. The traits that made Eadric so useful may have also been his biggest liabilities. Perhaps a clever, opportunistic streak that endeared him to Æthelred also made him hard to pin down when he was acting in his own best interest in the late stages of the conquest.

England was free from viking attack in 1007 and 1008 – the tribute payment had done its important but ignoble job – and Æthelred used this time prudently. He ordered the assembly of a new fleet of ships to defend the kingdom, along with the systematic provision of mail coats and helmets. The new ships were ready in 1009, and the *ASC* marvels that there were more of them than 'had been in England in any king's time'. Based on supporting details from the *ASC*, historians like Richard Abels, Ryan Lavelle, and Marc Morris have estimated that the new fleet would have numbered at least 200 ships.[140] The *ASC*'s claim that there were more of them than ever before was apparently no hyperbole. This was not only a staggering number by English standards, but it also vastly exceeded the largest viking fleets of the last few decades. The fleet that attacked England in 991 was said to include ninety-three ships and the fleet of 994 had ninety-four, for comparison. Additionally, the armour and helmets that had been ordered as part of the same shipbuilding campaign would have been enough to equip 8000–9000 soldiers.[141] One estimate runs as high as 9000–10,000.[142] These were substantial figures in an era when England's population was likely no more than a couple of million. While such a program may have seemed overdue, it is a credit to the organisation of England that it could be undertaken at all. Even more significantly, a ship- and armour-building program like this may have been more expensive than the tribute payments themselves.[143] England clearly had not given up the fight in 1009.

Thorkell's Army

If Æthelred had kept himself away from military affairs in the preceding years, 1009 would be much different. When his mighty fleet assembled at Sandwich that year, the king himself was there to see it off. However, the factionalism that the king seemed so eager to prevent ended up dooming the endeavour. Eadric Streona's brother, Brihtric, accused another lord, Wulfnoth Cild, of treachery before the king. Wulfnoth decided to make his escape, probably knowing what Æthelred would do to him and well aware of Eadric and Brihtric's favour with the king. Wulfnoth managed to steal away twenty ships, which he used to raid along the southern coast. Eighty ships were sent after him, but they ran into a storm and were smashed to pieces along the shore. For good measure, Wulfnoth's rouge fleet then arrived to burn what was left of the eighty smashed ships. With a single accusation, Æthelred's court had self-destructed. Half of the king's great fleet was now gone.

After this, the remaining ships retreated from Sandwich to London – amazingly, just in time for a viking fleet, which the English called 'Thorkell's army', to appear at Sandwich that August. The Thorkell in question is Thorkell the Tall, a figure who would dominate English warfare and politics for the next decade and a half and arguably played just as large a part in the Danish Conquest as Swein himself.

Some later chroniclers thought Thorkell was a subordinate of Swein Forkbeard, but modern scholars think he was more of an independent Danish warlord, something akin to a free agent, and surely he knew that wealth and glory could be obtained in England. Thorkell may have been the chief leader of the invasion, but he was not the only one. John of Worcester says that fleets led by men named Hemming and Einlaf joined the main fleet at Sandwich, and it is likely that the combined forces were made up of soldiers from Denmark, Norway, and Sweden.[144] The inclusion of a 'Hemming' as one of the commanders is interesting. In the 1040s, the *Encomium* recorded that Thorkell began his campaigns in England because he sought revenge for the death of his brother at the hands of the English, and the much later Jomsvikinga saga says Thorkell had a brother named Hemming.[145] These may not be the same Hemming, given the chronological confusion, but it is possible that the Hemming who arrived to augment Thorkell was indeed his brother, and perhaps he was killed by Æthelred's forces sometime during the campaigns of 1009–12, the exact order of events misremembered by the encomiast decades later.

Regardless of its co-leaders' identity, Thorkell's army was unusually large for the time and place. After decades of back and forth on the matter, one recent estimate places Thorkell's composite army at roughly 5000–8000 soldiers, with perhaps 2700 of them serving under Thorkell himself.[146] A force with fewer than 10,000 soldiers may not sound particularly large from a modern perspective, or even when compared to some other ancient and medieval armies, but this was a significant sum for Scandinavia and the British Isles in the eleventh century. Levi Roach has pointed out that it may have rivalled William the Conqueror's army in size – hardly a ragtag coalition, and perhaps strong enough to overwhelm England entirely.[147] This combined force was likely larger than anything the English had seen to this point and may have approached the number of English soldiers that could be equipped under Æthelred's armour-making program of 1008–09.

Given that the English fleet had originally been amassed at Sandwich, and the viking fleet arrived at exactly that location, it may be that 'each side had some idea of what the other was doing'.[148] If each side did in fact have intelligence on the other, this could explain why Æthelred had the ships retreat to London just before Thorkell's army landed. To the *ASC*'s annalist, the move to London was exasperating, but if Thorkell's fleet was larger than what was left of Æthelred's, it was also strategic.[149] However, Thorkell exploited the situation for his own benefit: 'In forcing a landing at Sandwich in 1009, Thorkell was hindering the English fleet's deployment; in establishing his army on the lower Thames, he was in effect shutting it up in its home-base while permitting the free movement of his own ships'.[150] Thorkell's army made for Canterbury, which quickly paid him off with £3000. From there, Thorkell sailed to the Isle of Wight, which he used as a base to terrorise the southern English coast.

King Æthelred once again decided to raise levies and confront the vikings. Unlike the army the king had gathered in 1006, though, this force did manage to intercept Thorkell's army – and also unlike the army of 1006, this one was led by the king himself. After trapping Thorkell near the coast and blocking him from his ships, the English were ready for battle. John of Worcester even adds that this army was ready to 'conquer or die'. But just as they were about to fight, according to the *ASC*, Eadric Streona persuaded the king to hold back. We know nothing of the location or terrain where this took place, nor do we know the size of the respective armies in this particular encounter. Thus, it is hard to say why Eadric persuaded Æthelred not to attack or why the king listened. Interestingly, Thorkell also declined to attack. Both armies somehow managed to face off and then go their separate ways. For Thorkell, perhaps it was best to avoid direct conflict with an English army that was better equipped than it had been in years. For the English, containment may have been the overall goal.[151] After all, 'battles are rare in warfare; the Anglo-Saxon period is no exception'.[152] Entering battle with a large army was extremely risky for both sides, given that defeat could leave all of England up for grabs. For example, in 1014, the viking prince Cnut would see most of his support wiped out by Æthelred in a single blow, and in 1016, the English king, Edmund, would lose almost his entire army in one swoop against Cnut. With the benefit of hindsight, though, it is hard to see the 1009 encounter as anything but a missed opportunity for Æthelred, especially because Thorkell's escape meant that he spent the rest of the year raiding through Kent and Essex.

The *ASC* may imply that this was not the only time the king had caught up with a viking force in 1009, though, given that it characterises this as 'a certain occasion'. Ryan Lavelle speculates that the English army of 1009 may thus have been more competent than it is normally given credit for, and wonders if this 'particular near success was one event among many'.[153] There is another clue that the picture was more nuanced, this time from a law code from the prior year, 1008, which stipulates that penalties are steeper for anyone who deserts an army led in person by the king. This line hints that Æthelred himself may have been more militarily present in previous years than the *ASC* portrays him. If Æthelred had not personally led an army between 1000 and 1009, the reference to deserting an army led by him is curious in a document from 1008. If the king had been present with some of the levies of the preceding years, though, the warning makes more sense, and the *ASC* had previously omitted the king's army from an entry in 997 when other evidence shows it was in the field. These are mere hints and shadows, though. The English had some overt successes in 1009, too. The *ASC* proudly recalls that London repeatedly resisted the viking onslaught, perhaps thanks to the king's fleet, which would have still numbered around a hundred ships. The *ASC* also notes that 'an army was collected against them' at London near the end of the year, which Thorkell managed to avoid thanks to advance warning. Ryan Lavelle has called King Æthelred 'tenacious' for his ability to keep an army in the field so late in the year in 1009.[154] On the balance, the situation in 1009 was still dire, however. Oxford, for example, was not as lucky as London, and it was burned down by the vikings.

The royal administration's spiritual reaction to Thorkell's invasion is encapsulated in an edict known as *VII Æthelred*, typically dated to 1009. Drafted by Archbishop Wulfstan, the edict declares a 'general penance', where everyone must fast on bread, herbs, and water, and men must walk to church barefoot. Slaves were to be excused from work. Priests must offer masses 'against the heathen' and sing Psalm 3: 'Why, O Lord, are they multiplied?' *VII Æthelred* fits nicely with a similar work by Wulfstan from 1008, *V Æthelred*, which is likewise highly concerned with spiritual matters. Much has been made of Wulfstan's pronouncements against 'heathen practices' and apostasy in 1008's *V Æthelred* and 1014's *VIII Æthelred*. They have given an overall impression of societal decay late in Æthelred's reign, although a preoccupation with sorcery and backsliding can be seen in law codes dating back to the time of Æthelstan, traditionally regarded as a high point in early English history. The law code *II Æthelstan*, for example, has a section 'on witchcraft', showing that bishops and kings had long been fixated on magic and apostasy regardless of the state of the kingdom.

While the extent of spiritual or societal collapse is impossible to gauge based on the writing of medieval clerics, who are always eager to emphasise the need for repentance, there can be no doubt that *VII Æthelred* was created in direct response to viking invasion. It explicitly says as much: 'This was decreed when the great army came to the country. All of us have need eagerly to labour that we may obtain God's mercy and his compassion and that we may through his help withstand our enemies'.

Around the same time, and perhaps during the same overall program of spiritual renewal, Æthelred issued a new and highly unusual coin. It is now known as the Angus Dei (Lamb of God) penny, and it notably lacks a portrait of the king. Instead, it features a lamb on one side and a bird (possibly an eagle) on the other. The

Angus Dei coinage saw only limited circulation, increasing the likelihood that this was a temporary, special measure implemented in response to Thorkell's Army (and perhaps alongside pronouncements like *VII Æthelred*) rather than representing the regular re-minting of coins that had occurred every few years dating back to Edgar's reign.

These efforts seem desperate to modern eyes, and perhaps they were. As with earlier acts of penitential rulership, though, it was not the only solution, nor was it an act of giving up. Seeking God's help was just one weapon in the arsenal against the vikings, which also included armies, fleets, town defences, and tribute payments – all of which were used, with varying levels of success, during the invasions of 1009–1012.

If 1009 had seen some mixed success in resisting the vikings, the next few years would be far different. In 1010, the *ASC* records that Thorkell's army had repaired its ships and once again began terrorising the English countryside. In May, the viking army marched to East Anglia because they knew that Ulfcytel – the same leader who had dealt Swein Forkbeard such tough fighting in 1004 – had assembled an army. The vikings seem almost eager to confront Ulfcytel in the account, and the exact reasons for this are lost. However, this behaviour stands in contrast to the avoidant behaviour of 1009, when Thorkell had declined to engage Æthelred, then purposely avoided an army that had assembled at London. For reasons now lost, Thorkell's men were more willing to face Ulfcytel than Æthelred, and John of Worcester says the battle was fought at a place called Ringmere. The *ASC* accuses the East Anglian contingent of fleeing almost immediately, while the Cambridgeshire men fought well in spite of the East Anglian desertion. But the vikings were victorious, and the *ASC* names several thegns who perished on the field. The D and E versions of the *ASC* add that Thorkell's army was then granted horses and maintained control of East Anglia thereafter. From this point on, the *ASC* records a litany of destruction and no effective resistance. 'When [the vikings] were journeying to their ships, the English army should have come out again in case they wished to go inland', says the *ASC*. 'Then the English army went home', the chronicler adds dryly. The entry becomes more exasperated and more figurative as it goes on, although there is almost certainly an element of truth in its lines: 'And when they were in the east, the English army was kept in the west, and when they were in the south, our army was in the north'.

In 1011, Æthelred at last sued for peace. The *ASC* complains that he had not done so earlier, one of the few times the chronicler comes close to criticising Æthelred directly. Normally the king is presented as standing above the fray, coming up with sensible solutions only to be undermined by treacherous ealdormen, misfortune, or leaders who flee from battle. But in 1011, the *ASC* says that the tribute was not offered 'in time', but only after the worst of the destruction had been done. It is also a clue that tribute was not seen as universally negative in the early eleventh century, even though modern commentators have sometimes assumed it must have been. Perhaps the ordinary English people felt the same way the chronicler did, hoping the king would stop summoning his armies and simply sue for peace. As mentioned in earlier entries, like those for 1006, the English army could cause hardship for its own people, compounding the viking problem by simply adding another army to the field that likewise used up valuable resources. Ironically, from the vantage point of 1011, it may have seemed that Æthelred's main flaw was not his use of tribute, but his reluctance to offer it, instead raising army after army with diminishing returns.

By the time Æthelred finally admitted defeat, the vikings had overrun all or part of seventeen shires, consisting of most of southeast and central England. The great viking army of 1009–11 probably did not occupy all these territories at a single time, but the chronicler's point is to show just how widespread the damage had been over the preceding two years. After Æthelred's administration offered tribute to Thorkell's army, the vikings splintered into smaller, decentralised bands, continuing to pillage and plunder despite a supposed truce. There were practical reasons for the continued pillaging, however. Thorkell was going to receive a massive tribute payment of £48,000, the largest yet on record, and raising that kind of money was going to take time. The vikings in England obviously could not leave before they received their payment, but they would still have to supply themselves in the meantime. This is likely why they continued foraging and ravaging England in spite of the peace Æthelred and Thorkell had agreed to. Fragmenting into smaller groups gave them the advantage of mobility, but also reflected the ephemeral nature of large viking forces. Thorkell himself was just one leader among many in the coalition that came to bear his name, and just because one leader agreed to a truce, that did not mean they all had to.

In September 1011, one group of these vikings besieged Canterbury and successfully gained entry to the city, allegedly through the betrayal of an English archdeacon named Ælfmaer. The vikings took Canterbury's leading men and women captive, including Archbishop Ælfheah of Canterbury, Bishop Godwin of Rochester, Abbess Leofrun of St Mildred's, and Ælfweard, one of the king's reeves. Ælfmaer, the man who had allowed the vikings access to the city, was rewarded by being allowed to escape. It was a sorry state of affairs – the *ASC* notes the irony that the seat of Christianity in England, the place where Christianity had first arrived on its shores, was now held captive by Scandinavians, who were often stereotyped as heathens. In reality, many of them were also Christians by this point, but chroniclers and annalists, many of whom were clerics, rarely acknowledged this. The occupation of Canterbury in 1011 would foreshadow one of the darkest episodes in the entire Danish Conquest – the shocking murder of Archbishop Ælfheah the following year.

Ælfheah, noted as the most prominent captive from 1011, was still in viking custody in the spring of 1012. The tribute payment that Æthelred had offered in 1011 was finally ready to be turned over to Thorkell's army. The payment was to be made after Easter, and

Eadric Streona was yet again handed a prominent but undesirable task – handing over the then-record £48,000 tribute payment to some of the fiercest men in the western world. Eadric arrived in London early to oversee the payment, along with many other notable but unnamed leaders. Given that the payment was centred around Holy Week, a time of solemnity but also hope of renewal, maybe these English leaders felt they were finally crossing over into better times.

If so, they were wrong. In Canterbury, not too far from where the payment was being transferred in London, the situation spiralled out of control. The *ASC* provides an early account of what happened to Ælfheah, written just a few years after the events it describes: 'The army became greatly incensed against the bishop because he would not promise them any money, but forbade that anything should be paid for him. They were also very drunk for wine from the south had been brought there'. Soon after this, they began pelting the archbishop with bones and struck him with the blunt side of an axe, killing him.

This event was so stunning that it found its way into continental sources in short order, too. Thietmar of Merseburg, likewise writing just a few years later, provides his own account. It mixes up the archbishop's name, confusing him for an illustrious predecessor, Dunstan, and claims that he had eventually agreed to be ransomed rather than consistently refusing. It adds another flourish by claiming that Thorkell himself tried to intervene, promising riches if his unbridled men would stop their assault on the archbishop. However, it is unlikely that Thorkell himself was with the archbishop in Canterbury when this happened; as one of the senior leaders of the viking army, he was probably in London where Eadric was making the tribute payment. Thietmar and the *ASC* do agree that the vikings flung cattle skulls at the archbishop, showing that this oddly specific detail was already established as part of Ælfheah's martyrdom. Details about ransom payments also appear in both stories, suggesting Ælfheah's death did indeed have something to do with this, even though the sources disagree on whether the archbishop eventually agreed to be ransomed or refused it all along. The murder of such a high-ranking Christian sent shock waves through the medieval world, with Thietmar including his own resolution to the story to balance things out: 'For one of the [viking] leaders was suddenly crippled, thereby revealing through his own body that he had harmed the chosen one of Christ. So it is written: "Revenge is mine, and I will exact retribution, says the Lord"'.

Poetic words indeed. But instead of revenge, the English were left with a dead archbishop, a humiliated populace, and a scorched landscape. Thorkell's army of 1009–1012 is specifically linked with fire in the *ASC*, which often notes how it burned through shires and fens alike. As if all that was not bad enough, it had set the kingdom back £48,000, and oppressive taxes were among the most prominent complaints of those living during this time, such as Wulfstan and the anonymous *ASC* annalist. Rather than being a time of rebirth and renewal, it must have seemed that England was retreating further into death and darkness during Easter 1012.

3 Conquest

The greatest of all betrayals of a lord in the world is that a man betrays the soul of his lord...

Edward was betrayed, and then killed, and after that burned; and Æthelred was driven out of his land.

Archbishop Wulfstan II,
Sermo Lupi ad Anglos, 1014 CE

The years of Thorkell's army, 1009–1012, had been some of the bleakest in early English history. Only the kingdom's remarkable ability to raise cash had saved it from total collapse. The English did have one thing going in their favour in early 1012, though: after the tribute payment was completed, Thorkell the Tall, the menace of England, did something incredible. He switched sides. Demanding nothing more than to have his men clothed and fed, Thorkell brought forty-five of his ships into the king's service. Thorkell may even appear in one of the king's charters from 1012, which mentions a 'Þurkytel miles' (Thorkell, soldier) as a witness.[155]

Sometimes Thorkell's switch to Æthelred is thought of as penance for the murder of Archbishop Ælfheah, but as mentioned in the previous chapter, it is unlikely that Thorkell was personally involved or even present. There are two more likely possibilities. One is that with peace agreed and the money handed over, Thorkell or Æthelred made an offer that sounded attractive to the other. It would have been little different than the modern practices of a hacker offering to serve as a security expert or a poacher being turned into a gamekeeper. Who better to defend England from vikings than the one who had come the closest to toppling the entire regime? The second possibility is that Thorkell's change of sides was built into the tribute agreement of 1011–12 all along. Æthelred's previous experiments with viking mercenaries had not always worked out, as evidenced by the fleet of 997–99 and his efforts to purge mercenaries on St Brice's Day in 1002. But England had also seen substantial benefits from such arrangements in the past, such as when Æthelred became Olaf Tryggvason's Christian sponsor in 994 – a 'divide one's enemies' tactic that likely helped keep Swein away for several years. One of the most significant details about the successful alliance with Olaf is its Christian ceremony. Given that Thorkell did not require any further payment to switch sides in 1012 and that the tribute had been transferred at Easter, perhaps something similar was occurring; after a ceremony of much spiritual significance (and a hefty tribute payment), Thorkell would switch sides as part of the arrangement. Other major leaders, such as Einlaf, were presumably not extended this offer – the same method used on Olaf and Swein twenty years earlier. The other named viking commander, Hemming, was possibly dead by this point. Regardless, as Richard Abels had aptly put it, Æthelred 'somehow managed to persuade the viking captain that it would be more profitable to eat from a king's table than to steal food from it'.[156]

Under Thorkell's protection, England was safe from attack for over a year – a mere blip on the historical radar when looking back a thousand years later, but to those living during the time, those fifteen months must have seemed like a godsend. Some English leaders used the interlude to revive old pastimes. Eadric, for example, returned to more ordinary aristocratic behaviour by launching a raid into Wales from his nearby base in the Midlands. According to the *Annales Cambriae*, Eadric led this expedition alongside a mysterious 'Ubi' – perhaps a Scandinavian mercenary. Eadric's attack on St David's lined up with English raids into Wales in the comparatively more stable years of 983, 985, and 993.[157] Given that England had recently lost £48,000, though, perhaps there was more urgency to extract wealth from neighbouring territories in 1012. Coincidentally, the *Annales Cambriae* also records that a 'Swein father of Cnut' suffered a shipwreck in Wales that same year.[158]

A year later, Swein had recovered from his shipwreck and appeared in England with an invading army. Maybe Swein had sailed back to Denmark and Norway between his shipwreck and reappearance in England so that he could recruit more soldiers, because it is obvious from the events of 1013 that Swein's army was a particularly effective one. It is even likely that Swein's fleet was made up of some of the soldiers who had harassed England under Thorkell, men from the fleet that had 'dispersed as widely as it had been collected' the year prior.[159] Now, perhaps many of them were ready to take on a new master, just as forty-five of Thorkell's ships had accepted Æthelred as their new employer. Large viking armies could be nebulous in their composition, ebbing and flowing from year to year under different leaders. Their primary motivation was finding a lord who could provide them with riches and glory. From 1009–12, Thorkell attracted a massive following for this reason. Æthelred succeeded in prying some of them away in 1012, doubtless because few leaders could promise more riches than he could. And in 1013, Swein was the veteran of several campaigns in England over the preceding twenty years, a magnet who could attract some of the best and most ambitious vikings to his cause.

Explanations for why Swein reappeared at this moment are varied, but one thing is certain: the old Danish king still had the impeccable sense of timing that had served him well throughout his life. An older, more traditional explanation for Swein's reappearance is that he sought to punish Thorkell for his 'treachery' in turning to Æthelred.[160] This line of reasoning has mostly fallen out of favour, however, because it makes too many unwarranted assumptions. For example, it assumes that Thorkell, as a Dane, was subservient to King Swein. However, modern scholarship sees Thorkell as more of an autonomous warlord. As military historian and Æthelred biographer Richard Abels puts it: 'What seems certain is that [Thorkell] acted as an independent warlord, much like the viking sea kings of the ninth century. Like Olaf Tryggvason, Thorkell represented a potential threat to the Danish king's Scandinavian hegemony'. In other words, Swein was moved by Thorkell not because Thorkell was a traitor, but because he was an increasingly successful rival. The older view of Thorkell as subservient to Swein comes from the *Encomium*, which strongly implies that Thorkell's campaigns were conducted on Swein's behalf, although the *Encomium* obviously has a reason to portray Thorkell as subservient to Swein.[161] Thorkell was eventually one of Cnut's leading men in England, and thus was subordinate to him, but it could be too much of a stretch to assume that he was equally beneath Swein in 1009. Despite this, Swein's 1013 invasion was doubtless motivated by Thorkell's success, even if not by any sort of 'treason'. Swein had campaigned throughout England numerous times before, often unprompted, but Thorkell's coalition had shown just how far England could be pressed. Thorkell had overrun huge swaths of the kingdom and extracted unprecedented wealth. The time was right for Swein to strike and do the same – and if England could not or would not pay up, Swein could conquer entirely.

Thorkell was now in his way, however. The *ASC* notes that 'before August' 1013, Swein's fleet arrived at Sandwich, but then it 'very quickly' turned north, sailing around East Anglia. Thorkell's fleet, like the English fleets of 992 and 1009 before it, is known to have made its base in the Thames. Thorkell's 45 ships, combined with up to 100 of Æthelred's remaining ships, had done their job by serving as a deterrent and redirecting Swein to the north. London, Kent, and much of the English heartland were thus spared the immediate effects of Swein's invasion. As dominant as his armies were in the field, Thorkell was often at his most effective when he used his ships to blockade opponents. He had boxed in the English fleet in 1009 by landing at Sandwich, keeping his enemies contained, and now he and Æthelred were doing the reverse to Swein, keeping him on the outside.[162] At this point, with Swein diverted but sailing quickly, there was little Æthelred could do but hope his faraway northern lords were ready to fight, too.[163]

Æthelred was to be sorely disappointed. Swein reemerged in the north, sailing up the Humber and then into the River Trent, making his base at Gainsborough. From there, the dominoes began to fall quickly. Uhtred, the same leader who had utterly destroyed a Scottish incursion in 1006, submitted to Swein 'at once'.[164] The immediate submission of an accomplished military leader like Uhtred is telling, suggesting that Swein's army was far too large or unexpected for him to counter. It also highlights the damage Thorkell's army had done in England. By striking before England had any chance to truly recover, Swein found even its most capable leaders willing to submit. The *ASC* says that at the same time Uhtred surrendered, so did 'all the people of Lindsey, and then all the people belonging to the district of the Five Boroughs, and quickly afterward all the Danish settlers north of Watling Street'. The chronicler may seem to imply a cultural or ethnic divide by calling out those of Danish descent, but this was not merely the act of people longing for the ways of their heathen ancestors; more likely, these were the actions of an exhausted and defeated people, ready to submit to anyone who would spare them years of further chaos. If it meant submitting to Swein, so be it. Æthelred could no longer protect them. An argument could be made that he had not been able to do so in some time. The damage inflicted by Thorkell had been so severe that joining the enemy was a more appealing option than fighting on behalf of God's anointed king,

Æthelred, whose family had ruled parts of England for centuries. By 1013, England's willingness to fight back had been crushed.

Swein had obtained the submission of some of the kingdom's most important leaders, and he began asserting his authority right away. The *ASC* says that once he knew he had their submission, he began making demands of them, requiring horses and provisions. He also took hostages from these families at this time, passing them off to his young son, Cnut. So far, Swein had been demanding but had not inflicted any direct damage. That changed once he turned south. Leaving Cnut in charge of the ships and hostages, Swein and his forces marched past Watling Street, the ancient Roman road, and then 'did the greatest damage that any army could do'. Oxford and Winchester immediately surrendered and gave hostages once Swein arrived outside their walls. Two of England's most prestigious and important cities had surrendered without a fight. Swein then turned his army east, set on taking the most strategically important city next: London. There were no greater cities left to topple than London, and Swein was surely at his most confident following the fall of Oxford and the royal family's hub of Winchester. At London, Swein was in for a rude surprise. The Londoners fought back and successfully repelled Swein. The *ASC* says they resisted with 'full battle' thanks to the presence of Æthelred and Thorkell, both of whom were inside its walls and presumably organised the defence.

The network of lordship, which bound everyone from the king down to minor thegns, had failed in 1013; however, the resistance of London shows how important the presence of the king could be, even in this dire situation. This point would become even more pronounced in the next few years, when Æthelred was consistently able to draw support wherever he was personally present, even if the highest rungs of the nobility were unwilling to fight for him. After thirty years of viking onslaught, it may have seemed that England was too large and its nobility too independent to mount any united defence against their enemies. The later reign of King Edgar had shown that relative unity was possible, although he did not have to fight off any external threats, much less the massive invasions that Æthelred did. Later, Cnut would emerge as a successful ruler who managed to quell the divisive factions of England's nobility, at least during the middle and later portions of his reign, and command the allegiance of its often fickle ealdormen.

For Æthelred, despite his personal courage and resourcefulness, he obviously had a part to play in the disloyalty of his most prominent nobles. He had consistently purged and replaced leading men during his long reign, killing and mutilating noble families and promoting newcomers like Eadric above more established ealdormen. From the nobility's perspective, Æthelred must have looked like a tyrant. He succeeded in many of the most fundamental aspects of kingship, such as leading armies and making laws, but failed to command the loyalty of his leading men due to his own ruthlessness. By 1013, it was obvious that Æthelred could no longer protect his people, either. This was not necessarily due to a lack of martial ability or willingness – the *ASC* records the king ordering out armies constantly, sometimes leading them himself – but due to his failure to retain the trust of those who should have supported him. However, in a much more localised setting, such as London in 1013, the situation looks much more interesting. By this point, with Æthelred king in name only, the basic interaction between him and London may have ironically been more similar to that of a viking leader and his small fleet. In this microcosm, without the intervening layers of nobility between him and his people, Æthelred was the warlord of a city of a few thousand people, and they and Thorkell's men were willing to fight for him in spite of poor odds. They succeeded – Swein abandoned his siege and turned west. Swein's decision to withdraw from the siege of London was a strategic one, though. 'Rather than wasting time and troops in a long, drawn out siege, Swein turned westward to reduce to submission those who were still loyal to Æthelred.'[165]

As the sun set on Æthelred's long reign, Swein secured the support of the rest of the kingdom by taking hostages and receiving formal submission from many western lords at Bath – the site of Edgar's imperial coronation just forty years prior. When Swein tried to take London a second time, the city finally submitted out of fear. By now, Swein was 'full king', with Æthelred restricted to an unnamed fleet in the Thames.[166] Perhaps it was his own, given that he may have had close to 100 ships at his disposal, but this was still a dangerous place to be. He was trapped between Swein in London and Thorkell at Greenwich, each of whom demanded payment from the displaced king.

Æthelred in Exile

Perhaps sensing that time was running out, Æthelred reverted to his most basic role: protector of his family.[167] He was no longer a king (at least outside his own mind), nor a commander, but he was still a father and a husband. The *ASC* reports that Emma departed for Normandy after the fall of London, apparently on her own volition, but that her sons Edward and Alfred remained in Æthelred's care. Soon, though, they too went into exile. Æthelred sent them to Normandy under the protection of Bishop Ælfhun, who was instructed to look after them. Curiously, Emma and her children may not have been together in Normandy given that the *ASC* names Bishop Ælfun as the children's intended guardian, not Emma or Abbot Ælfsige (an abbot that Emma had fled England with).

While the *æthelings* were escorted to safety and Emma was reunited with Duke Richard II and the court she had grown up in, Æthelred stayed behind to handle the dangerous task of negotiating with two rival viking leaders. He was trapped between a soon-to-be conqueror and a mercenary whose men had killed an archbishop just a year prior. Yet again, though, Æthelred managed to escape unscathed, perhaps after securing an agreement with Thorkell. The ex-king found his way to the Isle of Wight, where he celebrated Christmas. The Isle of Wight had been a staging post for viking invasions of England in the recent past, most notably in 1006, but nothing made sense anymore – Swein, a viking king of Denmark, was now the fully-acknowledged king of England. Æthelred, king of the English for thirty-five years, was reduced to the role of an exile, perhaps hurling threats from his outpost just off the southern coast. But unlike with the vikings of 1006 on the Isle of Wight, no invasion was forthcoming. Late 1013 had shown the king's 'tenacity and desperation', but it had all been for naught.[168] During the bleak and dark days following the winter solstice, Æthelred left his final stronghold on the Isle of Wight and arrived in Normandy, disgraced and unsupported.

As for what Emma and Richard thought of this turn of events, we cannot know, although Emma had not been closely associated with her husband for some time. Her recorded appearances at court grow few and far between by the 1010s, and just before Swein's conquest, her sons Edward and Alfred begin attesting charters without her for the first time. This lines up with the *ASC*'s suggestion that Emma left for Normandy on her own and without her children, but that Edward and Alfred were in the king's circle before he sent them to Normandy with a separate party. If Emma had indeed been sidelined at court or had been acting independently of the king, perhaps her retreat to Normandy was, in some sense, a small relief for her – no more viking invasions, no more treacherous English factions, and no more Æthelred, at least until he arrived in the duchy several weeks later. As for the duke, did he harbour any ill-will toward the man who had tried to capture him a decade earlier? We cannot know. Most likely, thanks to the marriage with Emma, Æthelred would have been treated as an esteemed guest.

There were practical reasons to welcome Æthelred to Normandy besides purely familial ones. Richard could have seen Æthelred as a valuable political pawn who could be used against Swein. For all his military might, King Swein would never be able to claim a blood right to the throne in the same way Æthelred could, and Æthelred had proven himself to be a brave man on several occasions. He had led campaigns in and beyond England and stayed behind to negotiate with Thorkell and Swein in 1013, despite the fact that much of his family had already fled to safety. His last stand on the Isle of Wight in 1013 is also a sign of courage. Even over a century later, William of Malmesbury – one of Æthelred's most devastating critics – said he had been told that Æthelred was not a coward. Having Æthelred as an honoured guest might have been expensive and uncomfortable, but Richard surely knew that if Swein misbehaved, Richard could threaten to unleash a reckless but brave Æthelred, backing him with Norman support.

Although Æthelred and his family would have lived in relative luxury at the court of his brother-in-law Richard, the life of an exile could never be a totally pleasant one. He had joined a select but undesirable group: rulers who became ex-rulers. A medieval exile would have found some solace in the biblical tales of exile, as well as Anglo-Saxon ones like *The Wanderer* and *The Seafarer*.[169] Perhaps Æthelred related to David on the run, unaware that some of his contemporaries would have found a comparison to the erratic and paranoid King Saul more appropriate. There was also the tale of Moses lost in the wilderness in search of a land he would never reach, as well as the story of Mary, Joseph, and Jesus fleeing to Egypt before the wrath of King Herod could reach them. The life of an exile was expected to be a reflective and repentant one, ever-aware that one's own sins were to blame but also hopeful that God would see the exile's repentance and restore them to their rightful inheritance.[170]

If things looked bleak for Æthelred, they were worse for those still in England. Now subjected to a Danish usurper, the English nobility held its breath, wondering whether their new lord would purge them despite their pledges of support and transfer of hostages. Those of lower social standing must have feared for their lives, too, but for different reasons. Years of intermittent warfare had taken a toll on society. When estates and entire shires were decimated, famine could follow. Archbishop Wulfstan's famous sermon of 1014, *Sermo Lupi ad Anglos* (*The Sermon of the Wolf to the English*) makes it clear, in no uncertain terms, how dire the situation had become (Marc Morris memorably refers to the sermon as 'an apocalyptic tirade').[171] The text opens with such reassuring words as, 'Beloved men, know that which is true: this world is in haste and it nears the end'. From the top of society to the very bottom, Wulfstan emphasises the sins and wickedness of the English people. In other words, they had brought this on themselves. According to Wulfstan, writing at precisely the time of Æthelred's exile, England in 1014 was a kingdom dominated by crime and lawlessness, and it had been for some time; slaves killed their masters and men betrayed their lords. Sexual immorality was commonplace, people turned to heathen gods, and free men were sold into slavery. 'There has been military devastation and hunger, burning and bloodshed in nearly every district time and again', says Wulftsan, describing a dark world of 'stealing and slaying, plague and pestilence, murrain and disease, malice and hate, and robbery'. Crops were wiped out by ferocious storms, adding pure misfortune into the mix, although it may have seemed more like divine judgment.

Although Wulfstan viewed Æthelred's ouster as a grave sin, the ex-king and his administration were not immune to the archbishop's scathing rebuke. Wulfstan names excessive taxation as one of the many hardships the people had to endure under Æthelred, all while repeatedly coming back to the allegation that the laws are not properly enforced and that the English whisper rumours against each other and betray one another at the drop of a hat. Yet again, it is hard to look at these accusations and not wonder if the former king's behaviour had played a leading role in creating the atmosphere of mistrust and suspicion. By this point, Æthelred's purges would have been well known and represented a clear pattern. Writers like Ælfric of Eynsham believed the apocalypse was imminent, with viking attacks being a sign of the end times rather than punishment, and his pronouncements on just and unjust kingship do not need to be read as a rebuke for Æthelred in particular.[172] Wulfstan likewise believed the end of the world was fast approaching. But while factionalism and betrayal were nothing new to medieval English politics, nor to politics in general, any perception of Æthelred as an arbitrary ruler had surely weakened the bonds between the nobility and their king.

The Reign of King Swein

The exact moment when Swein 'became' king of the English is harder to pinpoint than one might imagine. If we start Swein's reign from the moment the English acknowledged him as 'full king', then it probably began in the autumn or early winter of 1013, although the *ASC* does not provide a date. Beginning Swein's reign from this point acknowledges the reality of the power balance in England – Swein had near-total control and had received formal submission from nearly the entire country; Æthelred, although he bravely remained in the kingdom, had virtually no remaining support. With Æthelred still at large in England until Christmas though, an argument could be made that Swein's reign technically started then, when Æthelred finally conceded that his situation was hopeless and went into exile in Normandy. Either way, Swein's reign would rank among the shortest in English history.

Little is known about Swein's actions as English king. The *ASC* records no activity for him as a ruler, skipping straight to 'the happy event' of his death in February 1014. The *Encomium* likewise skips straight from the conquest to his final illness.[173] This should not be a surprise, given the brevity of the reign, but there are some non-English accounts of Swein's actions as king. The German chronicler Thietmar of Merseburg, writing only a few years after these events, says that Swein 'compelled [the English] to pay an annual census'. Thietmar, though writing very early, seems to think Swein ruled England longer than he really did, referring to Æthelred as 'long-exiled' even though he had only been gone a few weeks. Similarly, the description of the census as 'annual' is confusing given that Swein did not survive even a year on the English throne. Thietmar also inaccurately portrays Swein as a pagan, so his account is obviously shaky.[174] Later writers made similar claims about Swein, though, such as the archdeacon Herman, who wrote in the 1090s that Swein imposed a 'universal tribute' in England. Herman may have been portraying Swein as a generic bad ruler who taxed his people too heavily, using Swein to illustrate the evils of Herman's own day.[175] However, the claims about Swein in these accounts are not entirely unrealistic. Conquerors frequently imposed heavy taxes. In 1017, Cnut paid off his invasion force by organising a tribute payment far larger than anything Æthelred ever raised. Harthacnut, who brought a large fleet with him to claim the English throne in 1040, imposed taxes so harsh that they led to rebellion. It is possible that before his unexpected death, Swein was making plans to tax England heavily, or perhaps had already begun the process, and that Thietmar and Herman are relaying a garbled description of such efforts.

Rather than York, London, or Winchester, Swein chose Gainsborough as his main headquarters. Swein's choice reveals some of his intentions as king. He was not merely trying to recreate the old kingdom of York, as Gainsborough was farther south, in a more centralised location.[176] There are even some clues that Swein was preparing for the future of his dynasty in 1013–14. His son Cnut married Ælfgifu of Northampton, who was from a powerful family in the Midlands, probably sometime around the invasion of 1013.[177] Ælfgifu's father, Ælfhelm, had been killed at Æthelred's behest in 1006 and her brothers blinded. A powerful and established family that was an enemy of Æthelred was a natural ally for Swein and Cnut. Perhaps the marriage took place in the summer of 1013 when the nobles of Lindsey, the Five Boroughs, and Northumbria submitted to Swein. The union produced a future English king, Harold Harefoot, who would rule from 1035 to 1040.

Thus, from the vantage point of early 1014, it must have looked like Swein would be there to stay, and surely he expected as much. He had gained formal submission from everyone of note, obtained hostages, and linked his son with the English nobility through a highly strategic marriage. Everyone acknowledged that he was now king. Even hostile continental sources like Thietmar of Merseburg agree that Swein's control was absolute at this point. Thietmar also conveniently summarises the 'vikings as divine punishment' mindset discussed at length in other parts of this chapter, which should reinforce that this was not solely an 'English' mindset. Thietmar sums up Swein's entire conquest in a few laser-sharp words that those in Æthelred's circle could not have put better themselves: 'The Lord agreed to this [Swein's takeover] and compelled the enemy to do it in order to punish the sins of certain non-believers'.[178] The era of King Swein had begun, and it was already resting on strong foundations for such a new regime. Swein's son and grandsons would indeed go on to rule as English kings, but their paths to succession would be anything but linear. The Danish dynasty of England was instead interrupted by something completely unexpected – Swein's untimely death.

Swein died on February 3, 1014, probably in his fifties. His death must have been sudden, as there is some evidence that he was planning a large assembly at Gainsborough in February 1014. He had also just concluded months of campaigning with no recorded evidence of illness or injury. The *ASC* provides no details about Swein's death, treating it as a straightforward and matter-of-fact event. A much later source, the Scandinavian *Heimskringla*, also presents Swein's death as ordinary, saying that he died at night in his bed. The *Encomium*, written just a few decades after the events it describes, says that Swein had enough time to advise his son Cnut on proper Christian kingship before he died, presenting Swein as an ideal God-fearing ruler. By the end of the century, though, more fanciful tales were beginning to circulate. Osbern of Canterbury wrote that God killed Swein in 'a terrible manner', while Herman the Archdeacon is more specific, saying that Swein was killed by the spirit of St Edmund as punishment for heavy taxation. John of Worcester takes the St Edmund legend and combines it with the detail that Swein died after falling from his horse. John of Worcester's contemporary, William of Malmesbury, also claims that Swein was killed by the saint, although he maintains that this happened while Swein was asleep.

Swein, conqueror of England and ruler for only a few weeks, was buried about fifty miles away at York.[179] It was a location at odds with previous burials of English kings who had often been buried at Winchester, a throwback to the old Scandinavian rulers in Northumbria, even though Swein had obviously aimed to control far more than the old kingdom of York. His burial there reflected York's importance as a major city and Christian centre, but it may have been borne of necessity as well. With Swein's unexpected demise, the kingdom was open to a threat from the south in the form of Æthelred, and the great city of London was not known for its sympathy to vikings – the martyred St Ælfheah was buried there, and London had been the only place to successfully resist Swein in 1013. York was a similarly prestigious site that would pose fewer problems.

Æthelred's Restoration and Capture of London

The sudden death of Swein was a lifeline for both Æthelred and the English people. After Swein died, the nobles sent word to Æthelred that 'no lord was dearer to them than their natural lord'.[180] The tide had changed and the West Saxon nobles wanted their old king back. Æthelred sent Edward, his eldest son by Emma, back to England with a favourable response. The former king's decision to send Edward as his representative has raised more than a few eyebrows over the centuries. This episode is sometimes cited as evidence that Æthelred favoured his children by Emma over his older offspring, but this can be readily dismissed. The eldest *æthelings*, Æthelstan and Edmund, are not mentioned at all during this time, so it is possible that they did not follow Æthelred, Emma, and their half-siblings to Normandy. Perhaps they stayed in England, or maybe they sought refuge elsewhere. This points to a possible rift in the royal family, but does not mean Edward was Æthelred's chosen heir. Edward was simply the eldest *ætheling* available to him at the time.

The bigger mystery is why Æthelred himself did not return to negotiate. Why send a party that was nominally led by a 12-year-old boy? There are sensible reasons for the decision. First, it allowed Æthelred to prove that he was acting in good faith. Sending an *ætheling* – even though Edward is not openly presented as a hostage and Æthelred had many sons – was still a vulnerable act. Secondly, it allowed Æthelred himself to stay out of harm's way if the West Saxon *witan's* motives were less than honourable. It could be that this is one more example of Æthelred's paranoid streak, that 'dark vigilance' that 'facilitated his survival through two and a half decades of danger'.[181] Somehow, despite periods when he must have been deeply unpopular, Æthelred repeatedly managed to kill his enemies before they could kill him. It was a pattern that would continue as the restored king grew older.

The English were well aware that Æthelred could be a suspicious and vindictive lord, and after a period of exile, perhaps he would be angrier than ever. According to the *ASC*, they explicitly sought their protection against him as part of the restoration negotiations, all while ensuring that his most hated practices would be remedied. The king agreed to forgive everything that had been done against him and amend his most 'hated' practices, which are not explicitly named. 'They pronounced every Danish king an outlaw from England for ever. Then during the spring King Ethelred came home to his own people and he was gladly received by them all'.

This remarkable entry is the first known agreement between an English ruler and his people that was committed to writing. It has sometimes been called 'the Anglo-Saxon Magna Carta', given that it was an attempt to reform the behaviour of an allegedly tyrannical monarch.[182] However, the restoration agreement of 1014 probably has little to do with Magna Carta, and neither one has much to do with modern constitutional developments, as much as textbooks might like to portray these pacts as part of a gradual trend toward representative democracy. Æthelred's repentant nobles had no thoughts of republics and constitutions, only of finding a way to restore their exiled king without repercussions. And while other early English kings sought to mend their sinful ways (like Alfred and Edgar) or agreed to renounce hated practices (Cnut), the circumstances around Æthelred's agreement of 1014 were unique.[183]

The *ASC* does not say that any other candidates were considered for the throne during the restoration negotiations, although it is possible that such discussions took place. Maybe some of them wished to submit to Cnut, given that his father had been king, so they could simply put an end to the warfare that had plagued England for years. Others still may have preferred Æthelred's adult sons, Æthelstan and Edmund, who may not have gone into exile. They were younger and less experienced, but they were also part of an anti-Eadric faction at court, which would have appealed to those who resented the upstart ealdorman and his grasp over national affairs. Furthermore, there was precedent for an *ætheling* supplanting (or joining) an older ruler as king. It had happened when Æthelbald had revolted against his father Æthelwulf in the 850s, and much more recently, Æthelred's father Edgar had become king of Mercia and Northumbria in spite of the older Eadwig already being king of the English.

It was not a given that Æthelred would prevail in early 1014, and surely he was wary of the ambitions of his grown sons. But even with all that said, Æthelred obviously had the advantage. He was the anointed king of the English and his sons were not. Neither was Cnut. Even Swein, though he had been acknowledged as 'full king', did not live long enough to be consecrated. The exiled king had the best credentials and had thirty-five years of leadership experience, and he had proven himself to be brave and ambitious on occasion. The downside to Æthelred was his ruthlessness and arbitrariness, traits that the agreement of 1014 was designed to muffle. In spite of his flaws, the old king apparently made a good enough impression during negotiations to bring the fragmented elements of his administration back together. Æthelred had been described as well-mannered and graceful when he was young, and perhaps some of those traits could still shine through in 1014. In the end, the councillors decided to go with the devil they knew. Æthelred came home and was reinstated as king. It was a new beginning for both ruler and ruled.

However, even at this point, when it seemed that Æthelred was at the mercy of the English nobles, he was not without support. He presumably still had some kind of contract with Thorkell and had been working to get another mercenary on side: Olaf Haraldsson. Later sagas have much to say about Olaf's alliance with the restored king, boasting that the two reconquered England together. The saga of Olaf Haraldsson says that as soon as Æthelred landed in England, he sent out a call to anyone who would join him in reconquering the kingdom. Olaf Haraldsson was an upstart Scandinavian warlord who would have known how well Æthelred paid. He and his men signed up to help the old king, and together they were about to execute a stunning comeback.

The saga says that Æthelred and Olaf first marched on London, where they laid siege to the city that had once been Æthelred's last stronghold. London Bridge was lined with Danish warriors who were still loyal to the previous regime, that of Swein and Cnut. Æthelred commanded an assault on the city, but Cnut's soldiers resisted fiercely, driving Æthelred's men back. Æthelred then sought the advice of his council, where Olaf devised an ingenious plan: he would cover their ships with wicker shields and sail up to London Bridge, where they tied ropes around the bridge's supports and rowed backwards. London Bridge came toppling down, bringing many of the Danish soldiers with it. Olaf's men then overcame the nearby town of Southwark. At this point, the Danish soldiers in London submitted to Æthelred. 'The true friend of warriors was thus your debtor', said Ottar the Black of Olaf's assistance to Æthelred.[184] In Scandinavian tradition, Æthelred was not the unready and hapless king of modern English popular culture. England was part of the Scandinavian political world, and its king was 'a true friend of warriors', who was 'feared as a God'. To them, Æthelred was one ruthless North Sea ruler among many, a worthy master who paid well and won battles – in other words, little different than his viking opponents.

The remarkable details from Olaf's saga sounds like fiction, but they likely have elements of truth to them. Æthelred, as previous chapters have borne out, made frequent use of Scandinavian mercenaries throughout his reign. He also routinely sought council before acting, as the *ASC* and the king's own charters constantly remind us, so the detail about the king retreating and then seeking advice seems surprisingly (if accidentally) fitting. Finally, the details from the saga help fill a glaring hole in the *ASC*, which says that London was held by Swein in 1013, but the next time it is mentioned, Æthelred is in charge of it. The *ASC* says nothing about how the city changed hands, and it is virtually impossible to imagine that Swein and Cnut left England's most strategically critical city undefended. This still leaves a crucial problem, though. If Æthelred and Olaf retook London in dramatic fashion, why does the *ASC* not mention it? The *ASC*, after all, is heavily biased toward London's affairs, often recording its successful resistance to viking attacks when other cities fall without a fight. It may actually be this bias toward London that best explains why Æthelred's recapture of London (however it may have happened) is omitted. Sometime between 1014 and 1015, Æthelred reestablished control of London. But it does not suit the chronicler's biases to show London under Danish control, resisting its own rightful king. London is supposed to be the bulwark of English resistance, not a city that tries to repel God's anointed king. Thus, it was left out of the account.

However it happened, Æthelred regained London after his reinstatement, and in the absence of any other evidence, the saga's version of events fits quite snugly into the framework established by the *ASC* – even if the *ASC* is too embarrassed to mention anything of the sort. Furthermore, there are probably elements of London's recapture that are not mentioned by any source. For instance, if Thorkell was still in the king's pay in 1014 (as some of his biographers think he was), it would be surprising if he did not have some part in London's reclamation too. Perhaps Æthelred, Olaf, and Thorkell were all part of an effort to reclaim London.

London may have been in Æthelred's hands again, but he had an even bigger problem farther to the north: Swein's son Cnut was still in England, and he had his father's forces at his side. Æthelred's restoration agreement had proclaimed that every Danish king was now an outlaw in England, but words alone do not expel enemy forces. The English would have to face Cnut head on.

Æthelred Versus Cnut

The *ASC* says that after Swein's death, Cnut made Gainsborough his base just as his father had. Swein's former fleet declared Cnut king, and he was their logical choice if the conquest of England was to become permanent. Although Adam of Bremen says that Cnut's brother, Harald, was also in England at some point, it is more likely that he was far away in Denmark.[185] Besides proximity, Cnut had many other advantages. Swein had chosen to bring him along for the conquest, so Cnut had already been intentionally associated with England, its geography, its people, and Swein's viking army. Additionally, the *ASC* says that Cnut still had the hostages his father had taken the year prior, a vital insurance policy. And most importantly, he already had a link to one of England's most prestigious families through his marriage to Ælfgifu of Northampton. Cnut would be able to draw on support from not just his father's forces, but from some of the native nobility as well. No viking had ever had such strong support at such an early stage in his career, and Cnut had every reason to believe that he was his father's designated successor in England.

As previous succession disputes had shown though, there was more to kingship than being the predecessor's preferred heir, and there was more to it than having a paid fleet. A king must also have the assent of the most notable thegns, ealdormen, and bishops. The powerful factions that had unmade previous kings could unmake him as well. Through his marriage to Ælfgifu, Cnut had a strong start, but there was still work to be done. And if some of the most important people had extended an olive branch to Æthelred, they would have to be brought back into line by force.

In the spring of 1014, the young Danish prince struck a deal with the people of Lindsey, whose territory roughly corresponded to modern Lincolnshire – they would supply Cnut with horses and then they would join his harrying army and plunder the countryside with him. The end goal, presumably, was to obtain formal submission of the local magnates and become 'full king', just as Swein had done with his army a few months prior. The 'people' of Lindsey who supported Cnut (the local thegns and nobles) must have felt they had few other options remaining. They had readily turned to Cnut's father the year prior when faced with a large army, although their disillusionment with Æthelred meant that their support of Danish rulers might not have been entirely unwilling. While the hostage situation was not enough to deter the southern English from inviting Æthelred back, the people of Lindsey were directly confronted with Cnut and the great army he commanded in early 1014. The choice of Cnut over anyone from the old dynasty must have been fairly straightforward. Cnut probably hoped that Æthelred's return to England, just like his last stand in 1013, could be taken care of with a little persistence.

The dynamic between Æthelred and the other nobles had changed, though. Whereas Æthelred had found himself completely lacking in support in 1013 (aside from Thorkell, who was paid to be there), in 1014, the southern English appear united. Æthelred likely had an additional ally in Olaf. With Æthelred's restoration agreement complete, England now had two rival kings, each of whom could rationalise their claims and had significant support. The advantage would go to whoever moved against the other first.

Contrary to his reputation for reactionary behaviour, it was Æthelred who opportunistically struck first. It was the latest in a series of decisive moves by the old king, starting with his successful negotiations to be reinstated, followed by his hiring of Olaf Haraldsson. Now the king capitalised on his triumphant return by amassing a large army, with the *ASC* crucially noting that it was at 'full strength'. The comparison to Ulfcytel's forces in 1004 is unmistakable – the king had not arrived to help Ulfcytel in 1004, leaving the East Anglian army at less than full strength. This time, to the *ASC*'s approval, Æthelred was present and his levies were large enough to make a serious stand against a viking army in the open field. Cnut and his followers may have expected the old king to raise levies and chase him at some point – Æthelred always seemed to sooner or later – but a northern springtime campaign may have been a surprise. In recent years, viking fleets had often arrived in the summer and typically did their worst damage during late summer, autumn, and early winter. Perhaps unexpectedly, given Æthelred's (mistranslated) nickname, the Unready, his main advantage in 1014 was his earliness. Even with London possibly already taken, the wronged king unleashed his fury in 'a savage offensive'.[186] The aggressive Æthelred, the same one who had terrorised his neighbours in 1000, had returned: 'Then, before [Cnut's supporters] were ready, King Æthelred came there with the whole army into Lindsey, and then all human kind that could be got at were raided and burned and killed. Cnut himself went out with his fleet – and thus the wretched people were betrayed through him'.[187]

Æthelred had at last directly defeated one of his enemies. The *ASC* describes the onslaught in the sort of language usually reserved for viking attacks, making the severity of Æthelred's northern invasion painfully clear. With a fresh start for both ruler and ruled, Æthelred is depicted 'as a warrior with the strength of the nobles behind him' in 1014.[188] Although the *ASC* had noted the king leading armies before, such as in 1000 and 1009, Æthelred had seldom been portrayed as overtly martial until the entry for 1014. The *Encomium Emmae* provides an airbrushed account of the Lindsey campaign, having Cnut return to Denmark for advice after being expelled by an unnamed but massive English army that amounted to 'all the forces in the kingdom'.[189] Ironically, the *Encomium*'s failure to identify the English leader helps confirm that it was indeed Æthelred himself. The encomiast is infamous for never referring to Æthelred by name, only obliquely referencing him as an anonymous 'prince' of London.[190] This is understandable given that the *Encomium* was written in honour of Emma and her second husband, Cnut, who had been the enemy of the first. The solution was to avoid mentioning Æthelred at all, simply bypassing this uncomfortable predicament. The *Encomium* also hints at the losses Cnut suffered in Lindsey, saying he returned to Denmark with noticeably fewer ships than he and his father set out with, but stretches credulity with its explanation that this was because Thorkell was using them.[191] On the balance, the *Encomium* largely supports the *ASC*'s account, though. Something had gone disastrously wrong for Cnut that made him 'quite unequal' to the task of holding England, even if some of the details are fudged.[192]

Despite being one of the more detailed accounts of armed conflict in the *ASC*, supplemented by confirming information from the *Encomium*, historians have interpreted this confrontation between Cnut and Æthelred in different ways. Richard Abels follows the *Encomium*'s lead by assuming Cnut fled before Æthelred could reach him, interpreting the widespread slaughter as only affecting the English allies that Cnut had left behind. This interpretation turns

Right: 1. Artwork on the Jelling runestone in Denmark, which celebrates Harald Bluetooth's dynasty and boasts that he converted the Danes to Christianity. (Photo by Niels Elgaard Larsen; public domain image via Wikimedia Commons)

Below: 2. The Trelleborg ring fort in Denmark, which was constructed around the time of Harald Bluetooth's reign (*c*.980s). (Photo by Thue C. Leibrandt; public domain image via Wikimedia Commons)

Left: 3. Contemporary depiction (966) of King Edgar of England on the *New Minster Charter*. (Public domain image via Wikimedia Commons)

Below: 4. Pharaoh depicted as an English king surrounded by advisers. From the *Old English Hexateuch*, likely created in the early eleventh century, during the reign of Æthelred II (978–1016). (Public domain image via Wikimedia Commons)

Above left: 5. Modern statue in Maldon, UK commemorating Byrhtnoth, the English leader at the Battle of Maldon. Statue by John Doubleday, 2006. (Photo by Oxyman; public domain image via Wikimedia Commons)

Above right: 6. Æthelred of England in the thirteenth-century *Historia Ecclesie Abbendonensis*. (Public domain image via Wikimedia Commons)

7. English gold coin showing Æthelred as a warrior king. Early eleventh century. (Public domain image via Wikimedia Commons)

8. Swein Forkbeard conquers England while Emma of Normandy flees. From *The Life of King Edward the Confessor* by Matthew Paris, mid-thirteenth century. (Public domain image via Wikimedia Commons)

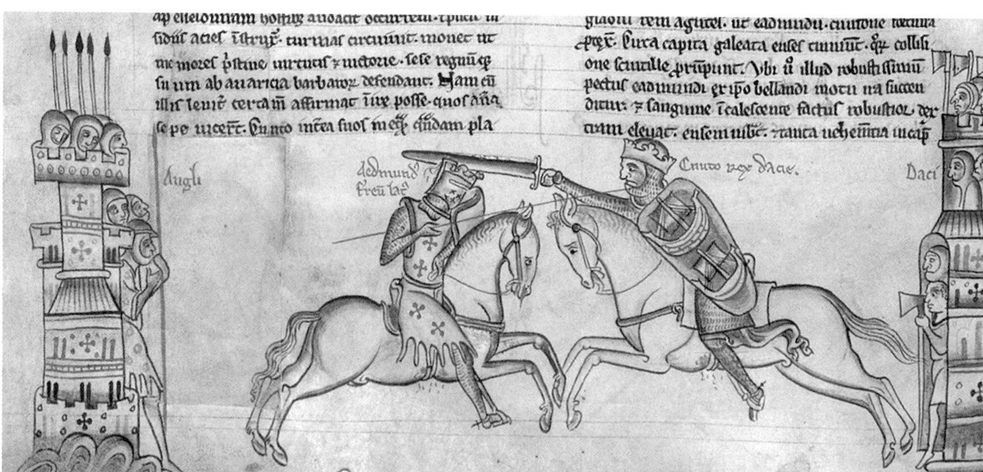

9. Edmund Ironside (left) and Cnut (right) in combat. From *The Life of King Edward the Confessor*. (Public domain image via Wikimedia Commons)

10. Contemporary depiction (1031) of Cnut and Emma in the *New Minster Liber Vitae*. Emma is listed by her English name, Ælfgifu (not to be confused with Cnut's first wife, Ælfgifu of Northampton). Note the similarities to King Edgar in plate 3. (Public domain image via Wikimedia Commons)

Left: 11. Harold Harefoot in *The Life of King Edward the Confessor.* (Public domain image via Wikimedia Commons)

Below: 12. Harold Harefoot depicted, fittingly, with a hare in a genealogical roll of the kings of England, MS Royal 14 B VI. Early fourteenth century. (Public domain image via Wikimedia Commons)

Right: 13. Emma being presented with her work of history, the *Encomium Emmae Reginae*, while her sons Edward and Harthacnut look on. *Encomium Emmae Reginae*, mid-eleventh century. (Public domain image via Wikimedia Commons)

Below: 14. The death of Harthacnut in *The Life of King Edward the Confessor*. (Public domain image via Wikimedia Commons)

15. King Edward the Confessor on the Bayeux Tapestry, eleventh century. (Public domain image via Wikimedia Commons)

16. William the Conqueror (centre) on the Bayeux Tapestry. (Public domain image via Wikimedia Commons)

Æthelred's Lindsey campaign into more of a revenge story, where Cnut leaves, but Æthelred satisfies his lust for blood by slaughtering those he perceives as traitors.[193] Others, like E. A. Freeman, Alice Sheppard, and M. K. Lawson believe that Æthelred and Cnut's forces met in battle. Freeman writes that 'Cnut's defeat must have been decisive', while Sheppard refers to the encounter as 'the battle of Lindsey'.[194] Lawson likewise refers to 1014 as a rare instance when a large English army 'brought the enemy to battle ... which saw Æthelred drive Cnut out of Lincolnshire'.[195] Of course, it is not always clear what differentiates a battle from a skirmish in early medieval warfare, especially considering that battles themselves were rare.[196] As seen in previous chapters, avoidance and ravaging were far more common.

Whether it is classed as a battle, skirmish, rout, or something else, the *ASC*'s structure suggests something closer to the idea put forth by Freeman, Sheppard, and Lawson. Æthelred was clearly aiming to directly confront Cnut, given that he targeted Lindsey, where Cnut had set up his headquarters, which is a sharp departure from the largely avoidance-based warfare seen on both sides up to this point. Crucially, the *ASC* also places Æthelred's great slaughter before Cnut's departure, not after it. Finally, Cnut's own actions are the most telling. If Cnut had escaped Lindsey with a large contingent of his forces, unharmed by Æthelred, we might expect him to restart his campaign from a different location.[197] Perhaps he would run from Æthelred initially and then sail far to the south in order to avoid the English army and resume his raiding after being resupplied by whichever nobles he could intimidate by his presence. However, this is not what happened. Cnut did resurface father south, at Sandwich, but only to drop off his mutilated hostages. After this, he sailed directly back to Denmark. As Cnut's future endeavours would show, he could be a formidable warrior king who was determined to wrest England from the House of Wessex. It is unthinkable that he would set up local agreements and amass a harrying army of Danes and English, only to flee to Denmark at the mere sight of an English army. Æthelred and Cnut almost certainly met in some kind of clash, meaning that Æthelred's great slaughter did not apply solely to unlucky peasants or disloyal English lords, but to part of Cnut's army as well. In 1009, Æthelred's army had reportedly vowed to conquer or die, but did neither. In 1014, though, Æthelred had conquered.

Æthelred's return showed that he could be a decisive and effective warrior king. Even E. A. Freeman, one of the king's harshest and most influential critics, seems to respect Æthelred's comeback of 1014: 'Æthelred engaged in righteous and successful warfare... Æthelred had thus for once shown real spirit and vigour, and had done a real service to his country'.[198] This would be a good time to make the case that we should stop calling him 'the Unready'. However, despite Æthelred's steadily-improving reputation (at least among academics) and much evidence of his competence, such a catchy nickname is unlikely to disappear at this point. Perhaps the best we can do is put a mental asterisk next to the name and remind ourselves that, just as with Edward the Martyr, it has little basis in reality. Originally, the nickname was *unraed*, meaning ill-advised – a slightly better fit for this energetic, if mercurial, monarch. However, it is one that significantly understates the trials he went through in his long reign, as well as his triumphs in 1014.

Following the debacle at Lindsey, Cnut arrived at Sandwich. This was the traditional starting point for Scandinavian invasions, but it was to be Cnut's final stop before heading back to Denmark. Once he landed there, he abandoned his English hostages on the shore – but not before cutting off their hands, ears, and noses. These hostages were most likely young thegns, and given that some might live on for several more decades, their mutilation would be a grisly reminder of the Danish wars for generations to come. One victim of such a mutilation was known by name, a certain Æthelwine whose hands had been cut off while a Danish hostage.[199] The parallels are so close to the *ASC*'s account that it is hard to imagine poor Æthelwine as anything but a victim of this exact episode on the beaches of Sandwich in 1014, watching a Danish fleet disappear over the waves. Cnut doubtless would have hoped that his possession of these hostages would deter anyone from inviting Æthelred back. When this was not the case, Cnut had only one option left: if he was serious about asserting his claim to England, he would have to harm the hostages. This episode is one of the most brutal of Cnut's life, but it was also an expected political statement from someone in his position. By leaving his maimed hostages on the shore, he ensured that the nobility could have no doubt as to their fate. England had formally severed its ties with the Danish dynasty, so Cnut was also finished with the hostages. England had been false to its pledges, and it was highlighted in terms no one could miss.

According to the *Encomium Emmae*, Cnut was back in Denmark in 1014–15. The *ASC* likewise has no more to say about Cnut in 1014 after he leaves Sandwich, suggesting the *Encomium* is correct that he was no longer in England. In Denmark, Cnut's brother Harald had succeeded to the throne, apparently without difficulty.[200] Historians think Harald was the firstborn of Swein's sons, even though the *Encomium* claims Cnut was actually older.[201] Harald's task of governing Denmark – the home kingdom – while Swein was away is a hint that his status was higher than Cnut's. England may have been extraordinarily rich in silver, but as conquered territory, it was also less stable. A generation later, Cnut himself would mirror this arrangement by appointing his most prestigious son, Harthacnut, to oversee Denmark, relegating the other sons to the more recently acquired England and unstable Norway. Despite the *Encomium*'s (probably embellished) claims that Cnut was the senior son, even it is forced to acknowledge that Harald was in no mood for sharing power. Following the loss of England to Æthelred, Cnut asked Harald to divide the kingdom of Denmark with him – a proposal that Harald, unsurprisingly, rejected.

While in Denmark, Cnut occupied himself with other things, such as helping Harald recall their mother from exile. Apparently Cnut's mother had been repudiated or driven out at some point, and her exact identity is unclear. This is because there is a great deal of confusion over Swein's marriage, or marriages, with Theitmar of Merseburg and Adam of Bremen saying that his wife was an unnamed Polish princess, whereas later Icelandic sagas say he married a (possibly legendary) figure named Sigrid the Haughty. The *Encomium* says that Swein's one-time wife was living in 'the land of the Slavs' when Cnut and Harald brought her back to Denmark in 1014. It is unclear which of these women should be equated with each other or exactly how many marriages Swein had. Whoever Cnut's mother was, she was clearly important to him and his brother, and it is a rare glimpse into the personal side of Cnut and Harald that one of their very first acts after Swein's death was to bring their mother home.

Harald also helped Cnut prepare for another campaign in England, doubtless because he had no use for an ambitious but landless brother at court who had already indicated that he wanted to share the rule of Denmark with him. Cnut knew that with Harald unwilling to share Denmark, his only hope for real power rested with England.[202]

Meanwhile, Æthelred set about reclaiming the rest of his kingdom. The toughest work had already been done; Cnut was gone and London was in English hands again, but doubtless there were pockets of resistance throughout the kingdom. Scandinavian sagas outright say as much. According to the *Saga of Olaf Haraldsson*, Olaf and Æthelred co-led an army to victory at a place called Ringmere Heath, defeating the English lord Ulfcytel.[203] Ringmere Heath is often taken to be a confused reference to the Battle of Ringmere in 1010 between

Ulfcytel and part of Thorkell's army. It may simply be that and nothing more. However, it could also be a confused reference to Cnut's defeat in Lindsey, which may have been remembered more favourably in Scandinavian sources that praise Cnut for making 'war in green Lindsey'.[204] It is even possible that the saga of Olaf records a battle not mentioned in English sources, attaching the incorrect name to it. The saga's Battle of Ringmere Heath may simply be a composite of what happened throughout England in 1014 as Æthelred, backed by his lords and mercenary captains, reestablished control. It certainly suits the reality of the situation, as many of the lords who had submitted to Swein and Cnut cannot have been happy to see Æthelred return. They had pledged hostages and their loyalty to the Danish line. In a more extreme case, Ælfgifu of Northampton had not just pledged loyalty to the Danish dynasty, but married into it. Furthermore, if Swein and Cnut's coalition of 1013–14 was as diverse as Thorkell's had been in 1009–12, not all of them would have followed Cnut back to Denmark. Just like the remnants of Thorkell's army, they may have fragmented back into smaller, more autonomous groups once they realised their chief leader was no longer in the fight, pursuing more plunder even if others had thrown in the towel.

As Æthelred and his mercenaries chipped away at the last resistance, those loyal to the House of Denmark took drastic measures to ensure Swein's remains were not desecrated. The earliest account of these efforts comes from Thietmar of Merseburg, who says Æthelred gathered his forces and aimed to destroy Swein's remains, a clue that Æthelred's campaigns of 1014 may have aimed much farther north than Lindsey – all the way to York itself, where Swein was buried. An undated grant likewise places Æthelred at York, one of the rare times he is ever found this far north, and Æthelred's biographer Ann Williams reasons that 1014 is the most probable dating for it.[205] Having been warned ahead of time, an unnamed English woman arranged for Swein to be disinterred and sent back to Denmark before Æthelred's approaching army could harm it. Curiously, the *Encomium* includes a similar tale of 'a certain English woman' who arranged to have Swein's body embalmed and sailed back to Denmark with it. There, according to the *Encomium*, she sent for Cnut and King Harald of Denmark, who graciously retrieved the body from her. Whoever this woman was, she obviously had 'an extraordinary degree of access to the Danish royal family – both living and dead'.[206] Although she is never named, the prime candidate for this mystery woman is Ælfgifu of Northampton, who is one of the only figures who can meet Thietmar and the encomiast's criteria of being an English woman with access to Swein's body, access to the Danish court, and the means to transport a royal body overseas.[207] As an English noble who had married into the Danish royal family (and whose father had been assassinated by Æthelred), she must have urgently needed to flee England in any case. Taking King Swein's body with her may have been secondary to self-preservation.

In England, we might at first imagine that the mood was triumphant following Æthelred's restoration, and the *ASC* does say that Æthelred was 'gladly received' by all his people. But that joy was only skin deep. England was a war-torn country, and Æthelred's victories came at a steep price: the *ASC* records that he ordered £21,000 to be paid to his mercenaries that same year. To add to the misfortune, a devastating flood swept across much of the kingdom in September 1014, wiping out 'many villages and a countless number of people'.[208] The royal court did not return to harmony either, even after the last pockets of Danish resistance had been stamped out. The king was no stranger to misfortune at this point in his life, and he was dealt a serious blow just after his triumphant campaigns: his eldest son, Æthelstan, had died on June 25, 1014. His cause of death is not known, but it is possible that he had been on campaign with his father throughout the spring; it is known from Æthelstan's will that he had a large collection of swords and armour, a rare glimpse into the world of an eleventh-century prince, so it would not be unexpected for him to be on campaign with the king. More interestingly, his will makes no reference to a wife or to children. Despite being about 30 years old, Æthelstan apparently had not married, a clue that suggests the king kept his sons under his thumb well into their adulthood. When one of the *æthelings* does finally marry a year later (Edmund in 1015), it is treated as an act of open defiance rather than a cause for celebration. Æthelred came from a long line of short-lived kings, so he must have been glad to have many sons, but perhaps he did not anticipate living long enough for them to become a threat to him. Æthelred had used marriage alliances strategically, first with Emma of Normandy and then by marrying off his daughters, so he knew his sons could theoretically use them to their own advantage as well.

Æthelstan's will provides rare details about the life of an *ætheling*, revealing that in addition to numerous swords, the prince also had many horses and stallions, 'penally enslaved' people, and a wide range of estates. His younger brother Edmund was given a sword that 'belonged to King Offa' – perhaps the powerful eighth-century English overlord – while another brother, Eadwig, received a silver-hilted sword. A Godwin son of Wulfnoth is also a beneficiary, and this may be the future Earl Godwin who would dominate English politics from the 1020s until the 1050s. The prince made bequests to Sigeferth, too, an important figure of the Five Boroughs area who was later associated with Edmund Ætheling. Future events would show that Edmund, Sigeferth, and Sigeferth's brother, Morcar, were all part of a loosely 'anti-Eadric' faction, suggesting that Æthelstan himself may have been opposed to the powerful ealdorman as well. Another curious feature about the will is an omission: Æthelstan's mother is not mentioned at all, not even prayers for her soul, but instead it makes reference to his grandmother, Queen Ælfthryth, 'who brought me up', and had died about a decade and a half earlier. The prince also mentions his foster mother, an otherwise unknown woman named Ælfswith, who was still living. The *ætheling* may not have mentioned his biological mother at all, but Æthelstan refers to his father constantly and with great deference in the will. He even went so far as to send messengers to the king before the will was drawn up, asking for permission to make his bequests as he thought appropriate. The king wrote back to say that this was fine. This exchange has sometimes been seen as a sign that the prince feared that his father would object to some of his wishes. It could also be that Æthelstan simply chose to refer to his father in formal terms in what was by its very nature a formal document and that seeking the king's permission beforehand was only a safeguard. In any case, Æthelstan died shortly after hearing back from his father.

Æthelstan's death must have been a significant loss for the restored dynasty. He was Æthelred's firstborn child, and he had always been listed before his many siblings in charter witness lists. His will reveals that he was extraordinarily well-connected and held much land, with everything suggesting that he had long been groomed as Æthelred's heir. Only the lack of a wife and children held him back from further prominence. The king had many throne-worthy sons, of course, but he had spent thirty years setting up Æthelstan as the first among his potential successors. For the wider court, Æthelstan's death meant that those who were not aligned with Eadric had lost a powerful ally. In the final years of Æthelred's reign, Eadric's influence reached new heights, and Æthelstan's death may have helped create that situation.

Two of Æthelstan's allies were left especially vulnerable. Morcar and Sigeferth (the latter of whom is mentioned in Æthelstan's will) were two of the leading nobles in the Five Boroughs region, an area encompassing the eastern parts of Mercia and possibly as far north as York when referred to as the 'Seven' Boroughs by the *ASC* and John of Worcester. These were areas that had long been troublesome for the royal administration, sometimes referred to as part of 'the Danelaw', and they had submitted to Swein and Cnut without resistance. The king may have seen Sigeferth and Morcar's loyalty as suspect, but he had promised to set old grudges aside during his agreement of 1014.

This would seemingly protect Sigeferth and Morcar, whatever their past actions had been, but during a 1015 assembly at Oxford, they were murdered. The *ASC* blames Eadric for their assassination, noting that Æthelred then confiscated their property. The king even ordered Sigeferth's widow to be seized. Either the king felt safe enough to disregard his agreement of 1014 or he had found new reasons to suspect them of disloyalty. Æthelstan Ætheling's death the year prior may have also made the move possible, as he had been closely associated with Sigeferth. Most telling, the king's failure to punish Eadric for the crime and his subsequent confiscation of property reveal where he stood.

The murders of Sigeferth and Morcar sent shock waves through the court and had an effect the king did not foresee: the rebellion of his son Edmund. In Æthelstan's will, Edmund appears as a close member of his circle, and he took up Æthelstan's role as an ally of the Five Boroughs. The *ASC* recalls that Edmund dramatically seized Sigeferth's widow and married her, in direct defiance of the king's wishes. More scandalous (at least among Churchmen) is that the marriage was of dubious legality, given that widows were supposed to wait one year before remarrying.[209] Then Edmund recovered Sigeferth and Morcar's properties, which had earlier been seized by Æthelred, and set himself up as the new ruler of the Five Boroughs late that summer. The entire situation, from the marriage to the occupation of the property, was an act of outright rebellion against an unjust killing. 'All the people [of the Five Boroughs] submitted to him', the *ASC* adds, almost as though Edmund Ætheling was a viking warlord.

Edmund's brazen defiance stands in contrast to his older brother's deference to the king. Æthelred was clearly not someone who took resistance, or even the hint of it, lightly. Normally the king would be expected to confront his rebellious son and bring him back into line, but in 1015, he was prevented from doing so by a serious downturn in his health. The *ASC* says that 'the king...lay sick at Cosham' in 1015, after Edmund's rebellion is detailed, but it is possible that Æthelred was already known to be ailing when Edmund made his move, striking when he knew his father could not respond. Turning to the illness itself, while we do not know what it was, it is still remarkable that Æthelred's illness is actually mentioned in the *ASC*. Normally, the *ASC* flatly notes that kings died and offers no additional information, with kings' illnesses instead recorded in other sources.[210] For Æthelred, it is the other way around, and the *ASC* is the only source we have for his affliction in 1015. Perhaps the strain of the previous two years had finally caught up to the aging king. Since 1013, he had defended London, gone into exile, returned from exile, and led at least one major campaign – and probably several more if Scandinavian sources are to be trusted. The last time he had been involved in such extensive campaigning, around the turn of the millennium, he had been in his early thirties. Now he was in his late forties – young by modern standards, but old by the standards of his dynasty. Among the West Saxon kings of all England, only his son Edward the Confessor lived notably longer, making it to his early sixties. One of Æthelred's predecessors, Eadred, had been so ill that he did little direct governing by his thirties. With this family history in mind, maybe the surprise is not that Æthelred was ill to the point of incapacity in 1015, but that such incapacity had not happened sooner.

England's loyalties were split between Æthelred and Edmund by late summer 1015, but the situation grew even more confused with the return of a third candidate. Cnut, who had been preparing for a fresh invasion for the past year, was back with his new fleet. Just as his father and Thorkell the Tall had recruited co-leaders for their great fleets, Cnut had a powerful helper in 1015. According to the *Encomium*, Erik Hakonson, an experienced Norwegian magnate, assisted Cnut in his invasion, an assertion that aligns well with Erik's prominence early in Cnut's reign. The *Encomium* also says that Thorkell was assisting Cnut at this time, and it has traditionally been thought that the forty ships that Eadric eventually 'seduced' to Cnut's cause belonged to Thorkell. However, some of Æthelred's modern biographers have argued that Thorkell instead remained loyal to Æthelred until the latter's death in 1016, making Thorkell's exact alignment unclear in 1015. Either way, with the help of Erik and possibly Thorkell, Cnut's ships landed at Sandwich and then sailed around the southern coast, eventually ravaging in Wessex and south-western England. As usual, the *ASC* says little about what the viking incursion itself entailed, but it does single out Dorset, Wiltshire, and Somerset as regions decimated by Cnut. With this sudden change of affairs, both Æthelred and Edmund's circles prepared to confront the invaders. With Æthelred ill, the king's party was led by Eadric, who gathered an army. Edmund likewise gathered his own army from 'the North'.[211] The factions met up, two uneasy rivals uniting to confront a mutual opponent. But the unlikely coalition between Eadric and Edmund crumbled almost immediately. The *ASC* says that Eadric wished to betray Edmund, so the two forces separated without having confronted Cnut. Eadric, of course, is the scapegoat for nearly everything that goes wrong in England in the eyes of the *ASC*, and given that the *ASC* was written in hindsight, it may be relaying the events of 1015 in light of Eadric's later actions. Rather than Eadric solely being responsible for the armies' dispersal, it is just as likely that mutual distrust was to blame. Edmund, after all, had married the widow of Sigeferth, a man Eadric was accused of killing. Eadric may have feared Edmund even more than Edmund feared him.

But Eadric can only be given the benefit of the doubt up to that point, because after he and Edmund went their separate ways, he did something shocking. Eadric, the king's right-hand man and son in-law, who had proven his loyalty to Æthelred in the most grisly ways imaginable, suddenly changed sides. He submitted to Cnut, taking forty ships with him over to the Danish side. At that point, Wessex submitted to Cnut, supplying him with hostages and horses, meaning Cnut now had the cooperation of the West Saxon heartland and Eadric's west Mercian power base. On the king's side, there were no longer any obvious candidates to take charge of the deteriorating situation. Æthelred's sphere of influence was shrinking as quickly as his allies were vanishing. Æthelstan was dead, Edmund was in revolt, and Eadric had betrayed the king. With Æthelred sick at Cosham, it is not known who was calling the shots for the ailing king, if anyone.

Cosham was dangerously close to the ongoing war, and Æthelred probably had not intended to stay there for any length of time, suggesting his illness had flared up rapidly and severely. Ryan Lavelle has suggested that the king may have been in Cosham because he was planning to go into exile once more.[212] Æthelred's subsequent actions suggest otherwise, though, as he then made the difficult journey to London instead – the same place that had been his refuge in 1013. If he was planning to go into exile, Æthelred was again going to make London's fall a prerequisite. He was in no shape for fighting this time, but Æthelred, in his typical fashion, was going to make things as difficult as possible for Cnut, even in the face of long odds.

In early 1016, Cnut and Eadric's combined forces turned north, crossing the Thames. They ravaged in Warwickshire, in Mercia, but tellingly avoided Eadric's sphere of influence to the west. The *ASC* records that in Mercia, Cnut and Eadric 'ravaged and burnt, and killed all they came across', not unlike Æthelred's actions against Lindsey in 1014 or Thorkell before him. Edmund again assembled an army of his own, and at this point John of Worcester records Edmund's immortal nickname: 'Ironside'. But Edmund was unable to spur his new army into action, as it refused to fight without Æthelred's involvement. John of Worcester blames this reluctance specifically on the Mercian contingent. Without the king's presence, Edmund failed to keep the army together and it dispersed, having accomplished none of its goals.

Like his father, Edmund was not always a successful general, but he was a persistent one, and the army was again assembled shortly afterward, with 'full penalty' threatened, requiring 'every man ... who was capable of service' to report.[213] This time, Edmund wisely took the precaution of notifying Æthelred of his intentions, a concession that the rebellious *ætheling* still needed his father's help. Word was sent to Æthelred in London, 'begging' him to bring the London garrison out to meet with Edmund.[214] In spite of his deteriorating health and Edmund's recent disobedience, Æthelred managed to lead an army into the field one last time. He met with Edmund's forces, but the *ASC* says that he was soon informed that he would be betrayed 'by those who should support him' – a frustratingly ambiguous allegation. John of Worcester is only marginally more helpful, clarifying that some auxiliary troops were the source of the threat. Even though he was mere months from death, Æthelred still had the same tenacious drive for survival that had seen him through so many threats in the past. The king abandoned the army and hurried back to London to escape his impending betrayal, whatever it may have been.

Modern historians have wondered whether Æthelred was reacting to a real threat in 1016 or whether his mind was beginning to break down alongside his body. Æthelred had been paranoid even when in better health, after all, so perhaps he was beginning to chase shadows in the closing chapter of his life. That said, the *ASC* portrays the king as reacting to a credible threat in 1016, not as being out of his mind, and it would hardly be surprising to see England turn against its hardworking but unfortunate king one last time. He had been subject to plots as early as 994 and 1002 and was abandoned by the entire country in 1013; following his comeback of 1014, he had been abandoned by Edmund and Eadric. Sometimes the king had a hand in his own betrayals, hastening his downfall through his own recklessness, but at other times, such as in early 1016, he appeared to be at the mercy of others.

Edmund's army seems to have broken up yet again following the plot against Æthelred. The ailing king had fled to safety in London, but Edmund instead went in the opposite direction, riding far to the north to meet with Earl Uhtred. With Uhtred's help, Edmund collected another army, this one recruited largely from Northumbria. Initially, 'every one thought that they would collect an army against King Cnut', but the *ASC* reveals the widespread disappointment with Edmund and Uhtred's subsequent actions. Instead of marching against Cnut, the English army resorted to the largely avoidant, ravaging-based warfare that dominated early English strategy. While battles were romanticised in poems like the *Battle of Maldon*, direct engagements like Maldon or Æthelred's 1014 rout of Cnut at Lindsey were exceptions – dramatic exceptions, but exceptions nonetheless.

Edmund and Uhtred's decision to embark on a ravaging campaign was strategic. They targeted the strongholds of the treacherous Eadric, with Chester, Shropshire, and Staffordshire named as places that fell victim to the marauding Northumbrian army. The aim was simple: destroy Eadric's resources and potentially even force him to abandon the field and return home. 'But it was, unfortunately, a game that two could play.'[215] Cnut and Eadric did not fall for the gambit, instead using the same tactics against their opponents. Cnut and Eadric left a trail of destruction on their way north to Uhtred's territory, finally arriving in Northumbria and setting their sights upon the vital northern city of York.

Uhtred took the bait. He abandoned Edmund and hurried north with the Northumbrian contingent of the English army, which may have left Edmund with a mere fraction of his original army. The *ASC* extends some sympathy to Uhtred, acknowledging that the decision to leave Edmund was probably not one made lightly – his flight north is noted as one 'of necessity', not one of cowardice or foolishness. Uhtred arrived in Northumbria and submitted to Cnut, which he surely hoped would spare him and his people from further bloodshed. He was only partially correct. The Northumbrian people do seem to have been spared further violence, as Cnut planned to appoint his important ally Erik Hakonson as its new earl. Erik would have no incentive to destroy his newly acquired base. But with Erik about to receive a promotion, this left Uhtred as a loose end, a redundant and dispossessed figure whose allegiance was no longer needed.

Cnut executed Uhtred, allegedly on the advice of Eadric. However, given that the *ASC* is universally hostile to Eadric, there is no good reason to assume Eadric was the catalyst for the assassination. It is more likely that he was blamed simply because he was present, and Cnut's prior and future actions show that he was capable of icy cold pragmatism without Eadric's influence. His mutilation of the hostages in 1014 and Uhtred's execution stand out as some of the most callously violent actions of his life; normally, like Æthelred, Cnut only harmed prominent figures who had directly acted against him or were rumoured to have done so. Uhtred had done nothing against Cnut personally; he only submitted when he realised he had been bested. Uhtred was simply a liability who was killed to make room for Erik. It was a shocking ending to an honourable life. The assassination of Uhtred also reveals the height of Cnut's ambitions, where honour could take a back seat to brute force when needed.

Edmund must have been devastated. His original strategy may have been to force Eadric out of the game by ravaging in western Mercia, but instead, Eadric and Cnut had used the same idea to lure Uhtred away from the field. Now, Uhtred was not just absent, but dead. At this point, Edmund's military record was looking particularly bleak. He was no more victorious than his father had been, and at least Æthelred had enjoyed isolated successes. The parallels are striking when compared to Æthelred's energetic but fruitless pursuits of Swein and Thorkell in the 1000s and early 1010s. Æthelred and Edmund each called out army after army and marched up and down the country, only to have success elude them in painfully ironic ways, such as how Æthelred's own fleet destroyed itself in 1009 or how Edmund was undermined in 1016 by having his own tactics used against him.

After establishing Erik as the new earl of Northumbria, Cnut was back on the move. He took his army south, and the *ASC* notes that he took a western route, a tacit admission to the advantage Cnut gained from having the morally dubious ealdorman Eadric on his side. Eadric's allegiance allowed Cnut's forces to move between Northumbria and Wessex without leaving friendly territory. Cnut's army had reached its ships by Easter, at which point Edmund fled to the safety of London, where he joined his father. After Easter 1016, the *ASC* says that Cnut 'turned with all his ships toward London', ready for a final encounter with Edmund and Æthelred.

The Death of Æthelred

Æthelred succumbed to his illness before Cnut's ships arrived. His death occurred on 23 April 1016. He was about 50 years old. The *ASC* notes his passing with some compassion, eulogising him as one who 'held his kingdom with great toil and many difficulties as long as his life lasted', while John of Worcester relays that he was given an honourable burial in St Paul's Cathedral. He had been an active and resourceful leader, but one whose best efforts could not stem the tide of viking incursions indefinitely.

Partly because of his unfortunate, mistranslated nickname, 'the Unready', and partly because he was on the losing side of the Danish Conquest, Æthelred has suffered from a disproportionately poor reputation for the last thousand years. In spite of contemporary sources like *The Life of St Oswald* going out of its way to show Æthelred favourably, at least on a personal level, later writers like William of Malmesbury recorded dubious and unflattering legends about Æthelred that portrayed him as a lazy, debauched drunkard. These late legends did irreparable damage to his reputation, even though they had little basis in reality.[216] However, for the last fifty years, academics have been gradually revising their opinions of Æthelred. In 1970, Frank Barlow recognised Æthelred's strengths as a warrior and a survivor, summarising him as 'a vigorous soldier' who was 'fertile in schemes for victory, always trying, always experimenting, never giving up hope'. Geoffrey Hindley echoed this more recently, describing Æthelred as 'a warrior king'. Cnut's recent biographer, Timothy Bolton, also summarises Æthelred as 'a strong and effective ruler', while Tim Clarkson and Tore Skeie independently describe him as 'a strong king'.[217]

This sympathetic view is not universal among academics, however. There are still some holdouts. Marc Morris is a notable example of a modern historian whose view of Æthelred is predominantly negative, even if it is nowhere as moralistic as was common in past generations.[218] Richard Abels also views Æthelred as a failed king, largely due to his overall lack of military success, while conceding that he was an 'energetic ruler committed to the defence of his kingdom and willing to try whatever might work'.[219] M. K. Lawson is more blunt, holding to the view that Æthelred was 'a failure'.[220] Clearly there is still not much consensus on how the long and complicated reign of Æthelred II should be summarised.

However, I think it is safe to say that Æthelred was an ordinary Anglo-Saxon king in most ways, and certainly not a spectacular failure. He did almost everything his predecessors did, and even consciously imitated them, and he possessed many of the traits that made prior kings like Æthelstan and Eadred successful: he had a militaristic streak, punished enemies harshly, passed notable law codes, and devised all kinds of ambitious plans to solve the viking problem. This is why he was able to hang on to his throne for so long, despite being undermined by his own nobility at the worst possible moments. Æthelred was not an extraordinary king by any means, but neither was he was a pushover, despite how popular culture likes to present him. It simply is not possible to understand the Danish Conquest, which was an extremely close contest, without recognising Æthelred's own role in prolonging the conquest and even undoing it from 1014–16. The scholarly reassessment of Æthelred was well overdue.

Edmund Versus Cnut

It would be reasonable to think Æthelred's death simplified matters somewhat, considering that this meant one of the war's major players was gone. However, the English were yet again divided on the best course of action after this point, and their loyalties largely depended on their proximity to the remaining contenders. London proclaimed Edmund as their king – a logical choice, considering that Edmund and his father's body were both present there. As for those outside of London, John of Worcester records that many of England's most important nobles and churchmen chose Cnut as king at Southampton. John records their selection of Cnut as a mirror image of their negotiations with Æthelred two years earlier: at Southampton, they repudiated Æthelred's line (echoing how they had outlawed 'all Danish kings' in 1014), which was followed by Cnut promising to be a faithful lord to them – the same thing Æthelred had promised in 1014. We cannot know whether this is mere extrapolation on John's part, drawn from the existing template from 1014, or if it was genuinely a formula that the English nobles used multiple times. It may even be derived from the English submission to Cnut after Edmund's death.[221] In any case, it essentially reflected the situation as it existed in 1016; most of the country threw their support behind Cnut, but London remained a significant holdout that instead reaffirmed its loyalty to Æthelred's line.

Edmund was now a king, or at least one of two contenders for the title, but what of the rest of Æthelred's family? The whereabouts of Æthelred's other children from his first marriage are unclear. Likewise, it is not known how long young Edward, who had returned with his father's message in 1014, stayed in England after that point. However, Æthelred's widow Emma may have remained in London after her husband died. The *Encomium* would like us to believe that she was in Normandy in 1016 and 1017, but the encomiast had a motive for saying so. The author wanted to outright omit Emma's marriage to Æthelred, so he cannot place her in England yet. Thus the encomiast portrays her in Normandy as 'a famous queen', even though she cannot rightly be called a queen if she is the unmarried daughter of a duke. The *Encomium* tries to have it both ways, with Emma portrayed as both a queen and residing in Normandy in 1016, but earlier sources agree that she was in London. Ironically, the sources that contradict the *Encomium* on this matter may actually depict her as a stronger and more capable character. The *ASC* says she was there in its entry for 1016, someone Cnut wanted to deal with directly so that he could marry her, and Theitmar of Merseburg gives her a leading role in the city's defence, tasked with negotiating with Cnut's viking army. Rather than being the virginal, disinterested queen of the *Encomium*, it seems that Emma may instead have been acting as a quasi-war leader and negotiator in London.

Two weeks after Æthelred's death, Cnut's ships arrived at London. Cnut and his forces hunkered down for a long siege, digging ditches and sealing off the city from outside contact by surrounding it on all sides. At some point, Edmund had left London, although the *ASC* does not say exactly when or how. However, it implies that Edmund fled sometime before the city was sealed off, perhaps immediately after his father's death and his proclamation as king. In the meantime (and perhaps unaware that Edmund had escaped), Cnut ordered several assaults on the city walls, but was rebuffed each time.

Edmund's flight from London was not intended as a way for him to stay out of danger. He did not go into hiding or exile; instead, it was a way for him to continue the fight. While Cnut was preoccupied with London's stubborn defences, Edmund used his time to rally support. He rode into Wessex, the traditional base of the native dynasty, and it submitted to him. It was both a strategic and symbolic move by Edmund, resembling Alfred's call to Egbert's Stone or Æthelred's triumphant return from exile. The West Saxon dynasty was not out of the fight yet. It would be understandable to see patriotic overtones here, but Edmund's acquisition of Wessex may have involved considerable intimidation, or even force. Wessex had just submitted to Cnut, after all, so Edmund 'may not have been received with unqualified enthusiasm'.[222] The weary nobles of Wessex had been forced to submit to various lords over the last few years, from Swein and Æthelred to Cnut and Edmund. It mainly depended on whose marauding army had been there most recently. Now it was Edmund's turn, and he used Wessex's submission to kick off some of the most relentless campaigning of the entire war.

With the backing of his newly assembled West Saxon army, Edmund fought a series of battles in quick succession against Danish forces, although the *ASC* is not always very detailed about what took place at each one. John of Worcester clarifies that before any of those battles took place, Edmund first brought his West Saxon army to London and lifted the siege. Cnut then left London to pursue Edmund, but kept a portion of his forces to guard his ships on the Thames. Erik Hakonson may have been in charge of the troops at London, judging by the *Encomium*'s detail that Erik was instructed not to harry, but to remain at London. Erik's court poet gives him the same role.[223]

The *ASC* and John agree that Edmund met a Danish army at a place called Penselwood, which is near Gillingham in Dorset, and this was the first of Edmund's battles. According to John, Cnut was the Danish leader at Penselwood, but the earlier *ASC* does not identify a leader. The *ASC* likewise has no information on who won the battle, merely recording that it was fought, but John names Edmund as the victor and says the Danes were driven away.

The *ASC* provides slightly more detail about Edmund's next battle, which took place 'after midsummer at Sherston'. Eadric is named as one of the leaders this time, but the *ASC* again does not name a victor, nor does it specify if Cnut was present. The *ASC* does say that each side suffered such severe casualties that they mutually withdrew from the fighting. This would imply that Sherston was essentially a stalemate. John again has more detail, but may be less reliable than he was about Penselwood, because his account of Sherston is dripping with dramatic and florid detail. His version of the story has Edmund personally exhorting his men by name, giving dramatic speeches, and fighting on the front lines while also overseeing the English forces' strategy. There is also a dramatic scene where Eadric holds up the head of a man who resembles Edmund and claims the English king is dead, which causes panic among the English until Edmund reveals himself to be alive. John also claims that the battle lasted two entire days and was essentially even, but that Cnut and the Danes retreated before the third day of fighting. This would make Edmund, in effect, the winner of the battle, as victory was usually ascribed to whichever army maintained control of the battlefield when the fighting was over.[224] In practice, though, the *ASC* is probably more or less correct to call Sherston a stalemate with the armies 'separating on their own accord'. John then says Cnut went back to London to attack the city again, even though this meant he was viewed as the 'loser' of Sherston for leaving the site. Cnut was quite literally willing to lose the battle to win the war, and he surely hoped the move to London would help him regain the upper hand strategically. As for Edmund, Sherston could be seen as something of 'a Pyrrhic victory for the English' due to such heavy casualties.[225] But even though the victory was more symbolic than decisive, it sent a clear and powerful message. Effective English resistance was still possible, and they had put a Danish army to flight. If John of Worcester is to be trusted about Penselwood, then Sherston represented the second consecutive English victory in 1016.

The Danish army returned to London, rejoining their colleagues who John of Worcester says had been left behind to guard the ships. Meanwhile, also according to John, Edmund fell back into Wessex rather than pursuing the Danes, hoping to assemble an even greater army to bring against Cnut. With his reinforced army, Edmund then made the march to London and lifted the Danish siege. Thietmar of Merseburg adds that Edmund had Welsh support and that these troops were crucial to breaking up the siege.[226] The Danes were driven back to their ships, according to the *ASC*, and two days later, Edmund caught the Danes across the river in Brentford. There, Edmund again forced a Danish retreat but was weakened by a large number of drownings from a 'careless' section of his army that rushed ahead of the main force. Edmund again fell back into Wessex after this, with the same goal of replenishing his army. The Danes, meanwhile, returned in his absence and renewed their siege of London.

For all of Edmund's struggles earlier in 1016, he was beginning to establish a winning reputation, which undoubtedly helped whenever he retreated to Wessex for new recruits. He had been unable to land a knockout blow against the Danes like Æthelred had in Lindsey, but he had managed to reclaim the English heartland and was repeatedly breaking up Danish sieges and forcing Cnut's armies to flee. Although the Danes were always able to resume what they had been doing once Edmund had to withdraw, Edmund was still proving to be more than just a nuisance. He was now known to be an effective and determined war leader, one Cnut would have to confront head on at some point.

After again failing to take London, the Danish army abandoned the siege and went into Mercia, where they burned the land and stole supplies and provisions. Judging by the brutal treatment of the land and the *ASC*'s detail of sailing up the River Orwell, the Danes were in the eastern parts of Mercia, not Eadric's more western base that was allied with Cnut. Then the Danish army 'drove their ships into the Medway', according to the *ASC*, moving southward. Edmund gathered yet another army, which the *ASC* calls his fourth, and pursued the Danish army into Kent. But the enemy fled before the English, allowing Edmund to kill only those he could overrun. John of Worcester adds the detail that this took place in Otford, Kent.

Edmund consistently had Cnut's forces on the run by this point, prompting Eadric to summon Edmund to a meeting at Aylesford, Kent, which was not far from the campaigning. At Aylesford, Eadric must have submitted to Edmund, because the *ASC* regards the meeting as a massive error in judgment on Edmund's part and has Eadric fighting on the English side at the next battle. Medieval chroniclers, of course, had already made their minds up about Eadric, reasoning that Edmund never should have allowed such a shady character to return to his favour. And with the benefit of hindsight, it could easily be argued that the chroniclers' judgment is valid. Edmund, however, had more to consider than Eadric's posthumous (or even present) reputation. Part of Cnut's success in 1015 and 1016 can be attributed to Eadric, who campaigned effectively, helped draw Uhtred away from Edmund, and allowed the Danish army a safe way to pass from north to south – and that is to say nothing of the resources, including fighting men, that must have been at his disposal as ealdorman of Mercia. Edmund needed someone as powerful as Eadric to help him deliver the final blow to the Danish army. Drawing Eadric back onto the English side would deprive Cnut of all those benefits by extension. It is possible that both Cnut and Edmund wished they could be rid of Eadric, but in 1016, there was simply no way to ignore Eadric's influence. His allegiance (or lack of it) could decide the fate of the war.

Cnut must have been desperately concerned for his position once Eadric, his most important ally, switched sides. The Danish prince now found himself in a similar predicament to 1014, which, like 1016, had started with the Danish army in a strong position but devolved into fierce English resistance and deteriorating Danish influence. Edmund, like his father, had managed to turn the tables despite starting in an exceedingly poor position – Edmund had controlled only London initially, while Æthelred began 1014 with no foothold in England whatsoever. In late 1016, Cnut must have feared a repeat of the 'second reign' of Æthelred, with a West Saxon candidate expelling him from the kingdom by force. Perhaps the Danish Conquest of England would have to be abandoned yet again and restarted in 1017 or 1018, after Cnut had time to regroup. Maybe permanent conquest itself was not to be and Swein's occupation of 1013 would go down in history as an anomaly. For all Edmund's momentum, Cnut did not seek any kind of rapprochement with the English – at least not yet. Neither did Edmund try to strike a deal, which is understandable given his recent successes. Edmund most likely hoped that he, like his father, could kick out Cnut with no English concessions necessary. But also like Æthelred, Edmund would likely need a direct confrontation with an especially large army to achieve this. He would get his chance on 18 October 1016, at a place known to early medieval writers as Assandun.

Assandun

After Eadric defected to Edmund, Cnut managed to escape to Mercia by way of Essex, and his viking army began harrying the countryside as usual. Edmund yet again called out his forces. The *ASC*'s wording suggests that this may have been the largest of Edmund's armies, or at least the one with the widest range of recruits, calling it 'all the English nation'. This distinctive phrasing is meant to highlight the uniqueness of this army, much as the *ASC* had clarified that Æthelred's triumphant army of 1014 was at 'full force'. The fragmented and factional English kingdom could only be described as militarily united in the rarest of times, but this was one of them: Edmund indeed had 'all the English nation' on his side, or at least something very close to it. In addition to his own West Saxon fighters, he was supported by a Mercian contingent, led by Eadric. An East Anglian force was led by Ulfcytel, the same leader who had dealt the Danes such heavy fighting over a decade earlier and earned the nickname 'Bold'. The soldiers of Lindsey were led by their 'ealdorman', Godwin. Hampshire was represented in the form of Ælfric, who had been accused of treachery in 992 and 1003 but was fighting loyally for Edmund this time. Edmund may even have had the support of the same viking mercenaries who had assisted Æthelred in 1014, and possibly even his Welsh allies from the second siege of London.[227] Edmund's massive army managed to overtake Cnut's forces in Essex, at a place called Assandun, which may be the modern location known as Ashingdon, Essex. Little is known about the viking force that Edmund fought at Assandun, other than that Cnut was its chief leader. A rare detail comes from the *Encomium*, which admits that it was smaller than Edmund's mighty army. Given how wide ranging Edmund's support was known to be from other sources, there is no reason to doubt the *Encomium* here.

At Assandun, the two armies faced off. The fighting was fierce – 'they stoutly joined battle', in the *ASC*'s words. John of Worcester is again more specific, saying that Cnut's forces entered battle slowly but that Edmund's rushed in quickly. John and the *Encomium* agree with the *ASC* that both sides fought hard. But the battle turned in Cnut's favour when Eadric and his Mercians began to flee. John of Worcester, like the *ASC*, blames Eadric whenever possible, saying that Eadric only began to flee when he sensed the English were winning. The implication is that Eadric somehow had incentive to let Cnut win. The *Encomium* goes further, saying that Eadric had previously agreed with the Danes to sabotage Edmund's army and that he fled before the battle began. John and the *Encomium* are unlikely to be correct here, given that Eadric had previously only switched sides when his liege was at a desperately low point, such as during Æthelred's illness in 1015 and after Cnut's series of defeats in 1016. Edmund, on the other hand, was at the pinnacle of his success. Helping someone on the losing side, like Cnut in autumn 1016, was not Eadric's *modus operandi*. Eadric's actions may reveal more about Assandun than meets the eye, though. If Eadric, the master of self-preservation, decided to flee the field, this could mean that Assandun was progressing in exactly the opposite way of what John says. Instead of the English gaining the upper hand, it is more likely that Cnut's forces gained the advantage at some point, which prompted the fickle Eadric to flee.

Whether it was before or after Eadric's flight, the battle turned in Cnut's favour. Our sources unfortunately say little beyond this about how the battle went, other than that the English were utterly annihilated. Ælfric, the supposedly cowardly ealdorman of Hampshire, died honourably on the battlefield that day. Ulfcytel likewise died for his lord at Assundun, along with Godwin of Lindsey. Two high-ranking churchmen, Bishop Eadnoth and Abbot Wulfsige, also died in the battle. John of Worcester reassures his readers that these men of the cloth had been there strictly for religious purposes, but it was not out of the question for early medieval clerics to fight in battle.[228] William the Conqueror's half-brother, Bishop Odo, is a particularly famous eleventh-century example of a warrior bishop, so perhaps the bishop pieces on our modern chessboards are not so far out of place. Returning to Assandun, the deaths of so many named ealdormen and even churchmen show that the very foundations of English leadership had been broken in a single battle.

> *There Cnut had the victory and won for himself all the English people ... all the nobility of England was there destroyed.*
>
> The *Anglo-Saxon Chronicle*, 1016

Rather than being the final blow to the Danes, it was instead a final blow for the English. The danger of amassing such a large army was that if things went south quickly, an entire regime could be nearly wiped out. One key figure managed to escape the slaughter, however – Edmund survived.

There are some hints that Edmund once again fell back to recruit more troops, and that a final skirmish was fought somewhere in the west, possibly near the Forest of Dean with Welsh support for Edmund.[229] A final battle, if it indeed happened, was evidently not significant enough to be mentioned in the main sources for the era, which treat Assandun as the climax of the Danish Conquest. Edmund's pool of fighting men must have been utterly depleted by this point, seeing as he had called out army after army in 1015 and 1016 and his largest one of all had been wiped out.

Edmund still had a card left to play, though – diplomacy – and Cnut gave him the chance to use it. Cnut sought out Edmund in Gloucester and brought his army with him, and possibly fought against Edmund one last time near the Welsh border, but the end result of the trip was a peace agreement. Everyone else was apparently ready for the fighting to be over too, with the *ASC* saying that Eadric and the other advisors who were present wanted the two kings to make peace. They met at a place called Alney, an island on the River Severn near Deerhurst. Islands were symbolic places for peace-making, representing neutrality while preventing either army from unexpectedly attacking. At Alney, Cnut and Edmund 'become partners and sworn brothers and established that both with pledge and also with oaths'.[230] The *ASC* also makes it clear that Edmund would have to pay up. Part of the agreement at Alney was that the English would make payments for the Danish army, showing that even a warrior king like Edmund could be forced to pay tribute after a serious defeat. Edmund was allowed to keep Wessex, while Cnut succeeded to Mercia, according to the *ASC*. John of Worcester says Edmund was also granted control of East Anglia, Essex, and London, although the *ASC* says that Danish soldiers were allowed into London at this time. Presumably Cnut succeeded to nearly everything else; his ally Erik was in charge of Northumbria, and if the *ASC* is to be believed, London was *de facto* Danish territory.

Perhaps the greatest sign of Edmund's strength as a ruler is not his tenacious series of battles against Cnut, but that he was able to retain the southern parts of the kingdom even after his army had been annihilated. Cnut knew how serious a threat Edmund was and that Wessex had been the source of many of Edmund's soldiers. Allowing Edmund to remain king of Wessex meant Edmund would keep his title and, hopefully, stay happy enough to abide by the agreement to be partners rather than enemies. Cnut and his allies had finally attained a great victory, but they knew Edmund could raise armies as well as anyone and that he was willing to drag the fighting on as long as possible. Appeasing Edmund was a far more appealing option. The agreement mirrored the division of England between Eadwig and Edgar in 957, where the candidate with the better 'claim' to England (the elder brother, Eadwig) kept the prestigious homeland of Wessex, but the other candidate attained more territory.

It is unclear exactly what was supposed to happen when one of the co-kings died. John of Worcester says that everyone who had been present for the agreement claimed that Cnut was supposed to succeed to the entire kingdom, but he adds that they were lying in order to gain favour with Cnut. Perhaps, though, this was really the arrangement. In 959, the surviving co-king of the English, Edgar, succeeded to all of England without difficulty once his older brother died, so it had happened before.

In any case, Edmund did not get to enjoy peace for long. He died barely a month after the Battle of Assandun, on November 30, 1016. He was probably no more than 30 years old. Early sources do not treat his death as suspicious, with the *ASC* simply acknowledging that it happened and the *Encomium* saying that God took away Edmund's life so that England could have lasting peace. Only later did Edmund's death attract fanciful details of murder and treachery. Some later writers blamed Eadric for assassinating him, with a particularly grisly version of the tale saying that Edmund was killed on the privy by an assassin who stabbed him from the cesspool below. Given how mundane the earlier sources are, though, Edmund's death was probably not suspicious. If Eadric were behind an assassination of Edmund (or even rumoured to be), then the *ASC*, *Encomium*, and John of Worcester would have been thrilled to blame him for it, yet none say anything about it. Edmund more likely died from battle wounds or natural causes.

Edmund Ironside is not one of the more famous medieval monarchs, but when he is remembered, it is often as one of the great 'what-ifs' of early English history – and it is certainly tempting to think in such terms. What if Edmund had won at Assandun? What if Eadric had not fled the field? What if Cnut was the one who died in 1016 and Edmund lived until 1035? If even one detail had been changed, English history would indeed be very different. But Edmund did lose at Assandun, and he did die a few weeks later, so he has mostly been relegated to obscurity, especially compared to Æthelred and Cnut. His reputation as a tenacious but ultimately unsuccessful defender makes him something of a tragic figure, someone like Harold Godwinson but without as much controversy, who won battles and inspired his men, only to fall short.

Edmund is also remembered as a polar opposite of his father. Whereas Æthelred is sometimes depicted by modern writers as unsuccessful and inactive, Edmund is remembered as the embodiment of everything Æthelred lacked. However, there was far more at play than mere personality differences, if such differences existed at all. The entire period from Æthelred's restoration to Edmund's death was one of renewed English resistance and more effective military leadership. The armies of Æthelred's 'second reign' and those of Edmund's reign benefited from the massive armour-building campaign that Æthelred had implemented. They were more effective not just because Æthelred and Edmund did a better job leading them, but because they were genuinely better equipped than any English armies before them. With new mail coats, helmets, and ships, it is hardly surprising that the forces of 1014–16 enjoyed more success against the Danes than those of the 1000s. Under both rulers, the English armies of 1014–1016 were also noticeably more aggressive than those of the 1000s. Rather than being viewed as opposite personalities, Æthelred and Edmund should both be remembered as tough, resilient rulers who were capable of fierce resistance, especially when their armies were at full strength and properly equipped. Both kings endured fruitless pursuits of their enemies, such as Æthelred's campaigns in the 1000s and Edmund's repeated musters in 1015 and early 1016, but both of them likewise inflicted serious defeats on Cnut, such as Edmund's series of victories in mid–1016 and Æthelred's re-conquest of 1014.

Rather than the Danish Conquest coming down to personality differences, it seems more accurate to say that these two kings did the best they could, but their fortunes depended on the loyalty – or lack of it – of those surrounding them. Eadric's defection from Æthelred in 1015 crippled English resistance, and Eadric's flight from Assandun was likewise viewed as a turning point by medieval chroniclers, whatever Eadric's exact motives may have been. Even the *ASC* eulogises Æthelred and Edmund somewhat similarly:

> *[Æthelred] held his kingdom with great toil and difficulties as long as his life lasted.*
>
> *[Edmund] stoutly defended his kingdom while his life lasted.*

By the end of 1016, both were dead. Cnut had conquered England. The illustrious House of Wessex had resisted ferociously but was still trampled underfoot by the Danish conquerors. The conquest itself was complete, but now Cnut would find himself in the same, difficult position as his rivals Æthelred and Edmund – a king who would have to fight hard to hold on to his possessions.

4

England Under Cnut

In popular culture, Cnut is one of the least understood early English monarchs and is best remembered for an apocryphal story about him and the tide. The story most often takes the following form: Cnut, believing himself to be all-powerful, gathers his advisors along the shore and commands the tide to stay back. The tide, of course, comes in anyway and Cnut gets wet, looking like a fool. Because of this, his name is often invoked to mean 'one who denies reality' or believes their followers' flattery to be true. The legend originally had a slightly different connotation, though: Cnut, wishing to prove to his fawning courtiers that he was not all-powerful, commands the tide to stay away, as a political exercise. The tide comes in anyway, and the point is made; no one, not even a king, is more powerful than God.[231] This form of the story, while still clearly legendary, does at least connect to a common medieval view of Cnut as a pious king. More importantly, it correctly links Cnut's power to the sea, a pattern it shares with other legends about him, such as the story that he called out to St Edith of Wilton (Æthelred's half-sister) during a ferocious storm at sea. Edith appeared and, through God's power, calmed the waters. The possibility of shipwreck loomed over Cnut and his growing territory, especially since he made numerous trips back and forth to Denmark. Stormy seas had thwarted Æthelred's mighty fleet in 1009, destroying eighty of his ships, and much later, the White Ship disaster of 1120 upended Henry I's succession plans and led to years of chaos and confusion. Although they are often thought of as merely stories, the legends of Cnut and the tide and Cnut and Edith contain a vital reminder that Cnut's power was built upon the sea, yet he himself was at its mercy.[232]

Tide story aside, Cnut's legacy as king of the English is multi-faceted and often contradictory among public historians. He is sometimes viewed as little more than a simpleminded but ruthless conqueror. Michael Wood once summarised him as 'an opportunist, malleable, but ruthless thug', who 'needed a Wulfstan [archbishop of York] to tell him what to say'. On the other hand, the controversial David Starkey viewed Cnut as a pious ruler who 'went native and became more English than the English'.[233] Although these quotes may seem irreconcilable, there are elements of truth in each. Cnut's academic biographers paint a portrait of a flexible but strong ruler whose pious, Christian image and tough, viking image were not contradictions, but rather two sides of the same coin.

Cnut Establishes Control

Cnut's conquest of 1016, though brutal, is sometimes still thought of as less traumatic than William's half a century later. There is no good reason to think this. While Cnut's reign proved stable compared to Æthelred's later years, it took a while to mature to that state. In a way, the reigns of Æthelred and Cnut are mirror images of each other: Æthelred's started with relative stability and descended into chaos, and Cnut's started with chaos and progressed to relative stability. Make no mistake, though – the early part of Cnut's tenure was full of turmoil and instability, murder and rumour. Many of the same chaotic measures employed by Æthelred were used by Cnut as he tried to find his footing. In this sense, it is hard to say that the Danish Conquest necessarily involved less displacement or trauma than the Norman one. It has merely been talked about less.

Cnut began his reign by initiating a purge of high-ranking nobles from the old guard, not unlike Æthelred's 'palace revolution' of 1006. One of them was Eadric Streona, the most infamous of Æthelred's advisors. His career had not been especially long, but it had been winding. The previous chapter detailed how he had served Æthelred from 1006–15, submitted to Cnut in 1015, switched allegiance to Edmund in 1016, and finally came back around to Cnut later that year. Although Cnut initially allowed him to maintain control of Mercia, Eadric's skill for self-preservation finally met its match when Cnut had him killed.[234] The *Encomium* contains a narrative about how this happened. Cnut asks him, 'Shall you, who have deceived your own lord with guile, be capable of being true to me?' He then gives the command to 'pay this man what we owe him: that is to say, kill him, lest he play us false', and Eadric is beheaded on the spot.[235]

It is hard to fault Cnut for his desire to be rid of Eadric, who repeatedly proved he could not be trusted, but others met their ends in similar ways. One of them was Uhtred, the lord who had fought well for Æthelred against the Scots. 1016 had been a busy year for Uhtred: he had campaigned with Edmund Ironside and then switched sides to Cnut, who rewarded his defection by having him killed. But according to the twelfth-century *Historia Regum Anglorum*, Uhtred fought a battle at Carham against two kings, Malcolm II of Scotland and Owen the Bald of Strathclyde, in 1018. Another twelfth-century source, *The History of the Church of Durham*, likewise mentions a battle at Carham in 1018, placing it after the appearance of a comet that was visible for thirty nights. The battle was a victory for Malcolm, who was said to have control of the surrounding area thereafter.[236] This obviously complicates matters if Cnut had Uhtred killed in 1016. While some historians have felt strongly enough in Uhtred's identification to move the battle of Carham up from 1018 to 1016, the *Historia Regum Anglorum* may instead be mistaken when it names

Uhtred as the English leader. The aforementioned comet of 1018 was spotted in other places in the world, complicating claims that the battle actually took place in 1016. Historians sometimes substitute Uhtred's brother and successor Eadwulf Cudel ('cuttlefish') as the English leader instead, conceding that 1018 is the most viable dating and that Uhtred had died in 1016.[237] It may simply be that the English leader against the Scots and Britons of Strathclyde is unknown, and Uhtred was mistakenly named because he had indeed fought a battle against Malcolm II – the only problem was that it was in 1006, not 1018.

The more important point about the battle of Carham is that it shows how vulnerable England remained, even with a viking warrior prince on the throne. As Cnut struggled to establish his hold on England, assassinating various members of the previous regime, old enemies popped up to pick at the scraps. Malcolm II had not lost his opportunistic sense of timing, which had seen him launch an attack on Durham in 1006 after years of viking raids and famine in England. He had lost in 1006, but the situation in 1016–18 was just as chaotic (if not more so), and his risk-taking was rewarded by an overwhelming victory. Cnut would not retaliate against Scotland for nearly a decade.

Cnut instead spent the years 1016–18 moving against enemies who were closer to home. Besides Eadric's death in 1016 and Uhtred's in 1016 (or 1018), Æthelred's son Eadwig was exiled and subsequently killed in 1017. The *ASC* also lists 'Ealdorman Æthelweard' and 'Brihtric' as notable victims of Cnut's killings. As much as Cnut worked to discredit his long-reigning predecessor, he had taken a page right out of Æthelred's book.[238] Among the ealdormen, only Leofwine survived the purge and retained his position, although his brother Northman was killed.[239] Leofwine is scarcely mentioned in chronicles compared to the more prominent Eadric, but perhaps it was better to avoid flying too close to the sun. When Leofwine died, he was replaced by his son Leofric, who would play an important role in the reigns of Cnut, Harold, Harthacnut, and Edward the Confessor. Some vacancies were filled by new Englishmen, such as Godwin, whose father, Wulfnoth, had been a lord during Æthelred's reign. Wulfnoth's claim to fame was being accused of treachery by Eadric's family in 1009 and fleeing with a large portion of the royal fleet.[240] Perhaps for Cnut, an enemy of Eadric and Æthelred was a friend of his, and Godwin quickly rose to prominence. Cnut initially held Wessex for himself, but soon yielded it to Godwin. Godwin and his descendants would remain at the centre of English politics for the next fifty years.

In other cases, purged nobles were replaced by Scandinavians. An earl named Hakon appeared at Cnut's side, the son of Cnut's ally and mentor Erik, and would go on to assist him in the battle at Holy River ten years later. Thorkell the Tall, the longtime rival of Swein and Cnut, was installed as earl of East Anglia, the same area he had occupied as a marauding viking commander during Æthelred's later years. He was among the most powerful men in England in the late 1010s and early 1020s. A subtle shift even occurred in the wording for the highest noble office, as the Old English 'ealdorman' was supplanted by the Old Norse 'earl' (or 'jarl') during Cnut's time.

The *ASC* provides a clue that the upheaval extended well beyond the noble classes, though. It notes that around this time, Cnut outlawed someone named Eadwig, who was called 'king of the *ceorls*' – in other words, 'king of the peasants' or 'king of the commoners'. Different versions of the *ASC* place his outlawing in different years, with the E text mentioning it in the entry for 1017 and C placing it with the events of 1020. John of Worcester followed the 1017 dating when mentioning Eadwig in his own history. In any case, Eadwig, king of the *ceorls*, was outlawed at some point early in Cnut's reign. The *ASC* purposely distinguishes this Eadwig from Æthelred's son of the same name who was killed in 1017, so we can be clear that Eadwig, king of the *ceorls*, was not one of the *æthelings*. It is exceedingly rare for the *ASC* to mention a 'commoner', as its entries are instead dominated by kings, nobles, ecclesiastics, and war leaders. Unfortunately, it gives us no clue what Eadwig was up to or exactly why he was punished. But based on his nickname, the most logical explanation is that Eadwig was the leader of a peasant movement or uprising that grew so strong that Cnut was forced to deal with it. This episode was then fossilised into the *ASC* as Eadwig, king of the *ceorls*, being outlawed in the same breath as much more traditionally powerful figures like Ealdorman Æthelweard. After years of devastation under Æthelred and continued chaos under Edmund Ironside, perhaps the ordinary people of England were at a breaking point. When Cnut imposed even heavier taxes than Æthelred had, the result is hardly surprising: loosely organised backlash under a charismatic figurehead who became known as 'king of the *ceorls*', who was then outlawed. His movement, whatever it was, vanished without further note.

Cnut's high taxes would have affected all classes in one way or another. The *ASC* says that the new king did not pay off his massive invasion fleet until 1018, and when he did, it came at the astounding cost of £72,000 – far larger than anything Æthelred ever organised. An additional £10,500 was secured from London alone, bringing the total to a staggering £82,500, which nearly doubled Æthelred's infamous payment of 1012. The steepest payment of so-called 'Danegeld' thus came, ironically, under Cnut himself.[241] After these men were paid off, most of them returned to Scandinavia, heavy with loot and boasting of their adventures. Some of them erected runestones to memorialise their adventures that referred to taking 'the geld' in England. Cnut did maintain a fleet of forty ships in England after 1018, which was pared down to sixteen at some point.[242]

Despite killing and ousting much of the old guard, Cnut also made significant efforts to link himself with the previous dynasty. He paid his respects to Edmund Ironside at Glastonbury and echoed the laws of Edgar, deliberately associating himself with what must have seemed like a golden era of peace and good kingship.[243] Any positive reference to Æthelred was avoided. He remained a threat to Cnut even from beyond the grave in the form of his living children. Two of his sons, Edward and Alfred, were in exile in Normandy. Cnut and his administration had a fine line to walk, but they did it masterfully. Edgar and his West Saxon predecessors were presented as good and righteous rulers, but it was dangerous to extend this honour to the more recent Æthelred, so he was instead avoided or obliquely referred to as an author of bad laws, who had presumably forfeited his right to rule through his own mismanagement and wickedness.

Cnut may have also felt that Edmund was 'safer' to honour because he had no known living children – at least, that is what Cnut thought. According to John of Worcester, Cnut had sent Edmund's infant sons away to Sweden to be killed, but the Swedish king, Olaf, had mercy on them and allowed them to escape into exile. They lived at the royal court in Hungary, apparently unbeknownst to anyone in England. Even the exiles' uncle, Edward the Confessor, did not learn of their survival until 1054. This helps explain why Cnut felt that it was too dangerous to explicitly honour Æthelred, but had no such reservations about Edmund – Cnut was under the impression that Edmund was a dynastic dead end.

Most significantly, Cnut married Emma of Normandy (Æthelred's widow) even though he was already married to Ælfgifu of Northampton. The *ASC* says that Cnut had Emma 'fetched', perhaps indicating that she had not fled from England and had been stuck in London during the final siege. The *Encomium*'s version of events, as usual, is a bit confusing because it does not align well with the *ASC*. The *Encomium* places Emma in Normandy at this time and portrays her as central to the negotiations – no male relatives were making decisions for her.[244] It does imply that she has a noteworthy political past, calling her a 'famous queen'. Cnut's youth is repeatedly stressed throughout the *Encomium* and in later Scandinavian sagas, and it is likely that Emma was significantly older than Cnut. She had entered the written record in 1002 and had children by the mid-1000s, whereas Cnut is depicted as being unusually young when he rises to prominence a decade later. 'You were of no great age when you pushed off your ships', says a *Knútsdrápa*, a poem written in honour of Cnut. 'Never, younger than you, did [a] prince set out to take his part in war.'[245] In the *Encomium*, Emma's past is left in the dark aside from vague references to her political standing and the implication that she is older than Cnut. The *Encomium* avoids directly associating her with Æthelred or the conquered dynasty, instead portraying her as solely Norman at this stage.

To Cnut's followers in Scandinavia, marrying his predecessor's widow signalled that he was a dominant king. It was common in Scandinavia for conquering warlords to marry the wives of dead or less dominant rulers, but there was more going on here than mere posturing and boasting.[246] Emma, despite growing more distant from Æthelred's court in the early 1010s, was valuable to Cnut. Just as Cnut's marriage to Ælfgifu around 1013 had been strategically important, so too was his marriage to Emma in 1017. Emma was a link to the old dynasty who was familiar with English administration and politics. Like Wulfstan, she could guide Cnut through the minefield of royal politics because she had been there before. Unlike Wulfstan, though, Emma had something in common with Cnut: she had also grown up elsewhere and adapted to a new political environment. It's possible that they both spoke Danish since Emma's mother spoke it.[247] Some have even claimed that Emma and Cnut enjoyed a love marriage, although this is an overreach.[248] It's understandable that some modern commentators have gleaned this from the *Encomium*, which speaks highly of Cnut and portrays him and Emma as an ideal royal couple, but the *Encomium* is also propaganda. We cannot know much of their inner lives. Her status seems to have been lower in the earlier years of the reign. In the 1020s and 1030s, though, she is ranked highly in witness lists of royal diplomas, sometimes just after the king himself. Whether the apparent closeness in the *Encomium* was the product of propaganda or genuine affection cannot be known. Perhaps it was a little of both.

Emma and Cnut had two known children: a son, Harthacnut, and a daughter, Gunnhilda, who later married the future German emperor, Henry III. Although this was not a high output by medieval standards, it should not be surprising given that Cnut and Emma were often separated from each other when Cnut travelled overseas. Another contributing factor is that Emma was older than Cnut, perhaps by as much as a decade, and could have been in her mid or late thirties when Gunnhilda was born.[249] Emma and Harthacnut made a prominent appearance in 1023 when they were present for the translation of Archbishop Ælfheah's relics. Supposedly Emma had secured a promise from Cnut that he would not promote any of his other children above those he had with Emma, and while the prestige bestowed upon Harthacnut may appear to confirm this, Cnut also entrusted the 'other' royal family – Ælfgifu and her children – with more authority than he gave to Emma.[250] Medieval chroniclers like William of Jumièges wrote that Ælfgifu had actually been married 'in the Danish fashion', although it is not clear what this entailed other than being of lower status than a full wife. But this 'Danish fashion' union is practically unknown outside of what William says about it, and modern historians have referred to it as a myth.[251] There is not much compelling evidence that Ælfgifu of Northampton was put aside, as much as Emma wished she had been, meaning Cnut spent the rest of his reign as a bigamist or something uncomfortably close to it.[252] Rather than viewing Emma as the only legitimate wife who superseded Cnut's earlier union with Ælfgifu, it instead seems that they operated within their own rival spheres of influence. Law codes from the time rail against bigamous unions and taking concubines, perhaps a veiled barb at the king himself, with no effect.[253]

Cnut also issued very English-sounding law codes through Archbishop Wulftsan, a survivor of Æthelred's administration. Indeed, much of Cnut's legislation is derived from the codes of prior kings, particularly those of Edgar and Æthelred. It contains many of the usual religious elements as well, warning against those who practice witchcraft, violate fasts, or work on feast days. But if Cnut's English laws hardly seem 'original', this in itself is significant – Cnut did not use the law to upend English practices. Instead, he conformed to and confirmed them. His administration's approach to English law greatly differs from his heavy-handed approach with Norway in the 1020s and 1030s, where his regents imposed new laws that were seen as harsh and radical.[254] Perhaps it was the influence of the eminent Wulfstan that spared England from a similar fate, or perhaps Cnut recognised that there was no need to overhaul an efficient and effective structure. After all, 'by the time of Æthelred, almost all that would make England run well under a king's control had been set up'.[255]

Cnut's reign saw a noticeable downturn in original literary output, which had often focused on religious matters in previous reigns. Material continued to be copied and revised, but there is far less surviving original material from English writers, aside from the late stages of Wulfstan's career. Later Scandinavian and Icelandic writers committed Cnut's reign to writing, as did continental writers like the encomiast, but it looks like the reform-minded writing that had been so common in the tenth and early eleventh centuries mostly fizzled out in Cnut's reign.[256]

King of Denmark

By 1019, Cnut was in the midst of his turnover of the English court when something unexpected happened. His brother, Harald II of Denmark, died after a reign of about five years. Harald was most likely only a few years older than Cnut, probably still in his twenties, and his demise may have been unexpected. Almost nothing is known about Harald's tenure in Denmark or, by extension, the political situation that Cnut would inherit. Harald and Cnut had brought their mother back from Poland during the latter's visit in 1014, and no Danish raids were launched against England after Cnut won control of it, something Harald probably had much to do with. Most likely, he would not tolerate further raids on what was now friendly territory. Another sign that the brothers were on good terms is a gospel book from Christ Church Canterbury, *c*.1018, that bears Harald's name, although this does not necessarily mean he was physically present in England at any point. Continental writer Thietmar of Merseburg goes so far as to say that Harald fought alongside Cnut during the conquest of England, although he may be ill-informed on this point.[257] Contemporary English sources name several viking leaders involved in the Danish Conquest who were not kings (such as Thorkell, Hemming, Einlaf, Erik Hakonson, and so on), so it seems surprising that all these sources would fail to mention the involvement of Harald II of Denmark. More likely, if Harald did indeed come to England, it was on friendly terms after Cnut had established peace, not during the conquest.

Another rare clue about Harald and Denmark is a late source from the 1200s, the *Annales Ryenses*, that claims Harald was briefly ousted for his 'effeminacy' and debauched lifestyle, although this is so much later than the events it describes that it may not be worth taking seriously. Nonetheless, Cnut's biographer, Timothy Bolton, does not outright dismiss the stories of instability in Harald's reign, and perhaps there is a kernel of truth to them. According to the *Annales Ryenses*, Harald was deposed in favour of Cnut, but was then restored after Cnut was away from Denmark for too long.[258] This late source may instead be remembering a perception that originated after 1019, not before it, when Cnut was indeed splitting time between his kingdoms. Much earlier sources like the *Encomium* and *ASC* give no indication that Cnut was ruler of Denmark twice. They give the opposite impression, with Cnut arriving in Denmark in 1015 not because he was chosen as its king, but because he had been seriously defeated by an English army. In the *Encomium*, Harald has such a firm grip on Denmark that there was nothing Cnut could do about it, no matter how much he pleaded. In any case, if there was instability in Denmark about Harald's quality of rule, it was resolved by Harald's apparent death and Cnut's accession in 1019.

Cnut had paid off much of his fleet in 1018, leaving him with forty ships. But crucially, when Harald died, Cnut took just nine ships with him to claim the Danish throne. The relatively small size of this fleet shows how confident Cnut was about succeeding to Denmark. Maybe Harald had designated Cnut as his preferred successor (Harald is not known to have had children), or perhaps the Danish elites had already negotiated Cnut's return. Either way, with Harald dead after a short and mostly mysterious reign, Cnut would be able to add a second kingdom to his ever-expanding territory. The *ASC* records that he spent 1019–1020 in Denmark as he established control there, although it does not tell us anything about what that entailed. As for Harald, Cnut had already honoured him by having his name entered in the aforementioned gospel book at Canterbury, and Cnut also named one of his sons Harold, surely with Harald II and Harald I Bluetooth in mind.

Unfortunately, the history of eleventh-century Denmark is poorly recorded, and little is known of Cnut's reign there except for his occasional mention in dramatic sagas that were written centuries later. The best early information about the transfer of Danish power from Harald to Cnut comes, perhaps unexpectedly, from Cnut himself. He sent a letter back home to his nobles in England in late 1019 or 1020, which provides a few rare details about the affairs of both kingdoms:

> King Cnut greets in friendship his archbishops and his diocesan bishops, and Earl Thorkel and all his earls, and all his people... Since I did not spare my money as long as hostility was threatening you, I have now with God's help put an end to it with my money. Then I was informed that greater danger was approaching us than we liked at all; and then I went myself with the men who accompanied me to Denmark, from where the greatest

> injury had come to you, and with God's help I have taken measures so that never henceforth shall hostility reach you from there as long as you support me rightly and my life lasts. Now I thank almighty God for his help and his mercy, that I have so settled the great dangers which were approaching us that we need fear no danger to us from there... If anyone, ecclesiastic or laymen, Dane or Englishman, is so presumptuous as to defy God's law and my royal authority or the secular law, and he will not make amends and desist according to the direction of my bishops, I then pray, and also command, Earl Thorkel, if he can, to cause the evil-doer to do right.

The sections of the letter quoted above provide valuable information about the political and military situation Cnut had to deal with following his accession in Denmark. Although he does not explicitly name the 'dangers' he refers to throughout the letter, he may be referring to military threats to England from Danish shores. He refers to deterring them with money earlier, perhaps a reference to his massive £82,500 tribute payment a year earlier, and indicates that he has deterred them again in 1019–20. Read in light of the possible peasant uprising under Eadwig, king of the *ceorls*, it almost looks like Cnut is desperately trying to explain what his burdensome taxes are being used for. But Cnut could do more than just solve problems with money. Thietmar of Merseburg writes that Cnut had destroyed a hostile fleet of thirty vessels in 1018, a detail not recorded by other sources, giving us yet another clue at the kind of protection Cnut could offer. Clearly Cnut was not bluffing when he claimed he could avert danger. Turning back to the unnamed 'dangers' in the letter specifically, perhaps after the death of Cnut's ally and brother Harald, Danish captains were again planning to raid in England, but Cnut's arrival in Denmark (and possibly his pocketbook) put a stop to any such plans. Cnut says that England will be safe from Danish hostilities as long as his life lasts, indicating that he secured some kind of assurance from his Danish subjects that England was off limits. England and Denmark were both under Cnut's control now, and anyone who dared cross him would be defying their own ruler.

The letter also tells us who was calling the shots in England while Cnut was away. Thorkell, Earl of East Anglia, is given the preeminent spot among the earls and is specifically tasked with maintaining order at home. Thorkell's prominent position did not last long. Cnut returned home in 1020 and outlawed Thorkell the next year. According to the *Vita Edwardi Regis*, Earl Godwin became English regent around this time because he had fought well for Cnut in a 1022 campaign in Scandinavia.[259] The *ASC* does not record any reason for Thorkell's banishment, but does note that he was restored to favour in 1023, when he and Cnut exchanged sons as *de facto* hostages. Perhaps Thorkell, with his fearsome reputation as a warlord, had been stirring up trouble elsewhere in Scandinavia. The name of Thorkell's son is unknown, and neither is it clear which son Cnut exchanged with him. However, given that Harthacnut was present in England for St Ælfheah's translation from London to Canterbury, it was probably either Swein or Harold. Ryan Lavelle has reasoned that the latter was likely too young, meaning Swein is the best candidate.[260] In a stunning reversal of fortune, Cnut then 'entrusted' Denmark to Thorkell, effectively making him a regent, although his exact level of control there has been questioned.[261]

Even more surprisingly, after his triumphant return to Cnut's inner circle, Thorkell vanishes from history. He had been one of the foremost players in English and Danish politics for a decade and a half, starting with his devastating campaigns in England from 1009–1012 and then transitioning into increasingly prominent roles – Æthelred's mercenary, earl of East Anglia, and eventually Cnut's regent in England and Denmark. It seems shocking that such an influential figure could disappear without a trace, but it illustrates just how threadbare the sources can be for early Denmark and England. The only clue about Thorkell's demise comes from Osbern of Canterbury, who alleges that Thorkell was killed by a mob in Denmark, a surprisingly common fate among Danish nobles and kings. If this account can be trusted, it was an inglorious end to a remarkable career. With that said, the silence in all other surviving sources means that a willing retirement or natural death is not out of the question. Even though Cnut obviously had a suspicious mind and had executed previous nobles seemingly at random, no one insinuated anything like this happened to Thorkell. Even Osbern's story depicts Thorkell being killed by commoners, not by the king. Whether he died violently or of natural causes, Thorkell disappears from recorded history after 1023, similar to the scores of thegns and ealdormen of the tenth century whose attestations simply cease at some point.

Although the ascendant Godwin may have been in charge in England by this time, Thorkell's death or retirement left Cnut with a glaring hole at court in Denmark. Cnut travelled widely in the 1020s, everywhere from Norway to Rome, so he needed someone he could trust to rule his native kingdom in his stead. The man chosen to succeed Thorkell there was Ulf, whose life is marginally better recorded than most of Cnut's mysterious inner circle. Ulf had been present in England at least once in the early 1020s, as his name appears on a charter from *c.*1022 known as S 980. His name also appears in the Thorney Abbey *Liber Vitae*, one of the most valuable sources for identifying members of Cnut's court, which also includes some very recognisable names like Emma, Ælfgifu (of Northampton?), Harthacnut, and Harold I. The list of names in the *Liber Vitae* was copied down in its existing form sometime around the year 1100, making it difficult to know exactly when each individual originally visited, but Ulf's name could have been written down around the same time he was in England to witness S 980.

With a paranoid streak to rival Æthelred's, Cnut needed to be sure he could trust Ulf to govern Denmark loyally. The king turned to a tried and true method he had used with success in the past: marriage alliances. Ulf married Cnut's sister Estrid, and Ulf's sister Gytha was married to Godwin, Cnut's fast-rising English earl. Ulf was now bound to the English court on multiple levels through Cnut and Godwin, mirroring the double marriages Cnut had to Ælfgifu of Northampton and Emma. In spite of this good planning, Ulf would not remain loyal to his new brother-in-law for long.

Holy River and Norway

By the mid-1020s, Cnut was undoubtedly the most powerful ruler in Scandinavia, especially thanks to his vast resources in England, so his Norwegian and Swedish counterparts began scheming against him. The Swedish king, Anund Jacob, and the Norwegian king, Olaf Haraldsson, hoped that their combined strength could check Cnut. Olaf in particular had history with Cnut – he had fought alongside Æthelred in 1014, helping to expel Cnut from England that year. Anund Jacob and Olaf secured the help of someone named Ulf, and this is generally thought to be the same figure Cnut had installed as the Danish regent, although this identification is not certain. That said, if there is one figure of Cnut's reign who could simply be referred to as 'Ulf' with no other explanation in English sources like the *ASC*, this is it. English sources also name an Einlaf as Ulf's counterpart in the affair, which was the name of Ulf's brother, who held an English earldom. Ulf the regent and his brother, the earl Einlaf, stand out as the prime suspects until shown otherwise.

This then begs the question: why would Ulf and Einlaf play such a dangerous game, risking the ire of their king by siding with his enemies? There is little in the surviving sources to betray their motives. One saga does portray Ulf as opportunistic, hoping to place Cnut's son Harthacnut on the Danish throne and rule through him instead, although the source could simply be reading into events that happened anyway; Harthacnut was eventually installed as

Danish king under Cnut. It is also difficult to see how this would be dramatically more beneficial for Ulf, given that either way, he would still be Danish regent. An argument could be made that Ulf would not have to answer to young Harthacnut the same way he did to Cnut, although he would end up in the same situation a few years later when Harthacnut came of age anyway (he would have been around 8 or 9 years old at this time). No matter the motive, Ulf's defection meant Cnut had fallen out with a regent for the second time in five years, following Thorkell's fall from power in England in 1021.

Matters came to a head in 1026, when Cnut faced off against his enemies at a place in Scandinavia known only as Holy River, resulting in a naval battle. Unfortunately, the many medieval sources that mention this evidently significant battle vary in detail about who was involved and who won. It is not even clear where 'Holy River' is, as there are two locations known by this name, one near Denmark and one in Sweden.[262] Saxo Grammaticus adds a detail about a land battle as well, meaning there could have been two components of the overall conflict – a naval battle and one on land. The *ASC* says that Cnut, with both English and Danish contingents, fought against Ulf and Einlaf, who were supported by Swedish forces. It also curiously mentions 'both a land force and a naval force', a detail that aligns with Saxo Grammaticus's details about an accompanying land battle. In the *ASC*, Holy River involved heavy losses on each side, but was a victory for Ulf, Einlaf, and the Swedes. Other sources include different details about the battle. The *Heimskringla* says that Cnut's opponents were led by the kings Olaf Haraldsson and Anund Jacob, and it adds that Cnut was supported by Earl Hakon, who was prominent in England. A *Knutsdrapa* poem (in honour of Cnut) reframes the battle more favourably, saying Cnut 'smote the Swedes at a place called Holy River', implying a victory or at least something close to it. This is the same poem that praises Cnut for 'making war in green Lindsey' – the site of his defeat to Æthelred in 1014 – so perhaps it is best not to take it too literally. Rather than reflecting clear-cut victories, it is probably more accurate to say the poet, writing expressly in praise of Cnut, is memorialising times when Cnut's armies fought hard, regardless of outcome. Scandinavian sources do mention Ulf being involved in some double-dealing, too – the source for the aforementioned story of Ulf trying to place Harthacnut on the Danish throne and rule through him.[263]

The battle at Holy River was clearly a significant event in Cnut's middle reign, given that it was referenced in so many sources, but it remains frustratingly unclear exactly who won (if anyone), why it happened, or even where it occurred. Nonetheless, this hodgepodge of sources seem to indicate that Ulf had been given control of Denmark and, left to his own devices, quickly got up to trouble when contacted by Cnut's enemies. He allied himself with the Norwegian and Swedish kings, possibly also supported by his brother Einlaf. Cnut arrived, supplemented by English troops, and was involved in a possibly inconclusive naval battle that left both sides weakened, perhaps with a separate conflict occurring on land. According to one legend, Cnut then dramatically had Ulf murdered in a church in Roskilde, Denmark (a predecessor of Roskilde Cathedral). His brother Einlaf was evidently forgiven, as he was in England as late as 1035.[264] It turned out that Cnut was no better at controlling his subordinates than his much-maligned predecessor Æthelred had been, but he was just as good at disposing of them.

According to a source known as the *Oldest Saga of St Olaf,* Cnut withdrew after Holy River but left his fleet in place, essentially trapping the Norwegians in the east. In the meantime, Cnut travelled to Rome, potentially leaving the Norwegian forces to return home via land, a rugged and dangerous journey considering they had only been planning on travelling by sea.[265] The next year, after his visit to Rome was complete, Cnut brought fifty ships with him to Norway and deposed Olaf Haraldsson, apparently without resistance.

It may seem surprising to learn that Cnut was able to conquer Norway after an inconclusive battle at Holy River, or worse, one that is characterised as a defeat in sources like the *ASC*. But if it is correct that Olaf's forces were decimated on their long trek through the harsh interior of Norway, this would have two significant advantages for Cnut that could make sense of his apparently bloodless coup. The first is obviously a reduction in the number of fighting men who could oppose him, but the second is that a disastrous loss of troops may have broadly weakened Olaf's support. John of Worcester also relays the dubious detail that the Norwegians despised Olaf because he was too gentle and pious, which is hard to square with Olaf's battle-hardened reputation. The battle was not Cnut's only move against Norway, though. He paired it with lavish gift-giving, where ruling men were wooed to Cnut's cause through bribes and promises (Cnut's son Harold would mimic these techniques a few years later when he laid claim to England). It also did not hurt that Cnut had brought a fleet of fifty ships with him, marvellously decked out in gold, as a show of both might and blinding wealth. The marvellous ships were not just a threat, but also a lure. Cnut could promise more spoils, loot, and prestige than Olaf could.

However, Cnut's most important asset may not have been bullion or a fleet, but a person. Hakon Eriksson, who had fought alongside Cnut at Holy River, was the son of Erik, the former Earl of Lade. Hakon was 'the last scion of his dynasty', and could lay claim to much of Norway through his late father. Hakon was also the son of Cnut's half-sister, Gytha, and Scandinavian sources refer to him as Cnut's nephew.[266] Hakon helped Cnut appeal to those who wished to return to the days before Olaf had taken over. Cnut and Hakon were a package deal, with the implication being that Hakon would return to his ancestral lands and rule them directly, and Cnut would serve as his overlord. The *ASC* flattens this arrangement somewhat, saying only that Cnut 'made good his claim' to Norway, skipping over Hakon, although in practice this is correct. Hakon had been installed as its governor, but Cnut was ultimately in charge of Norway. Olaf did not immediately resist Cnut and Hakon, instead seeking refuge in the mountains of Norway.

Cnut had added another territory to his ever-growing realm, a network of kingdoms that was beginning to look like something grander. For all its connotations, the term 'empire' has indeed been applied to Cnut's collection of kingdoms. There has been much hair-splitting over what constitutes an empire, but nonetheless, England, Denmark, and Norway under Cnut are sometimes collectively referred to as the North Sea Empire or, more rarely, the Anglo-Scandinavian Empire. Whatever one wishes to call it, Cnut had reached the zenith of his power. His prestige, though, reached its pinnacle not in Scandinavia, but in Rome, where Cnut attended the coronation of Emperor Conrad II and met with the Pope himself.

A Christian King

Amazingly, sandwiched between the battle of Holy River in 1026 and his conquest of Norway in 1028, Cnut managed to travel all the way to Rome to see the crowning of Conrad II, the new emperor – an event no English king had attended before. There is even some evidence that Cnut initially attempted to influence the election by backing a rival candidate from Aquitaine, Duke William V, although Cnut's prominent position at Conrad II's coronation means that he obviously assented to Conrad's eventual selection.[267] Cnut was dabbling in European politics at a level never seen before from an English king. However, to be fair to his predecessors, Cnut was not the first English king to travel to or interact with Rome. As early as the ninth century, the overthrown Mercian king, Burgred, had retired to Rome, and the West Saxon king Æthelwulf had visited Rome during his reign, bringing a young Alfred the Great with him. More recently, Æthelred had hosted a papal legate in England in 991 to resolve a dispute with Normandy. While these episodes reveal England's often unrecognised connections to Rome and mainland Europe, they pale in comparison to Cnut's international involvement. Perhaps for the first time in its long history, England (and by extension, Denmark and Norway) was emerging as a power on a European scale. Edgar and Æthelred had aspired to be emperor of the British Isles. Cnut had extended English influence further than either of them could have imagined.

Cnut's presence at the coronation had multiple advantages for him. He got to forge a relationship with Conrad, whose realm may not have been a concern for the English but directly bordered Denmark. Conrad's son Henry and Cnut's daughter Gunnhilda were also married a decade later, and perhaps the close connection between the two houses originally began at Rome in 1027.[268] But the Emperor was not the only powerful ruler Cnut wished to parlay with; Cnut met with the Pope in Rome, as well.

It was an obscure time for the papacy, with little known about it beyond some colourful stories of wicked immorality. Most famously, Peter Damian, a contemporary reformer, accused all ranks of clergy of simony, sexual immorality, and violence, and other chroniclers like Rudulf Glaber echoed his concerns. As with previous scandalous stories, it can be dangerous to read too far into what reformers had to say about their opponents. But even if the stories of turning the Lateran into a brothel are exaggerated, there can be little doubt that papal politics were viewed as corrupt by onlookers. In the early eleventh century, Rome was controlled by a powerful family, the Counts of Tusculum, and they often succeeded in getting their own kinsmen placed on the papal throne. The Pope who greeted Cnut with a letter *c.*1018, Benedict VIII, was one of them.[269]

The Pope that Cnut met in 1027 was yet another member of the family, Benedict VIII's brother, John XIX. John was certainly no churchman – he was a layman when he had been chosen to succeed his brother as Pope, and he had to be rushed through the various ordinations before he could wear the tiara. Even though he was more politician than priest, John was one of the tamer Tusculan popes.

There are rumours of bribes and concerns about extortionate fees to pilgrims, but nothing like the rapes and murders that John's nephew, Benedict IX, would be accused of during his three stints as Pope (Benedict IX even allegedly sold the papacy itself at one point).

But even in this era, which 'may be justly called a historic nadir' for the papacy, Cnut was awed by what he experienced in Rome.[270] Some of this may be mere posturing for his audience back home, playing up the glory of a prestigious trip to the heart of Christendom, but it is also possible that it was indeed more splendorous than anything he knew of in Denmark or England. Cnut, as a bigamist, was probably also relieved that he did not have to fear a moral rebuke from the pragmatic John XIX. As two ruthless rulers with pious exteriors, perhaps John and Cnut made natural allies. According to Cnut's letter, he and John talked business first and foremost, with good results. The king knew that his English pilgrims were burdened by the high fees they paid to travel to and through Rome, and he managed to convince the Pope that the fees should be relaxed. There is some independent evidence that English pilgrims were indeed exempt from fees in Pavia (northern Italy) around this time, so apparently Pope John kept his word and enforced the agreement.[271] Cnut returned home to England with tangible results to show for his absence.

Outside of his visit to Rome, Cnut also went to great lengths to ensure he was seen as a pious Christian, just like the traditional West Saxon kings before him. He sometimes went by his baptismal name, Lambert, and gave lavishly to churches and monasteries.[272] The most famous surviving image of the king is a contemporary illustration depicting his gift of a massive golden cross on the New Minster *Liber Vitae*, with Queen Emma at his side. The encomiast mentions how he saw Cnut make a spectacle of his visit to St Omer's, beating his chest and sobbing, and was evidently impressed by it.

Perhaps this seems bombastic to twenty-first century eyes, but it ensured that no one could miss the message: Cnut was a pious, generous, and active Christian monarch who was so far removed from his pagan heritage that he was nearly indistinguishable from previous kings like Edgar. Fittingly, the most famous image of Edgar is also one of overt, almost flashy, piety – it depicts him rejoicing beneath Christ, flanked by St Peter and the Virgin Mary. The parallels are hard to ignore. More importantly, Cnut's displays of piety worked. Later chroniclers like William of Malmesbury portrayed Cnut as a good Christian king who returned England to stability after decades of misrule under the wicked Æthelred. While there is obviously far more to a ruler's success than their piety (or lack of it), Cnut made Christianity a core part of his identity in England, something that must have made his advisor Wulfstan proud.

Family Matters: Regents and Delegation

Ulf, Cnut's brother-in-law and governor of Denmark, had died in the late 1020s, allegedly killed on Church grounds. The location of Ulf's killing may raise eyebrows, but the fact that it was ordered should hardly be surprising. It was only the latest in a long line of purges Cnut had made throughout his reign. Ulf's betrayal may have particularly stung Cnut, because Ulf had married into the royal family yet still supported the king's enemies at Holy River. Cnut replaced Ulf with someone not just related by marriage, but by blood. Cnut's own son, Harthacnut, would serve as the representative of Cnut's power over Denmark from the mid-1020s onward, effectively a sub-king or under-king for his father. Harthacnut was still a child at this point, though. Harthacnut may have already been ruling in Denmark as a sub-king prior to Ulf's downfall, judging by the tale of Ulf seeking to rule 'through' him, but it is not known who was assisting young Harthacnut with the everyday affairs of his kingdom after Ulf's death. It cannot have been Cnut, who was in England far more often than Scandinavia during his last decade of life. As the 1020s rolled into the 1030s, perhaps Harthacnut gradually assumed more duties. That said, almost nothing is known of Harthacnut's early Danish reign.

Although Harthacnut had been established as king of Denmark, Cnut had another vacancy to fill a few years later. Hakon, who had received control of Norway in 1028, met his end in 1029. The *ASC* memorialises him as 'brave earl Hakon', adding that he had died in a shipwreck. Cnut mirrored the strategy he had just used in Denmark. There would be no more nobles governing kingdoms in his stead. He would only use immediate family members from this point on. With Harthacnut already present in Denmark, Cnut turned to his first marriage to help fill the void in Norway. Ælfgifu of Northampton and their eldest son, Swein, were appointed as co-rulers of Norway.

By this point, Cnut's family network was stretched thin. One wife was associated with the English government and one with the Norwegian regime, and two sons were now serving as sub-kings. Cnut was planning for his daughter Gunnhilda to marry the son of Emperor Conrad II, Henry, at this time as well, leaving only Harold Harefoot unoccupied. Perhaps Harold lived with his brother and mother in Norway, or perhaps he lived in obscurity in northern England, as Frank Barlow once reasoned that he 'was probably considered a native of Northampton'.[273] But no medieval source informs us of his whereabouts until 1035, when he suddenly bursts onto the scene in England. In 1030, Harold was looking like the forgotten middle child, but should any further turnover happen, perhaps Cnut had plans to deploy him as well.

It is interesting that Swein, who was at least five years older than Harthacnut, would be required to rule alongside his mother. Someone of similar stature was likely assisting Harthacnut as well, perhaps Ulf initially, but it was certainly not his mother Emma. There is no evidence she left England during these years. Perhaps Cnut wished to avoid a repeat of the Ulf-Harthacnut dynamic and reasoned that if he was going to entrust a conquered kingdom to another inexperienced son, he was going to send his more politically seasoned wife with him. That way, no external party could have inordinate sway over Swein. The decision to send Ælfgifu is also a hint of her significant political abilities, which she had demonstrated in securing a match to Cnut in the first place and remaining married to Cnut even after he married Emma. Ælfgifu would again demonstrate her political prowess in the aftermath of Cnut's death. Cnut may have genuinely thought Ælfgifu was the most capable ruler available to him, and Swein's presence could have even been secondary to this, as he was only about 15 and still had much to learn.

But for all the ability Ælfgifu displayed at other times in her life, her stint in Norway was a troubled one. She and Swein managed to hold on to power for half a decade, but those five years were so difficult for the Norwegians that it was immortalised in verse as 'Ælfgifu's Time', an era of such hardship that people were forced to eat the food of livestock and chew rind like goats. Ælfgifu and Swein also enacted unpopular laws, supposedly based on those in Denmark, such as requiring no ship to leave the country without their permission. It is hard to imagine how such an act would even be enforceable, but it serves as an illustration of how harsh and controlling Norway's government was perceived to be. Ælfgifu and Swein also lacked the appeal of Hakon; he had been the son of a powerful earl of Lade, someone with a direct claim to much of Norway, unlike the more distant Ælfgifu and Swein, who seemed more like symbols of foreign power than rightful rulers coming home. Hakon, Ælfgifu, and Swein were all related to Cnut, of course, and Cnut is who the Norwegians ultimately owed allegiance to. But it is important to recognise that they did not all possess the same advantages in the eyes of Norway's nobility.

It may also be significant that this era was remembered as 'Ælfgifu's Time', not 'Swein's Time' – a clue that Ælfgifu may have been perceived as the real decision maker between the two. As a foreign woman at the top of the political hierarchy during a time of famine and hardship, Ælfgifu also could have been an easier target for critics than her son, Swein. Male writers may have never been particularly sympathetic to an outsider like Ælfgifu, even in good times.[274] Indeed the greatest surprise about her stint in Norway may not be that she was eventually overthrown, but that she survived there for half a decade first.

The oppressive rule of Ælfgifu and Swein collapsed in 1035, when Olaf Haraldsson returned from exile and gained enough support to drive them from the country. Swein died at about the same time, but Ælfgifu found her way back to England. Norway was involved in a constant see-saw between factions by now, with Cnut's family on one side and ex-king Olaf on the other. Olaf's restoration was brief. He was overthrown again just months later, dying at the Battle of Stiklestad against a coalition of nobles who were more aligned with Cnut. The Olaf faction would remain in power through Olaf's illegitimate son, Magnus, however – a figure who, along with Harthacnut, would pass on the Danish-Norwegian power struggle to a new generation.

The British Isles and Normandy

For all his triumphs against Norwegian and Swedish opponents in the late 1020s and early 1030s, Cnut was not content with Scandinavian hegemony. He sought dominance over the British Isles too, a goal that would have been familiar to his English predecessors. Cnut went to Scotland at some point in this era, although there is some confusion over the year, with 1027 and 1031 both being possibilities. Several versions of the *ASC* say Cnut's journey to Scotland took place 'as soon as he came home' from Rome, which should mean 1027, but the E version of the *ASC* records this as being 1031. One way to resolve the discrepancy is to assume that Cnut visited Rome twice, and Cnut's biographer M. K. Lawson has argued that this is not as far-fetched as it may seem.[275] Given how widely and quickly Cnut was able to travel, maybe two visits to Rome are not out of the question. Cnut might have travelled more miles in some years than earlier English kings did in their lifetimes. With all that acknowledged, other historians instead prefer the simpler explanation that one of the dates is incorrect.[276]

Since Conrad II's coronation can be safely dated to 1027, this leaves the remaining year, 1031, for Cnut's Scottish incursion.

As is common in early English history, the motives and context for Cnut's Scottish campaign were left unrecorded. However, the Scottish king, Malcolm II, had attacked England in 1016 or 1018, and Cnut's journey north may have been a (very belated) way to return the favour. It could also be that following his journey to Rome and involvement in imperial politics, Cnut knew he was at the height of his power and could force any of his neighbours into submission if he wished. It is not explicitly stated that this was a military campaign, but it is reasonable to assume that Cnut was at the head of a large army or fleet. English kings rarely ventured too far north of Wessex without arms. Eadred led an army to Northumbria, and Edmund I and Æthelred II both did the same for Strathclyde, for example. But Cnut was going much farther than that, as far north in Britain as the great Æthelstan had gone in 934. It is almost impossible to conceive that he would go this far into unfriendly territory without a large army. After Cnut arrived in Scotland, three kings submitted to him, including Malcolm II and the Macbeth of Shakespeare fame. The other figure who surrendered, King Iehmarc (or Echmarcach), was a powerful figure in Dublin and the Isles. Cnut's biographer Ryan Lavelle reasons that no fighting likely occurred, due to Cnut presumably bringing an overwhelming show of force with him.[277] Rudulf Glaber asserts that Cnut once fought a war against Malcolm II, although this is more likely to refer to the aftermath of the Battle of Carham in 1016 or 1018 – perhaps an otherwise unrecorded detail about Cnut getting his revenge earlier than 1031. The submission of three kings invites comparisons to Edgar's famous outing on the River Dee and the submission of seven lesser kings. Cnut clearly aimed to imitate Edgar in his laws and deeds, and even contemporary art depicts them similarly.[278] Judging by the success of Cnut in Scotland, the comparison seems well-founded.

Unlike with Scotland, Cnut's relationship with north-western Britain is mostly unknown to us. If he ever directed campaigns to

Strathclyde or the Isle of Man like Æthelred had, we have been left no trace of them. Instead, it may be that Cnut, as a Scandinavian, preferred to direct his attention to the east and north, rather than to the northwest as his West Saxon predecessors had. Wales received some attention as usual, though, as normal raiding activity persisted into Cnut's reign. The *Annales Cambriae* records a 1022 incursion into Wales that was led by Einlaf, one of Cnut's earls who had land in Mercia, following the age-old tradition of Mercian earls campaigning in Wales.[279] Similar incursions had occurred in 983 and 1012, for example.[280] The *Annales Cambriae* also records that a 'Caradog ap Rederch was killed by the English' in 1035, at the very end of Cnut's reign or the very start of Harold Harefoot's.[281] Aside from the mere mention of these events, almost nothing is known about them, but they do fit the wider context of constant back-and-forth raiding between England and Wales in the tenth and eleventh centuries.

The king's relations with Normandy remained tricky throughout his reign, existing in an uncomfortable equilibrium. Cnut's wife Emma was from Normandy, and her brother Richard ruled as its duke until 1026. Despite these close ties, Normandy also sheltered Emma's sons by Æthelred – Edward and Alfred – who would become major players in English politics after Cnut's death. While Cnut was alive, they remained off-limits to him, but surely he was wary of their ambitions and ancestry. Cnut had been able to exile or pick off other sons and grandsons of Æthelred, such as Eadwig (who was killed in 1017) and Edward the Exile (a son of Edmund Ironside who spent most of his life in eastern Europe). But Æthelred's sons with Emma were protected through their connection to their mother.

Cnut and Emma took steps to lessen the tension, giving priority to the children they had together. According to the *Encomium*, children from their prior marriages would be passed over in favour of any new ones. Obviously, this source is heavily biased toward Emma, but it seems to be correct on this matter. The events that followed Cnut's death more or less confirm the loose hierarchy that these children and stepchildren fell into. Emma and Cnut's son Harthacnut was at the top, followed closely by Cnut and Ælfgifu's sons. Emma and Æthelred's sons were at the bottom. If Cnut had reservations about Edward and Alfred Ætheling's survival, they were well founded, although he would not live to see those fears realised. In the meantime, they lurked in Normandy, waiting in the long shadow that Æthelred cast over Cnut's entire reign.

The Death of a Conqueror

> *The skaldic praises about the Old North and a Viking way of life might have taken on a bittersweet quality when recited in the green and pleasant valleys of Wessex.*[282]
>
> Ryan Lavelle

In his final years, Cnut stayed relatively close to home compared to the distant journeys that had dominated his activity in the 1020s and early 1030s. He had made numerous voyages to Denmark and Norway, and he went to Rome at least once, while also becoming the first English king since Æthelstan to venture into Scotland. However, after 1031, there is no indication that Cnut left England again. His final four years were not entirely stagnant, though. In 1033, he travelled as far north as York, a considerable journey from his base in Wessex. However, it seems that he spent most of his time ruling from Winchester, much as the earlier West Saxon kings had. 'Getting subordinates to travel to you, rather than the other way around, has always been a way of showing superiority', but Cnut's sudden lack of overseas travel after 1031 is startling.[283] William of Jumièges also includes a story about Cnut being in poor health, and although the story itself is suspect, all three of Cnut's modern biographers have speculated that Cnut was indeed in worse health during these final years.[284]

He died at Shaftesbury in November 1035. The date was either November 12, as recorded by the *ASC*, or November 11 as mentioned in records from Exeter, which mentions a 'most pious king Lambert' – Cnut's baptismal name – dying on that date.[285] His body was then transferred to Winchester, where it still supposedly rests to this day. One of the mortuary chests in Winchester Cathedral bears his name, although the chests have had a troubled history and the bones have been jumbled up in the centuries since.[286] That said, Cnut's remains, or at least some of them, still exist in the West Saxon heartland, the place he adopted as his home.

Cnut's death would throw England into yet another tangled succession dispute, hinting that the apparent stability of Cnut's middle and later reign was only skin deep.[287] In this way, he unintentionally mimicked Edgar, the king he consciously sought to imitate in other ways. Like Edgar, Cnut had ascended to the throne through a highly confused state of affairs and enjoyed a calm later reign, but his death brought about a bloody succession dispute. The kingdom's leading figures were about to face off against each other in support of either Harold Harefoot, Cnut's son with Ælfgifu, or Harthacnut, his son with Emma. At least one important figure fled England altogether when Cnut died; a Welsh source claims that Earl Einlaf, who had opposed Cnut at Holy River and then been forgiven, took flight for 'Germania'.[288]

Significantly, though, Edward and Alfred, Æthelred's sons, do not appear to have been in play immediately after Cnut's death. Tom License, Edward's most recent biographer, has argued that perhaps they were considered, but this is not the view of most other historians. Frank Barlow, one of Edward's earlier biographers, lumps Edward and the rest of Æthelred's family into a group of 'potential pretenders' and 'pawns'.[289] From the early sources that survive, Edward and Alfred only become significant after Harold wins the throne, not before. Their involvement was a desperate last-ditch effort by Emma, who panicked upon realising that Harthacnut may never show up. Even when they do arrive at Emma's request, the English themselves are quick to dispose of them, with Edward being stoutly resisted by his own countrymen and Alfred being betrayed almost instantly. While their ultimate fates were far different, both of them were immediately rebuffed out of loyalty to Cnut's son Harold, whose victory was complete by that stage.

In this sense, perhaps the biggest success of Cnut's later reign was not its stability, but that he utterly succeeded in ensuring that someone of his dynasty would be the next English king. Whether that honour fell to Harthacnut or Harold is beside the point; more importantly, it was not going to be Edward or Alfred. Only a generation after Cnut's conquest, England was wholly devoted to upholding Cnut's descendants, even against claimants from the ancient West Saxon line. It is worth noting here that Harold too may have been regarded as 'English' first and foremost rather than Danish, given that his mother was English and that he was already living in England when Cnut died, but he could not claim the kind of illustrious pedigree that Æthelred's children could. Nonetheless, he and his half-brother Harthacnut (who was not English at all!) were the only serious contenders after Cnut's death, demonstrating Cnut's most under-recognised achievement: securing his dynasty's right to succession. For the claimants, a familial connection to Cnut was more important than any kind of national or ethnic identity.

The historical Cnut – at least as close as we can get to him – appears to defy many of the stereotypes applied to him today: ruthless barbarian, ideal Christian king, fool who tried to command the tide. The man who conquered England in 1016 could indeed be ruthless and bloodthirsty, and he was a good and pious Christian ruler, but there is so much more to the story than that. One thing is certain, though. Cnut was not foolish, and neither did he act in ways that denied reality. He was an astute, adaptable, and undoubtedly successful king. He possessed many of the qualities that ideal kings are made of: intelligence, strength, and generosity. It is unfortunate that today he is remembered less for being a conqueror (and perhaps something close to an emperor) than for the legend about him trying to control the tide.

5

Cnut's Sons in England

Cnut's network of kingdoms was already beginning to fragment when he died in 1035, but large swaths of it were still controlled by his sons. England remained much the same as it had for the past century: it was wealthy, organised, and sometimes targeted by invaders. The main difference is that it would never again share a ruler with Norway. Norway had broken away under its new king, Magnus, in 1035, and Cnut's son Harthacnut, who ruled Denmark, did not attempt to reclaim it. Neither did Harthacnut make any attempt to bring England back into the fold as it drifted away from him in 1035–37 and eventually chose another of Cnut's sons, Harold Harefoot, as its king. Aside from a brief period from 1040–42 when England and Denmark were both ruled by Harthacnut, the 'North Sea Empire' ceased to exist in any meaningful sense. This is not necessarily unexpected. It was common for rapidly acquired territories to break free after the death of an abnormally capable or charismatic conqueror. It happened after the deaths of other early medieval rulers like Charlemagne and Offa of Mercia, and can also be seen in more ancient (and extreme) examples like Alexander the Great.[290]

It might have even been what Cnut intended. There is some evidence that Cnut wished for his kingdoms to be divided after his death, much as Charlemagne had. Medieval writers like the eleventh-century Adam of Bremen and early twelfth-century Symeon of Durham outright say that Cnut intended for Harold Harefoot, not Harthacnut, to inherit England.[291] Although they could merely be interpreting events with the benefit of hindsight, these claims have given some modern historians pause. Pauline Stafford, for example, wonders if Harold's presence in England, rather than in Scandinavia, lends some credence to this idea.[292] Before 1035, there were three sons and three kingdoms, and they do appear to have been ranked in a loose hierarchy. Harthacnut, son of Emma, would inherit Cnut's native kingdom, Denmark, while Swein, son of Ælfgifu, was relegated to the less stable, recently acquired Norway. Harold's status is the least clear and is clouded by the fact that his older brother Swein died in 1035. On one extreme, Harold could have been first in line to inherit England, a wealthy and relatively centralised kingdom; on the other extreme, as a younger son of Ælfgifu, he may have been seen as a backup for Swein who was in England in 1035 only because Norway had fallen and Swein had died. Either way, Cnut's actions with Swein and Harthacnut do show that he knew his territory was too large to be directly controlled by one ruler.

Part of the reason it is so difficult to determine the place of Harold Harefoot is because his status was dependent on his mother's, and that it not abundantly clear either. Ælfgifu was Cnut's first wife, and they probably married during Swein Forkbeard's invasion of 1013. The marriage gave Swein and Cnut a direct link to one of England's most prestigious old families. Swein Cnutsson and Harold Harefoot were products of this union. When Cnut also married Emma of Normandy in 1017, though, the situation became muddled. Emma claimed that Ælfgifu was no more than a concubine to Cnut. It was a concession that her husband previously had sexual relations with this 'other Ælfgifu', as the *ASC* calls her, but implied that the resulting children were not legitimate. There isn't any evidence that Cnut divorced Ælfgifu or had their marriage annulled. Neither did he stop associating with her. He considered her a close enough confidant and an able enough administrator to appoint her as Norway's regent, along with her son Swein, in 1030 – long after marrying Emma. The prevailing scholarly opinion is now that Ælfgifu and Emma were both legitimate wives of Cnut, possibly simultaneously. It has also been suggested that Ælfgifu occupied a middle ground between full spouse and mistress that we have no modern term for but that did not negatively affect her status.[293] Even if Ælfgifu were a full wife who was set aside at some point, this makes her no different than many of the royal English wives of the tenth century. The fact that Emma would go to such great lengths to discredit Ælfgifu and her children (at one point, her *Encomium* even claims that they were commoners who had been smuggled into Ælfgifu's bed) shows how threatened she was by their existence.

However, Cnut's intentions, whatever they were, may be a red herring. As seen with previous succession disputes, the succession question was not the king's alone to answer. It was not as simple as appointing a successor who would take over when one died, nor was there a clear system of primogeniture in place. While it's hard to imagine that Cnut's wishes would have been dismissed entirely, they would not have been the only (or even the primary) consideration. The *ASC*, for example, says nothing of Cnut's wishes or prior planning during the succession crisis of 1035–37. It skips straight from his death to which factions were supporting Harthacnut and which were supporting Harold. Harold's eventual selection, as this chapter will illustrate, had less to do with Cnut's succession planning than it did with Harold being a more appealing candidate for much of the kingdom. It was expected that the powerful families of England would put forward the candidate who would best support and protect them, and Harold was the superior choice outside of Wessex, where Emma's influence was too strong to overcome. Even though Harold Harefoot was initially an obscure figure, one that chroniclers and sagas found unworthy of mention until his father's death, he was about to experience a meteoric rise.

The Rise of Harold Harefoot

Even if Cnut had known of his impending death and wished for Harold to reign in England after him, there were considerable obstacles to this within the king's own circle. Harold was opposed by two of the most powerful figures in the kingdom: Queen Emma and Earl Godwin. Emma's reasons for opposing Harold are straightforward – Harthacnut was her son and Harold was not. Godwin too had reasons for supporting Harthacnut. Harold, through his mother, was affiliated with the Midlands and the areas north of the Thames. These areas were dominated politically by Earl Leofric, who supported Harold and was the only earl in England whose power rivalled that of Godwin. Harold's accession could shift the balance of power away from Godwin and the south and toward Leofric, who may have even been related to Harold.[294]

Regardless of Harthacnut's powerful supporters, Harold knew he had a good claim. He had royal blood and the general assent of the leading nobles north of the Thames. The *ASC* reports that Harold was backed by Leofric, 'nearly all the thegns north of the Thames' and the fleet at London. The situation was beginning to look dire for Harthacnut's faction; Harold had the second most powerful earl on his side, near-universal backing in Mercia and Northumbria, and even had substantial military support in the form of the London fleet.

Harold was appealing to these groups for many reasons. Aside from the obvious Midlands connections of his mother, Harold's accession could allow England to break away from Scandinavia. Cnut's campaigns in Scandinavia may not have been popular, and by the mid-1030s, there was little to show for them anyway. Norway was independent again, and Cnut's influence over Sweden had been negligible to begin with (despite calling himself king of 'some of the Swedes'). Backing Harthacnut, who was already king of Denmark, reopened the whole question of whether England would be required to defend Denmark, or even go on the offensive to reclaim Norway. In short, Harold could save England from costly wars in Scandinavia and afford the northern and middle regions of England an influence that they had not enjoyed in some time.

This posed a serious problem for Emma and the pro-Harthacnut faction. Emma knew that since Harold was the son of Cnut and a royal wife, his claim could hold up against Harthacnut's if he could gain enough support, and support for Harold was not in short supply. For Emma, there was only one way to stop Harold. His claim would have to be destroyed – not just countered, but uprooted entirely. Efforts to do this have survived in the *Encomium*, which she commissioned, and have found their way into the *ASC*. Emma's supporters claimed that Harold had no royal blood whatsoever, and they said this was for two reasons. The first was that Ælfgifu was not actually Cnut's wife, but a concubine. This was still not enough for Emma, though, as it would still imply that Cnut had fathered Harold. The second, and more drastic, measure was an assertion that Harold was not biologically related to Ælfgifu or Cnut at all, but had actually been placed into Ælfgifu's bed while she was incapacitated, leading her to believe she had given birth. For good measure, the *Encomium* also goes to great lengths to portray Harold as unfit to rule, calling him a tyrant and an apostate who abandoned Christianity.

These claims, especially those about his parentage, may appear obviously fabricated, but some medieval writers took them seriously. The C and D texts of the *ASC*, which are highly biased against Harold, assert that it was 'not true' that he was Cnut's son. The E and F texts are more charitable to Harold, but only slightly. They say that 'it seemed incredible to many men' that he was Cnut's offspring, although the anonymous chroniclers never reveal whether they themselves agree with this assessment. Later chroniclers like

John of Worcester indicate that by the twelfth century, the rumours about Harold had snowballed. John reports that Harold was allegedly the son of a cobbler and that his 'brother' Swein had been fathered by a priest. As with the chroniclers for the E and F texts of the *ASC* though, John seems unsure about how seriously he should consider this. He confesses that he does not know whether the allegations are true, but the fact that he records even more specific details proves that the tall tale had gained significant traction in the century or so since its origin. As for the claims that Harold was irreligious, they can safely be dismissed as political slander.[295] Alistair Campbell, editor of a translation of the *Encomium*, writes: 'Such evidence as there is does not suggest Haraldr [*sic*] was particularly irreligious or even anticlerical', and some of this evidence will be dealt with in more detail in this chapter.[296] More importantly, the nobles in the Midlands and the North would have been more familiar with Harold and Ælfgifu, and they obviously did not regard Harold as illegitimate or unfit for power in any way.

A few chroniclers may have taken the bait, but the allegations against Harold's parentage were not enough to stop his inexorable rise. A great council was held at Oxford in 1035, where it was decided that Harold would rule England north of the Thames as a regent. Harthacnut's supporters would rule Wessex in his absence. The implication is that when Harthacnut arrived, he would become king of all England, and Harold's tenure as a placeholder would be over. This may appear to be a win, however small, for Harthacnut, but in reality, it had opened the door even wider for Harold. The E and F versions of the *ASC*, after all, place the start of Harold's reign two weeks after Cnut's death, in late 1035, rather than in 1037. John of Worcester likewise refers to Harold as king of Mercia and Northumbria from 1035–37 and king of all England from 1037 onward. The unstated but dangerous message is clear: Harold had been the rightful king all along. In the meantime, in late 1035, Harold was no longer just a popular claimant; he now had direct, legal control north of the Thames, and his supporters would get to experience his rule firsthand. This was also dangerous for Harthacnut because previous attempts to divide the English kingdom in this way had not gone well for those in Harthacnut's position of having a supposedly senior or more 'prestigious' claim.[297]

Meanwhile, the new regent had other matters to attend to. Harold had staved off Harthacnut's claims, at least for the time being, but now he had to deal with two other claimants: Edward and Alfred, the exiled sons of Æthelred. It seems that Emma, sensing her deteriorating influence, had reached out to her first children, whom she had abandoned to exile nearly twenty years earlier. Edward and Alfred had been living in Normandy since 1017 at the latest. They had been superseded by Emma's children with Cnut and also by Cnut and Ælfgifu's children. However, Harthacnut's inaction was becoming unbearable, and Emma astutely realised she could no longer depend on him. A letter in Emma's name went out to the *æthelings* in Normandy, who were now well into adulthood, begging them to return to England and take a stand against Harold Harefoot. The *Encomium* claims that this letter was a forgery that Harold had sent, a trap to lure the 'innocent' *æthelings* into his clutches. Modern historians doubt this, usually concluding that the letter was genuinely from Emma or that no such letter had ever been sent. Harold had little reason to encourage an exiled dynasty to reignite their claims and make an armed stand against him. Edward's biographer, Tom Licence, has gone so far as to compare the alleged forgery, which is copied into the *Encomium*, with a genuine letter sent by Emma to Germany and concluded that they share an author. She may have attributed it to Harold in hindsight because its arrival in Normandy had disastrous consequences. The *æthelings* responded to the letter in their own ways. Edward, who was in his thirties by this point, amassed a fleet and raided Southampton in southern England. If he expected to find support among locals who favoured the old dynasty, he was to be sorely disappointed. Edward quickly headed back to

Normandy, ships laden with booty, little different than the viking raiders who had plagued his father's kingdom for decades. Alfred, the younger brother, seems to have made a more sustained effort. He landed in England with 'many Norman knights', according to the *Liber Eliensis*, and met with Godwin in some capacity. Whether Godwin's intentions were friendly or not depends on the source. One version of the *ASC* says that Godwin's forces killed Alfred's men, apparently for Harold's benefit but without Harold's intervention. Another version of the *ASC* omits the name Godwin, slyly modifying the material to make Harold alone look responsible (italics used to highlight key differences).

ASC, C Manuscript

> Alfred...[wished] to go to his mother in Winchester, but *Godwin* did not allow him, nor did the other men who had great power, because feeling was veering very much towards Harold, although this was not right. But *Godwin* then stopped him and put him in captivity...

ASC, D Manuscript

> Alfred...[wished] to go to his mother in Winchester, but *those who had much power in the land* did not permit it, because feeling was veering very much towards Harold, although this was not right. But *he* then stopped him and put him in captivity…

This sleight of hand once prompted a historian, Eric John, to disparage the D Manuscript as a 'Godwin propaganda sheet'. Godwin had plenty of reasons to switch his allegiance to Harold, given that the alternative was no longer the Danish king, Harthacnut, but the restored dynasty of Æthelred: 'Godwine would have had everything to lose; for he was the archetypal "new noble", who had risen to power in the entourage of King Cnut, and who would have reason to fear the restoration of the native dynasty'.[298] After all, Godwin had been one of the few English nobles that Cnut trusted when he was systemically purging the kingdom of Æthelred's remaining sons and allies. Æthelred's surviving sons may not have been happy to see Godwin. The *Encomium*, as expected, contains a more unwieldy account, spun to denigrate Harold and absolve Emma and Godwin of any wrongdoing. The *Encomium* claims that Godwin treated Alfred hospitably, but that Harold's forces intercepted them while they all slept and killed most of Alfred's men. The sources do agree on the final outcome of the situation: Alfred was blinded and taken to Ely, where he died in the care of its monks.

The blinding of Alfred was regarded as a great tragedy, and it seems that there were some efforts to acclaim him as a saint, but his manner of death was sadly typical. Blinding and mutilation were common punishments for noble offenders. Alfred attracted more sympathy than previous mutilated nobles, though, because he was something greater than noble – he was royal. Harold or Godwin's decision to mutilate Alfred shows that they regarded him as a political or foreign opponent rather than a strictly royal one. From Harold's perspective, Alfred's claim was null and void, forfeited when his dynasty went into exile, and blinding was a suitable legal punishment for a traitor or criminal. It was even somewhat lenient, as hard as that is to believe, because it allowed for the possibility of repentance and survival, whereas assassination did not. Alfred did survive his ordeal, at least for a few months. He died in 1037; only the *Encomium* claims that Alfred died instantly, probably to emphasise Harold's brutality.

There are numerous earlier examples of kings (and would-be kings) behaving this way. Cnut had mutilated his English hostages in 1014 after he suffered a humiliating defeat against a resurgent Æthelred. Æthelred himself blinded numerous political opponents, including Ælfhelm, Harold's maternal grandfather. If Harold had given the command to blind the captured *ætheling*, the whole situation obtains a bleak symmetry: Æthelred had blinded Harold's ancestor, and now Harold had blinded Æthelred's descendant. With Alfred grimly dispatched, Harold's position was stronger than ever. Harthacnut, despite pleas to return to England and stop Harold, did nothing. The situation in Denmark was precarious, with Harthacnut perhaps anticipating a Norwegian invasion. However, neither kingdom made a move against the other. Even though England was slipping further away with each day, Harthacnut was involved in a staring contest with Magnus of Norway that he was unwilling to lose.

In England, the uncomfortable truce between Harthacnut and Harold ultimately crumbled in 1037, when the English nobles finally tired of Harthacnut's stalling. Perhaps conceding that Harthacnut would never arrive, no matter how much they begged him, the remaining holdouts joined Harold's faction. In the words of the *ASC*, Harold became 'full king' – the same phrase that had been used for Swein Forkbeard's conquest a generation earlier. The term represents a completeness of control, albeit one that seems to imply he was a forceful outsider.[299] In practice, though, Harold had already been in charge since 1035, leading some versions of the *ASC* to backdate his reign to that year. In 1037, however, Harold had the formal recognition that the *Encomium* says he so desperately wanted. The *Encomium* claims that Æthelnoth, Archbishop of Canterbury, dramatically refused to consecrate Harold in 1035, which caused Harold to become an apostate and harass the Church. The *ASC*'s version of events is far easier to stomach: Æthelnoth, whatever his original misgivings may have been, apparently assented to Harold's rule by 1037, along with the rest of the kingdom. Godwin had also somehow become so loyal to Harold, despite his original opposition, that he allegedly captured Alfred for him.

In 1037, Emma found herself in a desperate situation. Harthacnut had not responded to her pleas, Edward had failed to make any significant inroads, and Alfred was dead. From her perspective, perhaps it seemed like all three of her sons had failed her in some capacity. Despite her resourcefulness and inventiveness, Emma now found herself without a defender.[300] Even Godwin had thrown his lot in with Harold. Emma was exposed now, and Harold knew it. He moved against her after his consecration, exiling her 'without any mercy to face the raging winter', in the disapproving words of the *ASC*. She fled to Bruges, where it is thought that she commissioned the *Encomium* to tell her own version of history – one that would vindicate her decisions, bolster Harthacnut and Edward's claims, and destroy Harold's reputation. It would go on to be one of the most famous sources for this era of history. In the late 1030s, however, Emma must have known her chances of returning to any form of influence were slim. Harold Harefoot had bested her.

Harold hadn't done it without support, though. His mother, Ælfgifu of Northampton, was a large reason for his success. A letter from the priest Immo to Bishop Azeko of Worms describes how Emma's daughter Gunnhilda was informed of the situation. Ælfgifu is shown flattering and bribing her way to influence, promoting Harold's claim the whole time. 'Your wretched and wicked step-mother, wishing to deprive your brother Harthacnut of the kingdom by fraud, organized a great party for all our leading men, and, eager to corrupt them at times with entreaty and at times with money, tried to subordinate them with oaths to herself and to her son.'[301]

This flattering, however, is no different than how Cnut reportedly won and maintained influence in Scandinavia.[302] As with Harold, Ælfgifu is mainly known from sources that are hostile to her. Modern historians have sometimes followed this medieval line of thought, such as how Eric John considered her 'a total disaster'.[303] On the opposite extreme, W. H. Stevenson considered her 'stronger and more ruthless' than Emma.[304] No matter what one thinks about her tenure in Norway, there is no denying that Ælfgifu's efforts to acclaim Harold in England were impressive. Part of the reason for her success may have been sheer desperation. With Cnut dead, Swein dead, and

Norway lost, Ælfgifu knew that she needed to win with Harold at any cost. 'Defeat would mean oblivion for them both.'[305]

With that said, Ælfgifu's involvement in Harold's succession has led some historians to stretch her influence beyond what the evidence will support. The most famous example came from Frank Stenton, the highly-influential twentieth-century historian of Anglo-Saxon England. Stenton thought that Ælfgifu must have been Harold's 'power behind the throne' during his reign, which has been frequently quoted in the decades since. However, there is little indication of what happened to Ælfgifu after Harold's accession in 1037. We don't even know when she died. Only a handful of documents survive from Harold's reign, and none of them explicitly mention Ælfgifu. One mentions an unnamed 'my lady' alongside King Harold, which could be Ælfgifu, although it could be an unknown spouse or mistress of Harold. Whoever she was, she was notable enough to be referred to by 'my lady' alone, meaning that Harold's mother may be the strongest candidate for this mystery lady's identity. Until about a century ago, she would have been the only known candidate.

A Lost Royal Family?

The traditional line of thinking is that neither of Cnut's sons married or had offspring, which directly contributed to the collapse of the Danish line in 1042. However, an important but obscure 1913 article by W. H. Stevenson examined a medieval document that contains the only known reference to a possible son of Harold, as well as a spouse or mistress.[306] The son's name was Ælfwine, and he is described as an Englishman from London who was present in southern France with his mother, Ælfgifu, in the 1060s. The identity of the 'King Harold' in this source was the main question that Stevenson sought to answer in 1913, and he considered Harold II Godwinson and Harald II of Denmark the other main candidates for being Ælfwine's father, before concluding that the only feasible option was Harold Harefoot. Harald of Denmark cannot be described as an English king, and it would be surprising for him to have a son born in London and bearing an English name. Godwinson is a trickier case, and Stevenson conceded that it is 'chronologically possible', but this option comes with its own set of serious problems. Godwinson had two partners and eight children whose names are known, but frustratingly, there are no matches for an Ælfgifu and Ælfwine among them. More importantly, there is no reason one of his sons (even an unimportant one) would seek his fortune so far away from England, in Aquitaine, when Godwinson was at the height of his power in England in the 1060s. However, there are plenty of reasons for a son of Harold Harefoot to be so far away, given that his faction lost control after 1040 and was subjected to threatening spectacles from Harthacnut, namely Harold's grisly exhumation. More significantly, we have an exact match in the name 'Ælfgifu', in the form of Harold's mother.

Few historians have discussed the existence of Ælfwine, but those who do so accept Stevenson's conclusion that he is the son of Harold Harefoot, not of other figures of the same name. Ælfwine's father, 'given the date, must be the dead Harold Harefoot'.[307] It is also commonly assumed that Ælfgifu is a garbled reference to Ælfgifu of Northampton.[308] In other words, besides mistaking Ælfgifu for being Ælfwine's mother rather than grandmother, everything lines up for this being Harold Harefoot's son. Even Ælfwine's place of origin, London, aligns nicely, as it is one of two places specifically listed as Harold Harefoot's base (the other being Oxford, although a medieval English king would also be itinerant to a degree). Harold Harefoot is presented as ruling from London during the capture of Alfred Ætheling and was buried, exhumed, and reburied in London. John of Worcester even claims London was where Harold Harefoot died, although this is contradicted by the *ASC*. But Harold was clearly and frequently associated with London one way or another, making it a logical place for his son to come from.

There is another intriguing argument that can be made about Ælfwine and Ælfgifu from this source: it is possible, although not necessarily probable, that the Ælfgifu in question is not Ælfgifu of Northampton. What if the document is not in error when it calls Ælfgifu the mother of Ælfwine and faithfully records the name of Harold's onetime partner? After all, Ælfgifu was a name so common among royal women that it almost appears mandatory. From the 980s until 1052, there was virtually always a royal spouse or mother named Ælfgifu: we have Ælfgifu of York, who was Æthelred's first wife from sometime in the 980s until about 1000; Emma, who took the English name Ælfgifu and was present in England from 1002–37 and again from 1040–52; and, of course, Harold's mother Ælfgifu of Northampton, who was part of Cnut's circle from about 1013 until his death in 1035 and was alive until at least 1037. Would it really be too far-fetched to throw one more Ælfgifu into the mix as Harold's spouse? Even if this was not the woman's birth name, perhaps she adopted it in honour of Harold's mother, just as Emma had adopted it in reference to a royal predecessor. Could this woman be the mysterious 'my lady' of the diploma?[309] We will never know, and this argument is admittedly speculative. It is possible that the document refers to Ælfgifu of Northampton and that the identity of Harold's wife or mistress must remain unknown, although Bolton considered the options 'equally likely'.[310] Regardless of who Ælfgifu is, thanks to Stevenson's 1913 article, we can now say with relative certainty that Harold had at least one child. Harold, far from being a one-off usurper, is beginning to look more and more like a fully legitimate king who was building his own royal family.

The Reign of Harold Harefoot

Once Harold was established as full king in 1037, England returned to apparent harmony. The *ASC*'s entries for the reign are surprisingly mundane considering how much its authors disliked Harold. There was 'a great wind' in 1039. Bishops died and were replaced. There were no scandals worthy of note, no famines, no unpopular wars, no uprisings, and no high taxes worth complaining about. Any of the preceding events would have been notable enough for the chronicler to mention, and indeed they are frequently mentioned in other reigns. It seems to have been a calm time as much as it was a poorly recorded one. If part of Harold's appeal was that he would extract England from foreign wars, he seems to have acted accordingly. English thegns were never expected to campaign in Scandinavia, as they sometimes had been under Cnut.

That is not to say that the English were militarily dormant in Harold's reign, though. There was an English raid against 'the Britons' of Strathclyde in 1038.[311] This attack was led by a Northumbrian lord named Eadwulf and mirrors the royal expeditions to Strathclyde by Edmund I in 945 and Æthelred in 1000. It is unclear just how much influence the rapidly declining kingdom of Strathclyde had in 1038, meaning the 1038 attack could have been something akin to a proxy war with Scotland, or, more simply, an attempt to plunder a weaker opponent. Wales was another source of conflict. The *ASC* records that Edwin, a brother of Earl Leofric, was killed by the Welsh in 1039, but says little more about it. John of Worcester adds that Edwin had been killed in an ambush, but likewise says nothing about where this took place or which side instigated the conflict.[312] Interestingly, the famous Welsh king, Gruffudd ap Llwelyn, is known to have won a battle against English forces in 1039, according to the *Annales Cambriae*.[313] It is tempting to identify the two events with each other, but it is unclear whether this is the same event referred to in the *ASC*.[314]

While Harold's nobles engaged in both aggressive and defensive warfare, it is possible that Harold never personally led an army. This puts him at odds with many previous rulers, such as Æthelstan, Edmund I, Eadred, Æthelred, Edmund II, and Cnut. The closest Harold came to military action was in 1035 and 1037 against Winchester, when he deprived Emma of the treasury and exiled her, respectively. Both likely required some kind of armed presence, but there is no record of fighting. In all, it appears that Harold, once he had formally become king in 1037, was content to let his subordinates lead armies, either on his behalf or purely in their own interests.

After the succession crisis, there are few indications of political controversy while Harold was king. Aside from his clashes with Emma, the only other record of political conflict in Harold's reign comes from a diploma called S 1467. This document tells of allegations made against Harold by Christ Church, which claims that he appropriated its access to Sandwich for his own use. In the diploma, Harold's denial is recorded: he swears 'by God and his saints that it was neither his advice nor his doing'. The author of the diploma agrees, conceding that 'it was evident that it was the doing of other men, not of King Harold'. The document posits that the greedy abbot Ælfstan obtained the toll money from Styr, Harold's elusive household manager, without the king's knowledge. Upon learning of this, King Harold restores the Church's rights to collect its income. This remarkable document runs contrary to the accusations made against Harold in the *Encomium*. Whereas the *Encomium* portrays Harold as irreligious and tyrannical, S 1467 presents him as a pious ruler with a conventional religious outlook. He took no action against his accusers, except to ensure that they went away satisfied and with their rights restored, and reversed the actions of his favoured counsellor, Styr. John of Worcester, although writing much later, also contradicts Emma's claims that Harold was an enemy of the Church. He indicates that Harold was closely involved with the appointment of bishops (an unusually high number of them died between 1037 and 1040), and both John and the *ASC* record Harold promoting his personal priests to some of these vacancies, just as Cnut had. Harold may have been playing favourites, but he was not irreligious; on the contrary, he seems surprisingly interested in Church affairs.

Not everyone has accepted Harold's excuses about Sandwich so readily, however. Nicholas Brooks, who wrote perhaps the most detailed analysis of S 1467 available, seems to imply that Harold really did seize Sandwich by his own volition. But even if this is the case, there was a strategic side to this action. Sandwich was the staging post for many of the viking invasions of Æthelred's reign, and Æthelred himself made use of it when he assembled his massive fleet of 1009. Harold too was vulnerable to invasion, mainly in the form of his spurned half-brother Harthacnut, who was known to be assembling a fleet by 1039. If Harold feared that Harthacnut would land in England with this fleet, Sandwich was likely to be their first stop, and this is indeed where Harthacnut landed in 1040.[315] If it truly was intentional, Harold's seizure of Church property was more about having direct control of a vitally important harbour than it was about greed.

The Church dispute diploma is notable for another reason, though. It tells us that Harold was an ill man. The events in the diploma take place at Oxford, Harold's base, where he was 'so ill that he was lying in despair of his life'. However, the diploma ends with Harold apparently still alive and able to make decisions, giving the impression that these were not actually his final moments. If they had been, surely this would have been worthy of inclusion. Even if these were not the king's final moments, S 1467 could be relaying events that took place in the king's final weeks or months. The *ASC* reports that he did indeed die at Oxford, although it is worth noting that a varying account from John of Worcester claims the king died in London. Interestingly, the *Encomium* also provides a clue that Harold's ill-health might have been known outside England; it says that Harthacnut had a dream that Harold would die soon, which turned out to be correct. It could be little more than a detail added by the encomiast in hindsight. However, knowing the *Encomium*'s tendency to warp or exaggerate 'mundane intelligence', this might be news from abroad that was incorporated into the narrative to make

Harthacnut's accession seem divinely ordained.[316] Perhaps Harold was chronically ill or suffering from a prolonged disease. Judging by S 1467, he had clearly learned to conduct important business while ailing. The details of the diploma do not provide a clear enough description to suspect any illness or disease in particular, but Harold was clearly not a well man.

Whatever Harold's mysterious illness was, something finally got the better of him when he died on March 17, 1040. His exact age at death is unknown, although he was probably in his early or mid-twenties. His brother, Swein, and his uncle, Harald, had died at about the same age, as would his half-brother, Harthacnut. The dynasty of Cnut had many strengths, but longevity was not one of them. Ironically, perhaps Harold's early death is a sign that, contrary to Emma's allegations, he was indeed Cnut's legitimate offspring.[317]

Harold left behind his son, Ælfwine, and possibly a wife or mistress. Ælfwine cannot have been more than a few years old. Other than two brief references to him as an abbot in France in 1060 and 1062, it is unknown what happened to him or whether there were any half-hearted attempts to promote his claim. It is not known what happened to Ælfgifu of Northampton either. Most of the accounts of this era are more concerned with, and biased toward, Emma and her circle, so they do not seem to be interested in what happened to this lost royal house. The hard-fought victory of Harold's faction died with him.

When Harold's immediate family fell from influence after his death, there was no one who felt compelled to write in his favour. Almost all of the references to Harold written after his death are hostile, usually because they are sympathetic to Edward the Confessor, aligned with Emma's circle, view Cnut unfavourably, or some combination of these. In the decades and centuries that followed, Harold became a convenient stock villain in the few sources that bother to mention him. In the *Vita Edwardi Regis*, written primarily about Edward the Confessor and his queen, Edith, Harold briefly appears as 'an arrogant fellow of bad character'. This characterisation is hardly surprising considering that Edward had been on the outside looking in when Harold took the throne. Edward, of course, did eventually become king, and the momentum continued to swing in his favour in the following decades; he was formally canonised in 1161, not even a century after his death.

Another unflattering depiction of Harold comes from William of Poitiers, who portrays him as an unusually cruel ruler, writing that 'Harold obtained his throne and crown, but it was unworthy of him because of his love of tyranny'. He also says that 'the English either did not wish to desert Harold or (which is more credible) did not dare to… They had not forgotten that the noblest of their race had been exterminated by the Danes in their cruelty'. William portrays Harold as sadistic and psychopathic during an unusually detailed account of Alfred's capture and blinding: Alfred is betrayed by the Judas-like Godwin and taken to Harold in London, who makes it clear that he wants to personally to watch Alfred's men be executed. Harold then orders Alfred to be tortured and makes his life more miserable than death, and he does this with the intention of frightening Edward the Confessor with his incredible cruelty. Alfred dies not long after because he had suffered a knife point to the brain while being blinded. Perhaps the only figure who comes across looking worse than Harold is Godwin, who is subjected to a comically lengthy tirade. William of Poitiers was writing in honour of William the Conqueror, so Godwin (as the father of the William's biggest rival, Harold II) had to be denigrated. As an ally of Godwin, Harold Harefoot could not be depicted sympathetically either. Additionally, the depictions of Harold's unbelievable wickedness probably have more to do with his connection to the rival Danish dynasty than anything else, as there were still Scandinavian claimants causing trouble for William after 1066. Cnut and his memory remained a threat to William and those sympathetic to him, just as Æthelred's displaced line had been a threat to Cnut. In William of Poitiers' account, it is also notable that the tales of Harold's illegitimacy – the biggest obstacle in Harold's lifetime – are missing; Harold's cruelty is connected to his father's, according to William, so the questions over his parentage were, ironically, omitted. William of Poitiers' characterisation of Harold is memorable, but it tells us more about William's biases than anything truthful about Harold.

Despite these later tales that emphasise Harold's brutality and sadism, there is almost no trace of this in early sources. Only the blinding of Alfred could be considered vicious, at least until one realises how commonplace this punishment was in this era. As seen earlier, it was a favoured punishment of Æthelred's. If anything, in contemporary sources, Harold comes away looking mild compared to his predecessors, especially his father, Cnut. Cnut had mutilated an entire group of hostages in 1014, killed or exiled Æthelred's descendants, and had some of his own leading men killed – even those who had married into the royal family. Harold, meanwhile, is only known to have exiled a single person in his five year reign, Emma, who was spreading salacious lies about his mother, and only resorted to blinding Alfred because he had landed in England with a foreign army. Part of this apparent tameness may be due to the poorly-recorded nature of Harold's reign. But given the evidence we have, it seems safer to say that Harold, rather than being a bloodthirsty usurper, only employed violence when absolutely necessary, something even the most passive of early medieval kings were required to do. As a result, we are left with the impression that Harold Harefoot was not particularly ruthless or barbaric. His later reputation for cruelty had more to do with Edward the Confessor's developing cult, the Norman Conquest, and Harold's association with his undoubtedly ruthless father.

Harold Harefoot, despite myriad efforts to blacken his name and an obscurity almost unique among English kings, appears to have been a remarkable man. With help from his mother Ælfgifu and Earl Leofric, Harold rose from an obscure son of Cnut to claimant, to regent, and finally to undisputed ruler of England. He was a politically astute claimant who had quick reflexes and always seemed to be in the right place at the right time. Perhaps this is the origin of the mysterious nickname Harefoot.[318]

The Reign of Harthacnut

Harthacnut and Harold may have shared a father and lived short lives, but they were opposites in almost every other way. Whereas Harold was decisive, quick, and sometimes conciliatory, Harthacnut was cautious but deeply vengeful. He had tarried in Denmark for four years while Harold chipped away at England, while he also declined to make a move against Norway. By 1039, he had finally secured an agreement with Magnus of Norway, meaning that Norway and England had both formally slipped away without bloodshed. In 1039, he arrived in Bruges to meet his exiled mother Emma. Even then, armed with an invading fleet and positioned just across the Strait of Dover, Harthacnut was reluctant to challenge Harold; in the *Encomium*, which was written partly to promote his claim, Harthacnut is so cautious that he nearly abandons the whole expedition until God sends him a dream about Harold's impending death. Even in a source sympathetic to him, it literally takes divine intervention to spur Harthacnut into motion. Harthacnut's reservations may have been well-founded, though. Harold had shown that he was not to be trifled with, and perhaps Harthacnut feared that he would end up like the mutilated Alfred Ætheling if his invasion went poorly.

True to Harthacnut's dream, Harold died. And to Harthacnut's credit, he did move forward after this, albeit at his own pace. Harthacnut waited two and a half months to make the short voyage from Flanders to England. In the interlude, he sent messages back and forth with the English leaders who wished to make him king. These nobles were 'thinking that they were acting wisely', the *ASC* bitterly adds with the benefit of hindsight. Although English kings were selected through the assent of the nobility, it is surprising that negotiations took this long. There were few credible alternatives at this point. His chief rival, Harold, was dead, his half-brothers Swein and Alfred were dead, and his other half-brother, Edward, had found no support when he raided Southampton a few years earlier. Perhaps Harold's son, Ælfwine, was an obstacle, although he would have only been a few years old and cannot have been taken seriously compared to a claimant with sixty ships at his disposal. Nonetheless, Harthacnut's accession might be the event that prompted Ælfwine to flee England, given that he would resurface in Aquitaine two decades later.

Whatever caused these further delays, once in England, Harthacnut made it clear that he would take none of the soft measures that Harold and Ælfgifu had used to gain favour. Harold and his mother had been accused of winning support through flattery and bribery, but Harthacnut would rule by sheer intimidation and take no chances. He arrived with his full invasion fleet even though the English had already agreed to make him king. Thankfully for both Harthacnut and the English leaders, the massive fleet never had to be put into action, and Harthacnut went to work as English king.

One of his first and most infamous acts was to desecrate the body of his dead rival Harold, having him exhumed from Westminster Monastery. Later writers report that Harthacnut cruelly required Harold's chief supporters to personally conduct the exhumation, along with some leading ecclesiastics. These included the earls Leofric and Godwin. However, this allegation is fairly late and suspiciously specific, so it could be an embellished account meant to emphasise Harthacnut's brutal rule. That said, there may be an element of truth to it, at least broadly speaking, because Leofric and Godwin were in a bind. Leofric had been one of Harold's foremost supporters, although he had at least been uniform in his preferences. Godwin had switched sides, while even Emma's commitment to Harthacnut may have briefly wavered if she was indeed the one who invited her children by Æthelred to return.[319] According to John of Worcester,

Godwin had to smooth things over by presenting Harthacnut with a magnificent ship – a fine gift for a seafaring lord like Harthacnut.[320]

The fate of Harold's body is detailed in several medieval accounts, not all of which align with each other. The *ASC* reports that Harthacnut had it thrown into a swamp. John of Worcester adds that he then had Harold's body retrieved and thrown into the Thames. Apparently Harold's corpse, which had been rotting for at least a few months, was also beheaded at some point.[321] Finally, the whole grisly affair came to an end when some of 'the Danes' in London defied their new king by fishing out Harold's corpse (or, in some accounts, only his head) and burying it honourably in their church, St Clement Danes. All these sources do agree that Harold's exhumation involved being discarded in the water, while later accounts agree that he was retrieved and reburied in London. Given all this, it is little wonder that Harold's young son did not stay in England.

The shocking exhumation of Harold may seem irrational at first glance, but there was a strategic side to the act as well. Harthacnut was attempting to show that Harold was a false king, a tyrannical usurper whose accession had been illegal. The exhumation removed Harold's body from consecrated ground, associating him with outsiders like criminals and apostates. Just as Emma had spread rumours about Harold's parentage to completely uproot his claim, Harthacnut exhumed Harold for the same purpose. His message was simple: Harold had never been the rightful king and would not be remembered as such. Unfortunately for Harthacnut and Emma, neither of their attempts was successful. Medieval chroniclers remember Harold's exhumation in particular with disgust and surprise, associating the act more closely with Harthacnut's ruthlessness, rather than reflecting anything further about Harold's status.[322] After the exhumation of Harold, and the possible humiliation of Harold's leading men, Harthacnut does seem to have accepted much of the old regime into his circle. Godwin and Leofric remained entrenched, and even Styr, a mysterious but apparently influential counsellor who had been

Harold's steward, retained some influence under Harthacnut. So, after initial actions meant to intimidate and shock his new subjects, Harthacnut does seem to have kept much of Harold's administration in place.

A bigger problem was that Harthacnut refused, at least for a while, to pare down his mighty fleet. Whereas Cnut and Harold had maintained a fleet of sixteen ships, Harthacnut had at least sixty, and their upkeep was expensive. Eventually he did reduce them to thirty-two, but this was still double the size of Harold and Cnut's fleets. Harthacnut's high taxes coincided with inflation, according to the *ASC*, which marvels at how expensive wheat became in 1040 – the medieval equivalent of using a loaf of bread as an economic measuring stick. The economic situation and the king's oppressive taxes became unbearable in 1041 in Worcestershire, which rose in rebellion and killed two of Harthacnut's housecarls, who were acting as tax collectors, within the minster church. According to the *ASC*, Harthacnut responded by ordering the county to be ravaged, but apparently did not partake in the campaign himself.[323]

A noticeably more detailed account of the murders appears in John of Worcester's chronicle. Given that this is John 'of Worcester', he may indeed have had far more information about the event than other chroniclers did. Often John paraphrases the *ASC* with some minor differences, and the scholarly consensus is that John likely had access to a Latin version of the chronicle that has not survived, which accounts for these variations. In the case of Worcester's ravaging, though, it is possible that John, as a local, was not overly dependent on the *ASC* for his account, which greatly exceeds anything in any of the *ASC*'s versions. 'Hardacnut [*sic*]...sent his housecarls through all the provinces of the kingdom to collect the tax which he imposed. Two of them, namely Feader and Thurstan, were killed Monday, 4 May, by the people of Worcestershire and the citizens, in an upper room of a tower of the monastery of Worcester, to which they had fled to hide themselves when a riot had broken out.'

This above account fleshes out the *ASC*'s summary by naming the housecarls, giving an exact date, and even providing information about where in the minster the housecarls were killed.

His account reveals just how complicated ravaging campaigns could be, even though most other sources devote just a few words to such events. According to John, Harthacnut's campaign against Worcestershire took six months to plan even though the event itself was over in four days. It involved everyone from the familiar Godwin and Leofric to the most minor earls, yet John follows the *ASC*'s implication that Harthacnut himself did not show up, suggesting the *ASC* is accurate here. Instead, the king passively 'had it ravaged' and 'sent' his earls. John's account also reinforces that, aside from forcing one's will on others, a primary aim of ravaging was to obtain spoils. Whether the king was English or Danish, the leading figures of England were not always so different from their 'viking' counterparts after all.

Ravaging, like blinding, was an activity that appears unusually tyrannical to the modern eye but was actually common, and Harthacnut had good precedent for his orders. When English kings could not enforce their will through law or coercion, they often resorted to violence, even against their own citizens. John's account emphasises how serious a harrying campaign could be – something that will not be surprising to those who are familiar with William I's infamous 'harrying of the north', but which may be alarming to those who ascribe less meaning to Æthelred and Eadric's many harrying expeditions. Typically the king himself would lead the onslaught, but not always. Eadred personally led a ravaging campaign into Northumbria in 948, and Æthelred personally led them inside and outside England (Rochester in 986, Strathclyde in 1000, and Lindsey in 1014). Although less common, there was precedent for Harthacnut's absence in 1041, too. For example, Edgar had 'ordered' Thanet to be harried in 969, with the *ASC*'s distant wording suggesting he did not necessarily accompany these forces. Harthacnut, who was known to be sickly, may have already been suffering from the disease that killed him just seven months later, making his absence from the field more understandable.

John and the *ASC* agree that it was at this juncture that Harthacnut and Emma invited Edward, son of Æthelred, back to England – a decision that has puzzled historians for centuries. Because medieval sources place Edward's recall after the rebellion and ravaging campaign, sometimes historians have assumed that one must have caused the other – Harthacnut had become so unpopular that it was necessary to associate him with a figure from the old dynasty. However, this in itself would be perplexing. Edward had already tried to make a move in the 1030s and been rebuffed, and it is hard to imagine that anyone viewed Æthelred's reign nostalgically. Important families may, however, have turned to these older connections with the House of Wessex if their relationship with Harthacnut was strained or if the king was known to be deathly ill.

According to William of Poitiers, the pious Harthacnut was sick and thinking 'more of God and of the brevity of human life'. Although it is a common trope for medieval writers to emphasise the suffering of figures they think are holy (Alfred the Great and Alfred Ætheling are good examples of this), John of Worcester and the *ASC*'s vivid depictions of Harthacnut's death just a year later mean that William may need to be taken seriously about the king's poor health. With no wife or children, and deteriorating health, Harthacnut needed to have some kind of plan in place if he did not want Harold's son, Ælfwine, put forward as a possibility. It may not have been appealing to the nobility to bring back Harold Harefoot's line either, which would risk more backlashes and recriminations under a boy king and his regents. Harthacnut would not have been eager to leave the door open, even a crack, for Harold's son to emerge as a candidate. Edward, on the other hand, was an adult and had no connections with Harold, whose legacy was already being destroyed by Emma and her encomiast at this time. In other words, Edward was a political unknown who was technically throne-worthy and had a clean slate. Whatever the exact reasons, the English nobility assented to Edward's return, and he became some kind of co-king or sub-king with Harthacnut.

A few months later, on June 8, 1042, Harthacnut met his end while attending a wedding feast. He collapsed as he stood at his drink, convulsing and speaking no more. A staggering number of Cnut's immediate relatives died young; Harthacnut's demise was no anomaly. This has led to speculation that genetic defects were at play in the House of Denmark, stunting its growth. Harthacnut was about age 24 when he died, around the same age his half-brothers Harold and Swein had been at their deaths. His uncle, Harald, had also died at about the same age, as did Cnut's granddaughter Beatrice. Harthacnut's sister, Gunnhilda, also died at this age, but her demise was caused by an outbreak of contagious disease rather than anything she inherited.[324] It could be that some of these other relatives also died of contagious illnesses, rather than of genetic defects, although none of our sources explicitly say so. Amazingly, Cnut's daughter, brother, granddaughter, and three sons were all between the ages of 18–25 at their deaths. Even Cnut himself died at the relatively young age of about 40 (or 37, according to a saga). Historians Timothy Bolton and Eric John have brought up the possibility of strokes.[325] It is also significant that Harold, Harthacnut, and Gunnhilda (two years before she died of pestilence) are all explicitly referenced as being ill in medieval sources: the diploma S 1467 refers to Harold as so unwell that he fears for his life, William of Poitiers portrays Harthacnut as sickly, and Gunnhilda is said to have recently recovered from an illness in a letter from the priest Immo.

However, the English House of Cerdic also had its share of short-lived rulers, even when excluding those who died violently. Eadred and Edgar died in their early thirties, while Eadwig died in his teens. Perhaps further analysis on the bones in the mortuary chests of Winchester Cathedral will shed light on the issue. Among the bones in the cathedral are those of Cnut, Emma, and Harthacnut, as well as the aforementioned Eadred and Eadwig. However, the bones have been mixed up in the centuries since, and analysis has been slow, although Emma's skeleton has already been conclusively identified. Genetic defects aside, maybe these deaths are a symptom of living in this era of history, when any number of now-treatable ailments could end one's life, striking with a randomness that would make it ordinary to die at any age. However, the fact that Cnut's direct descendants uniformly died upon reaching young adulthood might be too much to be a coincidence.

With Harthacnut dead, Edward became king with no difficulty, which may be the one true success of Harthacnut's short reign. At the very least, he had paved the way for a painless succession, something that had not occurred in generations. The last straightforward succession had been in 955, when Eadwig succeeded his uncle, Eadred, although this too was disputed just two years later. Before that, one must go back to Edmund I's succession of Æthelstan in 939 for an example of an uncontested succession. This also stands in contrast to how Edward's own reign would end in 1066, given that Edward's 'rightful' successor (whether it was Edgar the Ætheling, Harold Godwinson, or William of Normandy) is still debated to this day.

As for the final Danish king of England, a couple of later stories shed more light on Harthacnut and his personality, although it is unclear how seriously they should be taken. William of Poitiers was a rare exception to the constantly negative depictions of Harthacnut, saying that 'he was more like his mother's family, and did not rule by cruelty as his father and brother had done; nor did he desire the death of Edward, but only his advancement'. Writing in honour of William the Conqueror and his family, William of Poitiers has incentive to be sympathetic toward Emma – a source of William's claim – and depicts Cnut and Harold Harefoot as bloodthirsty usurpers. He was in a trickier situation with Harthacnut, who was the son of both Cnut and Emma, and chose to resolve this tension by simply concluding he must have taken after Emma. Another rare exception to Harthacnut's negative reputation comes from Henry of Huntingdon, who relates how Harthacnut had his tables set for feasts four times a day, giving the much-hated king a more jovial, generous side. Though trivial, it is a rare depiction of Harthacnut as anything other than a brutal king who subverted the expectations of English kingship.

The vast majority of medieval chroniclers had little to say in Harthacnut's favour. The same is true for Harold, although their negative details often accidentally imply positive things about Harold, such as his ever-growing popularity and political effectiveness. It is hard to find any such details in between the lines for Harthacnut; in two short years, he managed to alienate both noble and commoner through his ghoulish exhumation of Harold and high taxation. Even the *Encomium* glosses over his unpopular reign, preferring to skip it rather than mount any further defence of him. The *ASC* has no trouble taking shots at Harthacnut, though. It summarises his reign by saying that 'all who had wanted him before were then ill-disposed towards him. And he did nothing worthy of a king as long as he lived'.

At the time of Harthacnut's demise in 1042, it had only been seven years since Cnut's death; the former master of England, Denmark, and (for a time) Norway had no more living sons. He did, however, have a living grandson through the male line: Harold Harefoot's son Ælfwine was still around, although he was probably still a young child in 1042. Perhaps ironically, this means that of all Cnut's children, it was Harold – the one others claimed was illegitimate – who offered the House of Denmark its best chance of long-term survival. Had Harold lived a few more years, outlasting Harthacnut, the throne could have conceivably passed to Ælfwine. The main obstacle that prevented the House of Denmark from having an enduring legacy, perhaps unexpectedly from a modern perspective, was the premature death of the otherwise obscure Harold Harefoot. Continued Danish rule was not to be. Ælfwine was pushed out of the way to make room for the heavily-armed Harthacnut, who had little time to live but managed to position Edward the Confessor as his preferred successor. Just as the male line of the House of Wessex would eventually flicker out of existence with the unrecorded death of Edgar the Ætheling sometime after 1125, the House of Denmark's male line likewise flickered out with Ælfwine's unrecorded death sometime after 1062.[326]

Conclusion: The Bridge to 1066

Harthacnut was little mourned, but his death brought about the end of an era. The Danish kings of England were no more. However, for those alive in 1042, it may not have been obvious that the era of Danish rule had permanently ended. The new king, Edward the Confessor, agreed to uphold 'the laws of Cnut and his children', linking him firmly to the dynasty that had once exiled him, although it was common for kings to reaffirm the laws of their predecessors.[327] But Edward was old compared to previous English kings. Thirty-eight at the time of his accession, he was already older than most tenth- and eleventh-century English monarchs had been at the time of their deaths. Some may have thought of him as a caretaker, stop-gap, or placeholder. It would not have been apparent that Edward would live another twenty-four years, ruling until 1066.

Emma was surely glad that her son Edward was somehow the last man standing in 1042, but if she expected to retain the standing she had enjoyed under Harthacnut, she was mistaken. Edward confiscated the treasury from her – the same thing Harold Harefoot had done to her in 1035. 'She might as well have plumped for Harold I in the first place', mused Eric John.[328] Eventually Edward and Emma were reconciled, but she never regained the prominence she enjoyed under Cnut. She mostly vanishes from history after this point, perhaps settling into a reluctant retirement, although the *ASC* found her important enough to mention her passing a decade later, in 1052. And how could it not? Emma's story wound its way around both sides of the Danish Conquest in a way no one else's did, having first been on the losing side as Æthelred's wife and then on the winning side as Cnut's; she then found herself involved on all sides of the succession disputes that followed Cnut's death, being a champion to one of her sons, an obstacle to her stepson, the accidental cause of death of another son, and the target of anger from yet another. Emma, wife of two kings and mother of two more, practically encapsulated the chaotic and winding story of the Danish Conquest and dynasty in the form of her own life.

Unlike Emma, who had been forced into semi-retirement for her final years, Earl Godwin retained his influence even after the Danish kings were gone. Godwin was the creation of Cnut who grew so strong that he played kingmaker for Harold Harefoot, allegedly killing Alfred Ætheling on behalf of the Danish line. Godwin's fears about the return of Æthelred's line turned out to be well-founded. King Edward eventually turned against him and, together with Earl Leofric and Earl Siward of Northumbria, drove him into exile. Leofric's stint as the dominant English earl was brief. Such was Godwin's ability that he managed to get himself restored to favour when he and his family returned to England; they faced off against the king and the other earls, ready for battle. For once, an English king's counsellors had the bigger picture in mind and realised that destroying themselves against Godwin would leave the kingdom open to external attack, and Godwin was restored. In 1053, after decades in power and probably well into his fifties, Godwin suffered a debilitating stroke, losing his strength and ability speak. A few days later, he died, paving the way for his son Harold to become the most prominent figure in England – and, briefly, its king in 1066.

A handful of other figures from the Danish era lingered on into Edward's reign. The powerful Earl Leofric lived until 1057 and is today best known for being the husband of Lady Godiva, who rode naked through the streets in protest of high taxes. While Lady Godiva's ride may be fictional, the taxes themselves may not be; it would not be hard to imagine that the legend developed out of tales of Harthacnut's oppressive taxes of 1041, which were so harsh that his people rose in rebellion. Leofric, who appears as the oppressive taxer in the Lady Godiva myth, was indeed tasked with plundering Worcestershire during Harthacnut's harrying campaign of 1041. That said, the historical Godiva (whose Old English name was Godgifu, or 'god's gift') was famous in her own time for her generous donations to the Church, as was her husband Leofric. Godgifu outlived her husband and died sometime after the Norman Conquest.

Some figures from the era of the Danish kings returned to the scene decades later, but only in hints and shadows. The Bayeux Tapestry depicts a woman labelled Ælfgifu interacting with a clergyman, and her identity and role have been subject to much speculation. She could be Emma of Normandy, whose English name was Ælfgifu, but she was dead by the events of 1066. But if it is Emma, the tapestry may be mocking her for her alleged affair with the Archbishop Stigand, especially given that the scene is directly above some grotesque marginalia depicting a naked man (who looks a lot like the clergyman) with comically large genitals. But identifying this Ælfgifu as Emma raises more questions than it answers. For example, why would the Bayeux Tapestry, a celebration of William of Normandy's triumph, mock his ancestor Emma, who was a source of his claim? This would not just be a cheap shot at a fallen dynasty; by extension, it would be a cheap shot at William himself!

Emma, however, is not the only candidate for being the 'Ælfgifu' on the tapestry. One of the most popular possibilities put forward is that it is Ælfgifu of Northampton, the first wife of Cnut and mother of his children, Swein and Harold. Could her association with the clergyman, right above a similar naked man, be a crass reference to Swein Cnutsson, who was said to be the son of a priest rather than of Cnut and Ælfgifu? If it is nothing more than a crude insult to a fallen dynasty, Ælfgifu of Northampton would make more sense than Emma. But if it is not simply meant as a joke, what could Ælfgifu of Northampton have to do with 1066, and could she have still been alive at that time? Even though her whereabouts after 1037 remain unclear, if still living, she would have been in her sixties or seventies in 1066, so it is indeed possible she was alive. But if we accept that Ælfgifu of Northampton is a leading candidate, what could she possibly be doing on the Bayeux Tapestry, and how does she fit into the complex web of 1066? It is hard to image her motives as late as 1066, when her sons Harold Harefoot and Swein Cnutsson had been dead for decades. By 1066, despite being the wife of one king and the mother of one more, she had been reduced to little more than a memory.

But when Edward the Confessor died in 1066, there were still Scandinavian claimants ready to swoop in. Harald Hardrada of Norway thought that he had a claim through his predecessor, Magnus. Harthacnut and Magnus had agreed that whoever survived longer would inherit the other's kingdom, which came to fruition when Harthacnut died, at least regarding Denmark. Denmark passed to Magnus and England to Edward. But for Harald Hardrada, this agreement was excuse enough to invade England, too. He was defeated and killed by the army of Harold II Godwinson in 1066 at the Battle of Stamford Bridge. Later, in 1069, Swein Estridsson, king of Denmark, arrived in England and William the Conqueror had to buy him off – an Æthelredian way to solve a problem, but one that sometimes worked. Swein did not return. As late as 1084, Cnut IV of Denmark (Swein Forkbeard's great-grandson) was making plans to attack England, although the invasion itself never occurred.

After Cnut IV's aborted invasion of 1084, there were no more serious Scandinavian claims on the English throne. By the end of William's reign, the Normans were clearly cemented as the ruling dynasty, and most resistance had centred around the English House of Wessex rather than the House of Denmark. By this point, the Danes were predecessors of predecessors and their mark on England faded into history.

This should not diminish the fact that the Danish line had done something truly remarkable. They were the first to conquer a united England, and they held sway for a generation through Swein Forkbeard (1013–14), Cnut (1016–35), Harold Harefoot (1035–40), and Harthacnut (1040–42). Their reigns were exciting and full of intrigue, but largely forgotten. This book has been written to help remedy this, and I hope that it has succeeded in illuminating a dark, dramatic, and often neglected corner of early English history.

Notes

Abbreviations

ASC — *Anglo-Saxon Chronicle* (accompanied by the year of entry)
EHD — *English Historical Documents*: *Volume I, c.500–1042*
END — *English and Norse Documents Relating to the Reign of Ethelred the Unready*
EUC — *England's Unlikely Commander: The Military Career of Æthelred the Unready* (Brandon M. Bender)

Introduction

1. 'Viking' is often capitalised, but it refers to an activity, not to an ethnicity or nationality, so I have followed historian Richard Abels' lead and left it lowercase except in reference to broad terms like 'Viking Age'. Richard Abels, *Æthelred the Unready: The Failed King* (Penguin, 2018), pp. 37–38.

Chapter 1: A History of Bloodshed

2. I am using the Dorothy Whitelock's translation of the *ASC* except where specifically noted otherwise. 'The Anglo-Saxon

Chronicles', *English Historical Documents: Volume I c. 500–1042*, (ed.) Dorothy Whitelock (Eyre & Spottiswoode, 1968).

3. Clare Downham, '"Hiberno-Norwegians" and "Anglo-Danes": anachronistic ethnicities in Viking-Age England', *Mediaeval Scandinavia* 19 (2009), pp. 141–42.
4. Ryan Lavelle, *Alfred's Wars: Sources and Interpretations of Anglo-Saxon Warfare in the Viking Age* (The Boydell Press, 2010. Reprinted 2012), pp. 26–30.
5. The use of fleets did allow Anglo-Saxons to 'go-viking'. Lavelle, *Alfred's Wars*, p. 200.
6. Ryan Lavelle, *Æthelred II: King of the English 978–1016* (Stroud: Tempus, 2002; 2004 reprint), p. 50.
7. See Lavelle, *Æthelred II*, pp. 54–56 for more on the Danish transition to Christianity.
8. Eric John, *Reassessing Anglo-Saxon England* (Manchester University Press, 1996), pp. 66–67.
9. Catherine Hills, 'Anglo-Saxon DNA?' in *Mortuary Practices and Social Identities in the Middle Ages: Essays in Burial Archaeology in Honour of Heinrich Härke*, (eds.) Duncan Sayer and Howard Williams (University of Exeter Press, 2009): pp. 123–40.
10. Marc Morris, *The Anglo-Saxons: A History of the Beginnings of England* (Pegasus Books, 2022), p. 174. The charter is known as S 134.
11. *The Anglo-Saxon Chronicle*, (trans. and ed.) Michael Swanton (London: J.M. Dent, 1996), p. 54, note 6. Morris, *The Anglo-Saxons*, p. 173.
12. *ASC* 794.
13. John, *Reassessing Anglo-Saxon England*, pp. 91–95.
14. *ASC* 934. Sarah Foot, *Æthelstan* (Yale University Press, 2012), pp. 164–69.
15. Foot, *Æthelstan*, p. 171.
16. The *ASC* is mess of confused chronology from 939–943, with different versions recording different years for the same events.

Whitelock places Edmund's accession in 939, despite the *ASC* identifying it as 940, because the writer viewed the start of the year as September instead of January. See also Downham, 'Chronology of the Last Scandinavian Kings of York', *Northern History*, *40* (1), p. 49, for her chronology.

17. The 'D' manuscript of the *ASC* lists Olaf's accession under the entry for 941, but Whitelock believes it should actually be 940. Downham has Olaf take the throne in 939 or 940.
18. For more on Norse Dublin's military capabilities, see Poul Holm, 'The Naval Power of Norse Dublin', in *Clerics, Kings and Vikings: Essays on Medieval Ireland in Honour of Donnchadh Ó Corráin*, (eds.) Emer Purcell, Paul MacCotter, Julianne Nyhan and John Sheeha (Four Courts Press, 2015).
19. 'East Lothian skeleton may be 10th Century Irish Viking king', *BBC News: Scotland* (2014).
20. Clare Downham, 'Eric Bloodaxe – Axed? The Mystery of the Last Scandinavian King of York', *Medieval Scandinavia* 14 (2004): pp. 51–77.
21. John, *Reassessing Anglo-Saxon England*, p. 97.
22. David Pratt, 'The illnesses of King Alfred the Great' in *Anglo-Saxon England* 30 (2001): pp. 39–90, at 74.
23. Nicole Marafioti, *The King's Body: Burial and Succession in Late Anglo-Saxon England* (University of Toronto Press, 2014), pp. 68–69. Dunstan's monastery, Glastonbury, shouldered much of the burden of producing charters.
24. Shashi Jayakumar, 'Eadwig and Edgar: Politics, Propaganda, Faction', in *Edgar: King of the English 959–975*, (ed.) Donald Scragg (The Boydell Press, 2008): pp. 83–103, at 102.
25. Jayakumar, 'Eadwig and Edgar', p. 88. Morris, *The Anglo-Saxons*, p. 296.
26. Levi Roach, *Kingship and Consent in Anglo-Saxon England, 871–978: Assemblies and the State in the Early Middle Ages* (Cambridge University Press, 2013), p. 10.

27. Frederick M. Biggs, 'Edgar's Path to the Throne', in *Edgar: King of the English 959–975*, pp. 125–39.
28. C. P. Lewis, 'Edgar, Chester, and Mercia', in *Edgar: King of the English 959–975*: pp. 104–23, at 106.
29. Abels, *Æthelred*, p. 72.
30. Morris, *The Anglo-Saxons*, p. 296.
31. Quoted in Jayakumar, 'Eadwig and Edgar', in *Edgar: King of the English, 959–975*, p. 103.
32. Lavelle, *Alfred's Wars*, p. 27.
33. Jeffrey James, *An Onslaught of Spears* (The History Press, 2013), p. 165.
34. James, *An Onslaught of Spears*, p. 165. Edward the Confessor lived into his early or mid-sixties, while Alfred, Edward the Elder, and Æthelred II made it to about fifty.
35. Ann Williams, *Æthelred the Unready: The Ill-Counselled King* (Hambledon & London, 2003), pp. 2, 5.
36. Marafioti, *The King's Body*, p. 74.
37. S 937. This charter is also translated in *EHD*, no. 123, pp. 537–539.
38. 'Life of St. Oswald', *EHD*.
39. *ASC* 946.
40. Simon Keynes, *The Diplomas of King Æthelred 'the Unready' 978–1016: A Study in Their Use as Historical Evidence* (Cambridge University Press, 1980), p. 172.
41. Ann Williams, *Æthelred*, p. 13. Kirsten A. Fenton, 'The Tale of Queen Ælfthryth in William of Malmesbury's *Gesta Regum Anglorum*', in *Gender and Historiography: Studies in the Earlier Middle Ages in Honour of Pauline Stafford*, (ed.) Janet L. Nelson, Susan Reynolds and Susan M. Johns (University of London Press, 2012), pp. 49–60.
42. Marafioti, *The King's Body*, p. 170.
43. Ibid., pp. 171–73
44. Ibid., p. 164.

Chapter 2: The Vikings Return

45. Andres Siegfried Dobat, 'The State and the Strangers: The Role of External Forces in a Process of State Formation in Viking-Age South Scandinavia (*c*.ad 900–1050)' in *Viking and Medieval Scandinavia Vol. 5* (2009), pp. 65–104. Lavelle, *Æthelred*, p. 53.
46. Timothy Bolton, *Cnut the Great* (Yale University Press, 2017), pp. 41–44.
47. Lavelle, *Æthelred*, pp. 56–60.
48. Ian Howard, *Swein Forkbeard's Invasions and the Danish Conquest of England 991–1017* (Boydell Press, 2003), p. 8. Howard gives the most probable years of Swein's birth as 958–962.
49. Bolton, *Cnut*, pp. 35–37, 58. Ryan Lavelle, *Cnut: The North Sea King* (Allen Lane, 2017), p. 9.
50. Williams, *Æthelred*, pp. 53–54 for Harald's children.
51. *Encomium Emmae Reginae*, Cambridge University Press (1998; 2004 reprint), (ed.) Alistair Campbell with supplementary introduction by Simon Keynes, p. 15.
52. Howard, *Swein Forkbeard's Invasions,* pp. 32–35. M. K. Lawson, *Cnut: England's Viking King 1016–35* (The History Press, 1993; 2011 reprint), p. 31. Lawson, however, warns that the identification of Swein Forkbeard is not certain (p. 31, note 43).
53. Else Roesdahl, *The Vikings: Revised Edition,* (trans.) Susan M. Margeson and Kirsten Williams (Penguin Books, 1998), pp. 250, 285. Peter Sawyer, 'The Age of the Vikings and Before', in *The Oxford Illustrated History of the Vikings*, (ed.) Sawyer (Oxford University Press, 1997), p. 16. Lavelle, *Æthelred*, 62.
54. Sveinbjorn Rafnsson, 'The Atlantic Islands', in *The Oxford Illustrated History of the Vikings*, pp. 110–33.
55. According to the saga, Erik believed 'people would be attracted there [Greenland] if it had a favourable name'. From 'Eirik the

Red's Saga' in *The Vinland Sagas* (Penguin Classics, 2008), p. 28, (trans.) Keneva Kunz.

56. Lavelle, *Æthelred*, p. 64.
57. 'Life of St Oswald', *EHD*.
58. Margaret Ashdown, 'The Saga of Gunnlaug Serpent's Tongue' in *English and Norse Documents Relating to the Reign of Ethelred the Unready* (Cambridge University Press, 1930; 2014 reprint).
59. Morris, *The Anglo-Saxons*, p. 357.
60. Williams, *Æthelred*, p. 22.
61. James Augustus St John, *History of the Four Conquests of England: Vol. I* (London: Smith, Elder, & Co., 1862), p. 418.
62. Morris, *The Anglo-Saxons*, p. 327, speculates that it came from Ireland.
63. Simon Keynes, 'The Vikings in England, *c*.790–1016', in *The Oxford Illustrated History of the Vikings,* p. 74.
64. Lawson, *Cnut*, p. 31. Morris, *The Anglo-Saxons,* pp. 327–28.
65. For example, Thorkell the Tall entered Æthelred's service with forty-five ships in 1012, while Eadric of Mercia took forty ships from Æthelred in 1015 and defected to Cnut. Æthelred's fleet of 1008–09 likely numbered in the hundreds.
66. *ASC* 982, emphasis mine.
67. *Annales Cambriae* as quoted in Lavelle, *Alfred's* Wars, p. 28.
68. The charter is known as S 876.
69. Levi Roach, *Æthelred the Unready* (Yale University Press, 2016), pp. 92–93.
70. Williams, *Æthelred,* p. 25.
71. Ibid., p. 24.
72. Brandon M. Bender, *England's Unlikely Commander: The Military Career of Æthelred the Unready* (Rounded Globe, 2019), pp. 12–13.
73. Howard, *The Reign of Æthelred II: King of the English, Emperor of all the Peoples of Britain 978–1016* (BAR British Series 522,

2010), p. 19. This is based on some of the witnesses to charters of this period being called soldiers ('miles') rather than ministers. However, this seems circumstantial at best, and I have not seen this used anywhere else to argue for a campaign led by the king in 988.

74. Jeremy Haslam, 'The late tenth-century defences of Oxford and the towers of St George and St Michael', in *Archaeological Journal* 178.2 (2021), pp. 252–79.
75. Whitelock, introduction to 'Old English charter of King Ethelred confirming the will of Æthelric of Brocking', in *EHD*. S 939. Italics mine.
76. Abels, *Æthelred*, p. 37; Keynes, *Diplomas*, p. 222; Niels Lund, 'The armies of Swein Forkbeard and Cnut: leding or lið?', *Anglo-Saxon England* 15 (1986): p. 113; Roach, *Æthelred*, pp. 112, 121–22. Williams, *Æthelred*, p. 45.
77. This is Whitelock's suggestion, found in the introduction to the charter in *EHD*.
78. *ASC* 991, A manuscript. Brackets mine.
79. 'The Battle of Maldon', *EHD*.
80. *ASC* 991.
81. Benham, Jenny. 'The earliest arbitration treaty? A reassessment of the Anglo-Norman treaty of 991 G'. *Historical Research* 93, Issue 260 (May 2020): pp. 189–204. I am grateful to Levi Roach for pointing me toward this newer interpretation.
82. *ASC* 992.
83. Lavelle, *Alfred's Wars*, p. 163. Hirokazu Tsurushima, 'The Eleventh Century in England Through Fish-Eyes: Salmon, Herring, Oysters, and 1066', *Anglo-Norman Studies* 29 (2007 for 2006), pp. 193–213. Quote from Lavelle.
84. *ASC* 994.
85. Abels, *Æthelred*, p. 51, referring to a similar observation made by Neils Lund.
86. Roach, *Æthelred,* p. 176.

87. Richard Abels, 'Household Men, Mercenaries and Vikings in Anglo-Saxon England', in *Mercenaries and Paid Men: The Mercenary Identity in the Middle Ages*, (ed.) John France (Brill, 2008), pp. 152–53.
88. Ibid., p. 161.
89. Leonard Neidorf, 'II Æthelred and the Politics of The Battle of Maldon', *The Journal of English and Germanic Philology*, Vol. 111, No. 4 (October 2012), pp. 451–473
90. 'II Æthelred', *EHD*.
91. Snorri Sturluson, *Heimskringla* Vol. 1: Second Edition, (trans.) Alison Finlay and Anthony Faulkes (Viking Society for Northern Research, 2016), p. 170.
92. 'Saga of Olaf Tryggvason: The Longer Saga', *END*, pp. 152–53.
93. Theodore M. Andersson, 'Viking Policy of Æthelred', *Scandinavian Studies* 59, no. 3 (Summer 1987): pp. 284–295, at 291.
94. Lawson, *Cnut*, p. 31.
95. Morris, *The Anglo-Saxons*, p. 335. Roach, *Æthelred*, p. 178.
96. Bender, *EUC,* pp. 21–22. Roach, *Æthelred,* p. 179.
97. Haslam, 'The late tenth century defences of Oxford and the towers of St George and St Michael', p. 255.
98. S 891. Williams, *Æthelred*, p. 50.
99. *ASC* 999. The detail about it being a siege is added by John of Worcester's account for this year.
100. Roach, *Æthelred*, pp. 162–67.
101. Roach, 'Penitential Discourse in the Diplomas of King Æthelred "the Unready"', *The Journal of Ecclesiastical History* Vol. 64 no. 2 (April 2013), p. 270. This is also a major theme throughout Roach's 2016 biography of the king.
102. Brandon M. Bender, 'Æthelred the Unready and William of Malmesbury: The Death of a Reputation' in *The Year's Work in Medievalism* 24 (2019), pp. 32–41.

103. There is a possibility that Ælfthryth returned as early as 990, although it is certain she was back by 993. Keynes, *Diplomas*, p. 187 n. 115
104. Ibid., p. 188.
105. Roach, 'Penitential Discourse', p. 265.
106. Ibid., pp. 269–70.
107. Roach, *Æthelred*, pp. 179–80.
108. 'The Saga of Gunnlaug Serpent's Tongue', *END*.
109. Clarkson, *Strathclyde*, p. 126.
110. Roesdahl, *The Vikings*, p. 251.
111. Williams, *Æthelred*, p. 48. Roach, *Æthelred*, p. 181. Clarkson, *Strathclyde*, p. 127. Fiona Edmonds, 'The emergence and transformation of medieval Cumbria', *Scottish Historical Review* 93, no. 2 (October 2014): p. 208.
112. Lavelle, *Æthelred*, p. 97.
113. Henry of Huntingdon, *Historia Anglorum: The History of the English People, Volume 1*, (ed. and trans.) Diana Greenway (Clarendon Press, 1996), p. 331.
114. Clarkson, *Strathclyde*, p. 127.
115. Ibid., p. 133.
116. Ibid., p. 127.
117. Lavelle, *Æthelred*, p. 97.
118. Ibid.
119. Eric John, *Reassessing Anglo-Saxon England*, p. 141.
120. Roach, *Æthelred*, p. 187. Lavelle, *Æthelred*, pp. 97, 99.
121. Williams, *Æthelred*, p. 55.
122. Ryan Lavelle, *Aethelred II: King of the English 978–1016* (Tempus, 2002; 2004 reprint), pp. 97, 99.
123. Lavelle, *Aethelred,* p. 89.
124. Keynes, *Diplomas*, p. 210 note 203. Levi Roach advised me that he considers 1001 most likely, based on a 1002 charter (S 904) that finds the king redistributing land formerly held by his mother.

125. Roach, *Æthelred*, p. 192.
126. Bender, *EUC*, p. 33.
127. Abels, *Æthelred*, p. 105. Pauline Stafford, *Unification and Conquest: A Political and Social History of England in the Tenth and Eleventh Centuries* (Edward Arnold, 1989), p. 64.
128. Howard, *Swein Forkbeard's Invasions*, pp. 52–53.
129. Eadwig remained a king after Edgar became his co-ruler in 957, with kingship only terminating upon his death in 959. From 1035–37, both Harold Harefoot and Harthacnut claimed to be king and received support from rival factions. Neither candidate had been consecrated as English king by this point, though, which the *Encomium Emmae Reginae* claims infuriated Harold.
130. Roach, *Æthelred*, pp. 208–15.
131. Ibid., p. 210.
132. Bender, *EUC*, pp. 37–39.
133. Niels Lund, 'Peace and Non-Peace in the Viking Age Ottar in Biarmaland, the Rus in Byzantium, and Danes and Norwegians in England', in *Proceedings of the Tenth Viking Congress: Larkollen, Norway, 1985,* (ed.) James E. Knirk (Universitetets Oldsaksamling, 1987), p. 258.
134. Lavelle, *Æthelred*, p. 116.
135. *ASC* 1006.
136. Entry from the *Annales Cambriae*, quoted in Lavelle, *Alfred's Wars*, p. 28. '1012: Menevia laid waste by the Saxons, namely Edric and Ubi. The shipwreck of Swein father of Cnut'.
137. Bender, *EUC*, pp. 37-39.
138. Lavelle, *Æthelred*, p. 9. Tore Skeie, *The Wolf Age: The Vikings, the Anglo-Saxons and the Battle for the North Sea Empire* (Pushkin Press, 2022), (trans.) Alison McCullough, p. 299.
139. Roach, *Æthelred*, p. 213
140. Abels, *Æthelred*, p. 91. Lavelle, *Æthelred*, p. 116. Lavelle, *Alfred's Wars*, p. 149. Morris, *The Anglo-Saxons*, p. 342.

141. Abels, *Æthelred*, p. 91. Lavelle, *Æthelred*, p. 116. Morris, *The Anglo-Saxons*, p. 342.
142. Lawson, *Cnut*, p. 43.
143. Ibid., pp. 42–43.
144. Williams, 'Thorkell the Tall and the bubble reputation: the vicissitudes of fame', presented at *Gregynog Medieval Colloquium (University of Wales): 'Heroes and Villains'*, 28 February to 2 March, 2011, p. 4.
145. *Encomium*, pp. 11, 73.
146. Roach, *Æthelred*, pp. 256–57.
147. Ibid., p. 256.
148. Lavelle, *Æthelred*, p. 118.
149. Ibid., pp. 119–20.
150. Williams, 'Thorkell the Tall and the Bubble Reputation', p. 6.
151. Tom Licence, *Edward the Confessor: Last of the Royal Blood* (Yale University Press, 2020), pp. 30–31.
152. Lavelle, *Alfred's Wars*, p. 264.
153. Lavelle, *Æthelred*, p. 121.
154. Ibid.

Chapter 3: Conquest

155. Williams, 'Thorkell the Tall and the Bubble Reputation', 3. The diploma is S 926.
156. Abels, *Æthelred*, p. 96.
157. Lavelle, *Alfred's Wars*, p. 28.
158. Ibid.
159. Lavelle, *Æthelred*, p. 125. Quote from *ASC* 1012.
160. Harriet O'Brien, *Queen Emma and the Vikings: The Woman Who Shaped the Events of 1066* (Bloomsbury, 2006), p. 83.
161. *Encomium*, p. 11.
162. Abels, *Æthelred*, p. 97.

163. O'Brien, *Queen Emma and the Vikings*, p. 78.
164. *ASC* 1013.
165. Abels, *Æthelred*, p. 98.
166. *ASC* 1013.
167. Ryan Goodman, *In a Father's Place': Anglo-Saxon Kingship and Masculinity in the Long Tenth Century.* PhD Thesis, University of Manchester (2019), p. 167.
168. William Roy White, *A Discourse of Exile: Representations of Restored Royal Exiles in Anglo-Saxon England.* PhD Thesis, University of York (2012), p. 212.
169. Alice Sheppard, *Families of the King: Writing Identity in the Anglo-Saxon Chronicle* (University of Toronto Press, 2004), p. 109.
170. Tom License, *Edward the Confessor*. Brandon M. Bender, 'Edgar the Ætheling: A Case Study in Medieval Exile', *Epoch History Magazine* 06 (2021).
171. Morris, *The Anglo-Saxons*, p. 352.
172. George Molyneaux, *The Formation of the English Kingdom in the Tenth Century* (Oxford University Press, 2015; 2017 reprint), p. 225.
173. *ASC* 1014. *Encomium*, p. 15.
174. Thietmar of Merseburg, *Ottonian Germany: The Chronicon of Thietmar of Merseburg* (Manchester University Press, 2001; 2008 reprint), pp. 332–33.
175. Eleanor Parker, *Dragon Lords: The History and Legends of Viking England* (I. B. Tauris, 2018), p. 46.
176. Stafford, *Unification*, p. 66.
177. Williams, *Æthelred*, p. 120.
178. Thietmar, *Ottonian Germany*, p. 333.
179. Marafioti, *The King's Body*, p. 198.
180. *ASC* 1014.
181. Tom License, *Edward the Confessor: Last of the Royal Blood* (Yale University Press, 2020), p. 37.

182. David Starkey, 'Ængla-Land', *Monarchy with David Starkey* (Channel 4, 2004).
183. Molyneaux, *Formation of the English Kingdom*, p. 221 for Cnut, p. 223 for Æthelred's 'unprecedented' situation, and pp. 227–28 for Alfred and Edgar.
184. *END*, p. 157.
185. Lavelle, *Cnut*, p. 15.
186. O'Brien, *Queen Emma and the* Vikings, p. 87.
187. *ASC* 1014.
188. White, *A Discourse of Exile*, p. 218.
189. *Encomium*, 15.
190. Ibid., p. 23.
191. Ibid., pp. 15–17.
192. Ibid., p. 15.
193. Abels, *Æthelred the Unready*, p. 101.
194. Edward A. Freeman, *The History of the Norman Conquest of England: Its Causes and Results – Volume I,* Second Edition (Oxford: Clarendon Press, 1870), p. 368. Freeman concludes that Cnut's 'defeat must have been decisive'. Alice Sheppard, *Families of the King: Writing Identity in the Anglo-Saxon Chronicle*, University of Toronto Press (2004), p. 110.
195. Lawson, *Cnut*, p. 44.
196. Lavelle, *Alfred's Wars*, p. 264.
197. Freeman, p. 368.
198. Ibid., p. 369.
199. From Hemming's Cartulary, quoted in Lund, 'Peace and Non-Peace', p. 257.
200. Lund, 'Why Did Cnut Conquer England?' in *Conquests in Eleventh Century England*, p. 40.
201. Lavelle, *Cnut*, pp. 8, 15. Bolton, *Cnut*, p. 51.
202. Lund, 'Why Did Cnut Conquer England?'
203. 'Saga of Olaf Haraldsson', *END*.

204. Brandon M. Bender, 'Æthelred vs Cnut', *Medieval World* 6, p. 50. 'Saga of Olaf Haraldsson' *END*.
205. Williams, *Æthelred*, pp. 133 and 222 (note 11).
206. Marafioti, *The King's Body*, p. 199.
207. Ibid., p. 203.
208. *ASC* 1014.
209. David McDermott, 'Wessex and the Reign of Edmund II Ironside', in *The Land of the English Kin: Studies in Wessex and Anglo-Saxon England in Honour of Professor Barbara Yorke* (Brill, 2020), p. 342.
210. Bender, *EUC*, p. 61.
211. *ASC* 1015.
212. Lavelle, *Cnut*, p. 17.
213. *ASC* 1016.
214. Ibid.
215. Williams, *Æthelred*, p. 137.
216. Bender, 'Æthelred the Unready and William of Malmesbury: The Death of a Reputation'.
217. Clarkson, *Strathclyde*, p. 125. Skeie, *The Wolf Age,* p. 53.
218. Morris, *The Anglo-Saxons*, p. 357. Morris writes that Æthelred's reputation seems 'richly deserved'.
219. Abels, *Æthelred*, p. 106.
220. Lawson, *Cnut*, p. 51.
221. McDermott, 'Wessex and the Reign of Edmund II Ironside', p. 343. Williams, *Æthelred*, p. 140.
222. McDermott, 'Wessex and the Reign of Edmund II Ironside', p. 343.
223. Williams, *Æthelred*, p. 139. The source is Þórðr Kolbeinsson.
224. McDermott, 'Wessex and the Reign of Edmund II Ironside', p. 346. Good examples of this can be seen throughout the *ASC*, where battles are concluded by recording who held possession of the battlefield or 'place of slaughter'.
225. McDermott, 'Wessex and the Reign of Edmund II Ironside', p. 346.

226. Ibid., p. 347.
227. Ibid.
228. Jonathan Sneddon, 'Warrior Bishops in the Middle Ages', *Medieval Warfare* 3, vol. 2 (2013): pp. 6–8.
229. James, *An Onslaught of Spears*, p. 193.
230. *ASC* 1016, D manuscript.

Chapter 4: England Under Cnut

231. Brandon M. Bender, 'Epithets, Legends, and Lessons: Early English Monarchs and the 21st Century', *Camedieval*, 2021. Bolton, *Cnut*, pp. 214–16.
232. Eleanor Parker, 'Pilgrim and Parton: Cnut in Post-Conquest Historical Writing' in *The Medieval Chronicle* 9 (2014), pp. 271–296.
233. 'In Search of Ethelred the Unready', *In Search of the Dark Ages*, presented by Michael Wood (BBC3, 1980).
234. *ASC* 1016–17.
235. *Encomium*, pp. 31–33. Brackets mine.
236. Lavelle, *Alfred's Wars*, p. 344.
237. Clarkson, *Strathclyde*, pp. 133–37.
238. For Cnut's desire to discredit Æthelred, see Stafford, *Queen Emma & Queen Edith: Queenship and Women's Power in Eleventh-Century England* (Blackwell Publishers, 1998), p. 227.
239. *ASC* 1017.
240. *ASC* 1009.
241. The term 'Danegeld' is a misnomer, however. See Lavelle, *Æthelred*, Appendix 'On Danegeld'.
242. *ASC* 1018 mentions the fleet decreasing to 40 ships. *ASC* 1040 recalls that in King Cnut's time, sixteen ships had been paid for, suggesting the fleet was pared down further.
243. For Cnut visiting Edmund's tomb at Glastonbury, see Van Houts, 'Cnut: and William: a Comparison', in *Conquests in*

Eleventh-Century England, p. 71. For Cnut associating himself with Edgar's 'golden age' rule, see Bolton, *Cnut*, pp. 106–08.

244. Stafford, *Queen Emma & Queen Edith, p.* 34.
245. 'Knútsdrápa: Poem in Praise of Canute', *END*. Brackets mine for clarity.
246. Stafford, *Queen Emma & Queen Edith*, p. 226.
247. Ibid., p. 229.
248. One prominent example is from David Starkey, who brought up this possibility in the *Monarchy* episode 'Ængla-Lond'.
249. Lavelle, *Cnut*, pp. 52–54
250. Cnut appointed Ælfgifu as governor of Norway in 1030, along with their son Swein. This is discussed in more detail in the 'Family Matters: Regents and Delegation' section of Chapter Four.
251. J. L. Laynesmith, 'Queens, Concubines and the Myth of Marriage *More Danico*: Royal Marriage Practice in Tenth and Eleventh-Century England', *The Reading Medievalist* (2014).
252. Bolton, 'Ælfgifu of Northampton: Cnut the Great's Other Woman', *Nottingham Medieval Studies* LI (2007). Lavelle, *Cnut*, p. 37. Stafford, *Queen Emma & Queen Edith*, pp. 233–34.
253. 'Law of the Northumbrian Priests', *EHD*. 'II Cnut', *EHD*.
254. Bruce O'Brien, 'Conquest and the Law', in *Conquests in Eleventh Century England*, pp. 50–51.
255. O'Brien, 'Conquest and the Law', p. 63.
256. Lawson, *Cnut*, pp. 200–02.
257. Lavelle, *Cnut*, p. 15.
258. Bolton, *Cnut*, pp. 130–32.
259. Ibid.
260. Lavelle, *Cnut*, pp. 50–51.
261. Ibid., p. 50.
262. Bolton, *Cnut*, p. 149. Lawson, *Cnut*, pp. 96–97.
263. Introduction to 'Poems on Cnut's dealings in Norway', *EHD*.
264. Lawson, *Cnut*, p. 169.
265. Bolton, *Cnut*, pp. 150–51. Lavelle, *Cnut*, p. 55.

266. Bolton, *Cnut*, p. 154. Lawson, *Cnut*, p. 93, n. 47.
267. Bolton, *Cnut*, pp. 164–67.
268. Lavelle, *Cnut*, pp. 55–56.
269. Nicholas Brooks, *The Early History of the Church of Canterbury* (Leicester University Press, 1996), pp. 287–90. Lawson, *Cnut*, pp. 87, 121.
270. Peter Damian, *The Book of Gomorrah and St. Peter Damian's Struggle Against Ecclesiastical Corruption* (Ite Ad Thomam, 2015), (trans. and ed.) Matthew Cullinan Hoffman, p. 16.
271. Lawson, *Cnut*, p. 185.
272. Lavelle, *Cnut*, p. 80.
273. Frank Barlow, *Edward the Confessor* (University of California Press, 1970; Yale University Press reprint, 2011), p. 43.
274. Lavelle, *Cnut*, p. 61.
275. Lawson, *Cnut*, pp. 99–102.
276. Lavelle, *Cnut*, pp. 62, 83. *ASC* in *EHD*, footnote 1 on 1027 entry.
277. Lavelle, *Cnut*, p. 62.
278. See the section of Chapter Four, 'A Christian King'.
279. Lawson, *Cnut*, p. 169.
280. Lavelle, *Alfred's Wars,* p. 28.
281. Ibid.
282. Lavelle, *Cnut*, p. 85.
283. Ibid., p. 83.
284. Bolton, *Cnut*, p. 194. Lavelle, *Cnut*, p. 84. Lawson, *Cnut*, p. 108.
285. Lavelle, *Cnut*, p. 80.
286. Cat Jarman's *The Bone Chests: Unlocking the Secrets of the Anglo-Saxons* (William Collins, 2023) is a recent book about these Winchester mortuary chests, which have been under scientific examination for the last decade. The book has more to say about the lives of those in the chests than the chests themselves, although some of the material does focus on the

bones and their analysis. At the time of writing, though, there is frustratingly little public information about the progress on analysing the remains in these chests.

287. Morris, *The Anglo-Saxons*, p. 370.
288. Lawson, *Cnut*, p. 169.
289. *The Life of King Edward Who Rests at Westminster*, (trans.) Barlow (Clarendon Press, 1992), p. xvii. Barlow, *Edward the Confessor*, p. 39.

Chapter 5: Cnut's Sons in England

290. E. A. Freeman made a similar observation in *The History of the Norman Conquest of England,* p. 321.
291. Lawson, *Cnut*, pp. 108–09.
292. Stafford, *Queen Emma & Queen Edith*, p. 234.
293. Bolton, 'Ælfgifu of Northampton: Cnut the Great's Other Woman', p. 258.
294. Stafford, *Unification and Conquest,* p. 77.
295. *Encomium,* pp. cxlv–cxlvi.
296. *Encomium,* p. cxlvi, footnote 1.
297. For example, in the 850s, Æthelwulf was king of Wessex and allowed his son Æthelbald to rule during his absence when on pilgrimage. When Æthelwulf returned, his son refused to give up power and Æthelwulf conceded much of his former territory. A century later, Edgar became king of Mercia and Northumbria even though his older brother Eadwig had already been consecrated as King of the English. Eadwig never regained power in these areas. In 1016, Edmund II had a much more ancient and established claim to the throne than Cnut, but had to divide the kingdom with him anyway after much protracted warfare. Edmund never got to rule all of England before his death.
298. *Encomium*, p. xxx.
299. White, *A Discourse of Exile*, p. 210.

300. Brandon M. Bender, 'Emma of Normandy: A Resilient Queen', *Team Queens*, 2022. Harold was one of only two people (the other being Swein Forkbeard) to significantly mute Emma's influence in England.
301. Quoted in the Introduction to the *Encomium*, p. xxxii.
302. Stafford, *Unification and Conquest*, p. 75.
303. John, *Anglo-Saxon England: A Reassessment*, p. 162.
304. W. H. Stevenson, 'An Alleged Son of Harold Harefoot', *English Historical Review* 28 (1913), p. 114.
305. Licence, *Edward the Confessor*, p. 65.
306. Stevenson, 'An Alleged Son of Harold Harefoot'.
307. George Beech, 'England and Aquitaine in the century before the Norman Conquest', *Anglo-Saxon England* 19 (1990): pp. 81–101, at p. 94. Bolton, 'Ælfgifu of Northampton', p. 267.
308. Cat Jarman, *The Bone Chests*, p. 262.
309. I discussed the identity of Ælfgifu and Ælfwine in more detail on my website in 2022. 'A Son of King Harold I? The Case of "Alboynus Son of King Heroldus"', https://brandonmichaelbender.com/2022/12/09/a-son-of-king-harold-i-the-case-of-alboynus-son-of-king-heroldus/.
310. Bolton, 'Ælfgifu of Northampton', p. 267.
311. Clarkson, *Strathclyde*, pp. 146–47.
312. John does not place this in his entry for 1039, but in the entry for 1052 while discussing a similar Welsh raid that made him remember the events of 1039.
313. Lavelle, *Alfred's Wars*, p. 28.
314. Rebecca Thomas, 'The View From Wales', in *Conquests in Eleventh Century England*, p. 292, note 26.
315. Brooks, *The Early History of the Church of Canterbury*, pp. 297-99.
316. John, *Reassessing Anglo-Saxon England*, p. 165.
317. Bolton, *Cnut*, p. 203.

318. The nickname is traditionally said to refer to his speed and huntsmanship. However, Marc Morris has argued that Harefoot is a garbled reference to a different figure, Harald Fairhair.
319. Stafford, *Unification and Conquest*, p. 79.
320. There is a similar story about Godwin presenting a ship to Edward the Confessor. Keynes and Rosalind Love, 'Earl Godwine's Ship', *Anglo-Saxon England* 38 (2010): pp. 185–223.
321. Marafioti, *The King's Body*, p. 144. William of Malmesbury tells the version with the beheading.
322. Ibid., pp. 144–155.
323. *ASC* 1041.
324. Bolton, *Cnut*, 171.
325. Ibid., p. 195. John, *Reassessing Anglo-Saxon England*, p. 166.
326. Bender, 'Edgar the Ætheling'. Edgar, a direct descendant of Edmund Ironside, was known to be alive *c.*1125, but his death went unrecorded.

Conclusion: The Bridge to 1066

327. This comes from a twelfth-century legal compilation known as *Quadripartitus*, as quoted in Molyneaux, *Formation of the English Kingdom*, p. 222.
328. John, *Reassessing Anglo-Saxon England*, p. 166.

Index